Home Recording
POWER!

Ben Milstead

Home Recording Power

Credits: Cover and interior design, Stephanie Japs, Michelle Frey, Cathie Tibbetts, and John Windhorst, *DOV Graphics*; technical editors, Denis LaBrecque, Duane Ford, and Pat Pickslay; index, Kevin Broccoli, *Broccoli Information Management*.

Library of Congress Catalog Number 00-106698

ISBN 1-929685-08-4

5 4 3 2

MUSKA&LIPMAN

Muska & Lipman Publishing
2645 Erie Avenue, Suite 41
Cincinnati, Ohio 45208
www.muskalipman.com
publisher@muskalipman.com

This book is composed in Melior, Columbia, Helvetica, and Courier typefaces using QuarkXpress 4.0.4, Adobe PhotoShop 5.0.2, and Adobe Illustrator 8.0.
Created in Cincinnati, Ohio, in the United States of America

About the Author

Ben Milstead

infinite@regress.com

Ben Milstead has been tooling with home recording, rock music, and computers for almost two decades. He has been identified as an "auditory person" in relationships, is orthogonal but not dangerous, and is fed up with all the books on the market by professional engineers pertaining to "home recording."

He has been developing, writing, editing, and publishing technical and computer books, articles, and Web sites for almost ten years and currently manages Web services for the SoundMAX division of Analog Devices, Inc.—in addition to prototyping audio software applications for the PC and audio tools for gaming. He has founded and played in several rock bands, produced two full-length CDs, composed game music, and scored music for video and the Web. He is currently on a crusade to legitimize Gibson and Moog as deities by the human race.

Dedication

To Diane for putting up with all the long nights and latte trips, the workaholism, and the Valley. And to Alex and Summer for giving me the mindfulness to ever want to teach anybody anything.

Acknowledgments

You've read this before, but it's really true: A book like this could never make it to print without the hard work and talents of a whole slew of people. Thanks to Hope Stephan, Allen Wyatt, and Andy Shafran at Muska &Lipman—they're a first-rate team of professionals who are publishing with passion. In addition, some of the details in this book were researched or verified with the help of a number of excellent resources online, including Harmony Central, ProRec.com, MP3.com, and the countless personal home pages and newsgroups created and maintained by home recording artists and musicians. My hat is off to all of you trying to make and keep your experiences and ideas accessible to Internet users and the music community at large.

A special thanks goes to Denis LaBrecque and Duane Ford for nailing every technical detail to the wall and for stepping up at the last minute to provide additional notes and tips for readers. Thanks also to Laddie Ervins, Nick Pryor, and Matt Cookman for giving me real-world feedback and keeping me mindful of the spirit of home recording (a subject we all hold near and dear), and for being such good friends. Thanks to Pat Pickslay for providing early additional source material to use. While their assistance was invaluable, any errors remain mine.

Finally, a heartfelt thanks to you for reading this book, and for wanting to do your art, spread your jam, and bring your music to the rest of us.

Contents

8–All Kinds of Other Instruments

9–Wading in MIDI

10–Diving Deeper into MIDI

11–Fun-Da-Mental Audio

12–Serious Audio

13–Recording and Mixing

14–Step-By-Step: Your First 8-Track Song

15–Tracking Tips and Techniques

16–Pack It and Ship It

17–Wired for Sound: The Internet

18–Promoting and Marketing Your Music

Appendix 285

Index 297

Introduction

Home Recording Power! is a problem-solving and practical book, filled with hands-on examples to help you learn about home recording and how to do it right without killing yourself or putting your PA in hock. The book is loaded with examples, starting from scratch, that you can follow, and it has tricks and techniques you can apply to get the most out of your music and your budget. Professionals and amateurs alike can easily follow the examples. At the same time, advanced techniques and tips will allow you to dive deeper when and where you need the details.

What You'll Find in This Book:

▶ **Tutorials** on digital audio recording using SONAR software, EQ, and digital recording and mixing

▶ **Hands-on examples** with illustrations that show you how to work with synthesizers, guitars, drums, MIDI, microphones, mixers, CD-R media, and more

▶ **Tips** on how to make your studio and your music work for you—not against you

▶ **Techniques** on how to create stunningly good mixes

▶ **In-depth knowledge** on the recording and mixing process in both the analog and digital domains

▶ **Recommendations** of software, sound modules, synthesizers, and studio gear that will give you professional results

▶ **Time-saving tips** for how to market, promote, and distribute your music

▶ **Recording tips** for individual instruments from piano to brass to vocal recording

▶ **Real-world information** about MIDI, how it works, and how to really use it

▶ **Companion Web site** with updates, links, and recommendations

Whom This Book Is For

Home Recording Power! is for anyone either considering setting up a home recording studio or who already has one. If you're just getting started, this book can help you make smart choices about what you need for your individual home recording situation and determine how well they will work for you. If you already have a home studio setup, it will help you get the most from your gear, processes, and mixes and take you into some of the deeper aspects of audio engineering and digital recording.

This book is for anyone who craves real-world, no-bones-about-it knowledge, with in-depth tips and techniques to show you not only the ropes of recording and mixing your work, but also marketing and promoting it so that it can be heard. At the end of the day, *Home Recording Power!* will enable you to realize more of your potential as an artist.

How This Book Is Organized

Home Recording Power! is divided into eighteen chapters plus an appendix. The appendix contains Web links and information on additional, quality resources online.

▶ **Chapter 1, "So You Wanna Be a Star?"**—This chapter will get you started examining who you are as a recording artist, what you want to achieve with your music, and what you can expect as you gear up for home recording in terms of commitment, effort, and cost. You'll learn the difference between recording devices and how to plan a home studio equipment list.

▶ **Chapter 2, "Choosing Your Space"**—This chapter focuses on how to set up your recording space. You'll learn how to evaluate your room's sound, use soundproofing properly, set up monitors, and know what kinds of cabling and connectors to use. You'll find a compromise you and your pocketbook can live with.

▶ **Chapter 3, "Assembling Your Digital Studio"**—The only way to truly and affordably achieve anything resembling a good sound is to use digital, computer-based home studio equipment, and this one walks you through picking and choosing your equipment to get it set up for use right away. You'll choose a sound card, learn how audio software works, and connect all the components.

▶ **Chapter 4, "Listen to You"**—If you plan on recording vocals, this chapter is for you. The chapter will walk you through finding the right microphone(s), help you understand your capabilities as a singer, and show you how to achieve stellar vocal mixes as well as use effects for vocals.

▶ **Chapter 5, "Keyboards & Synths"**—The synthesizer has come a long way from the Telharmonium, and you'll discover how and why. From how synthesizers work, what's available, and how to select the right synth for your style of music, you'll be a synth-head in no time without geeking-out.

▶ **Chapter 6, "Getting the Guitar Sound"**—This chapter will help you turn otherwise amateurish-sounding guitar tracks into recordings you can be proud of, by showing you how to get the most out of your setup. The key is evaluating your playing style, learning how to properly mic both electrics and acoustics, and how and when to record direct.

▶ **Chapter 7, "No More Drummer Jokes, Please!**—This chapter is not about "percussion" in the traditional sense; it's about working with a standard drum kit (hi-hat, kick drum, snare, cymbals, and toms) in the ways you need to get "the drum sound." You'll not only learn how to get that sound, but also how to best integrate drum kit pieces into your style. MIDI, sample-based, and loop techniques are also covered.

▶ **Chapter 8, "All Kinds of Other Instruments"**—Though most of this book focuses on electronic instruments, this chapter goes into both recording popular acoustic instruments, as well as emulating different instruments using sampling technology. Strings, acoustic piano, and faking it all with GigaStudio are discussed in detail.

▶ **Chapter 9, "Wading in MIDI"**—While it's possible to be a home recording artist without it, MIDI is a powerful tool that can save you time and money, and it can make it easier for you to write and record your compositions. This chapter is an introduction to MIDI, guiding you through the ins and outs of FM and wavetable synthesis, hooking up MIDI devices, common configurations, and basic sequencing.

▶ **Chapter 10, "Diving Deeper Into MIDI"**—This chapter is an in-depth discussion about the internals of MIDI and MIDI messages. You'll understand the types of MIDI messages and what they do, as well as learn how to record and edit tracks using a software sequencer, all centered around practical knowledge of how the MIDI file format and specification really work.

▶ **Chapter 11, "Fun-Da-Mental Audio"**—Chapter 11 will teach you the fundamentals of audio and sound in terms you can grasp and put to use. This chapter will take you to the heart of what makes a great-sounding recording by distilling the science of audio. You'll learn about the differences between analog and digital recording, choose the solution that works best for your music, and you'll be led through the process of installing a sound card on computer. You'll actually understand what a sound card really does before you finish the chapter. Headphone use and techniques are covered as well.

▶ **Chapter 12, "Serious Audio"**—From the RIFF file format to understanding what audio buffer data is, this chapter is an introduction into some of the advanced topics of audio and sound. Concepts like oversampling, dithering, and effects are presented in practical terms—without the math!

▶ **Chapter 13, "Recording and Mixing"**—There is both a science and an art to recording and mixing, and you'll learn both in this chapter. The chapter begins with recording and mixing fundamentals and moves on to monitoring, cabling, the actual mixing process, and EQ. Tips for pushing your software to the limit and using effects are covered in detail.

▶ **Chapter 14, "Step-By-Step: Your First 8-Track Song"**—This chapter is a single tutorial which will step you through recording, mixing, and mastering a simple 8-track song. Each section is a specific step in the process, from setting up your recording preferences to exporting the finished product as both a wave file master and an MP3 file.

▶ **Chapter 15, "Tracking Tips and Techniques"**—This chapter offers special tips and techniques for planning your recording session, an EQ "cheat sheet" for quick EQ, using a patchbay, and mastering.

▶ **Chapter 16, "Pack It and Ship It"**—This chapter will take you through the world of CD-R and CD-RW media for mastering and storing your audio data and master mixes. Available software and hardware are discussed without too much of the technical jargon, as well as the types of media you can use for both audio masters and computer storage. Putting together sleeves, liner notes, and graphics are here, too.

▶ **Chapter 17, "Wired for Sound: The Internet"**—The Internet is still the biggest thing to happen to music in a long time, and after reading this chapter, there is no way you'll miss out on it. You'll learn about the differences between online audio file formats, how to set up your music Web site without becoming an HTML programmer, and how to protect your music online.

▶ **Chapter 18, "Promoting and Marketing Your Music"**—If you want your music to be heard, you have to tell people about it. This chapter is a wealth of knowledge on where and how to market your music on the Web, including how to get in on advertising and affiliate programs that will get your music out there.

Conventions Used in This Book

The following conventions are used in this book:

All Web page URLs mentioned in the book appear in **boldface**, as in **www.urock com.**

Besides this typographic convention, the book also features the following special displays for different types of important text:

TIP
Text formatted like this offers a helpful tip relevant to the topic being discussed in the main text.

NOTE
Text formatted like this highlights other interesting or useful information that relates to the topic under discussion.

Keeping the Book's Content Current

Everyone involved with this book has worked hard to make it complete and accurate. But as we all know, technology changes rapidly and a small number of errors may have crept in besides. If you find any errors or have suggestions for future editions, please contact Muska & Lipman at this Web site:

www.muskalipman.com/homerecording

You can also find updates, corrections, and other information related to the content of the book.

1

So You Wanna Be a Star?

This chapter is designed to get you started examining who you are as a recording artist, what you want to achieve with your music, and some of what you can expect as you gear up in terms of commitment, effort, and cost. You may want to skip this one if you're already comfortable with the direction you're headed as an artist or if "the ropes" are all-too-familiar to you, in which case Chapter 2 is a better place to begin.

For the rest of us, we'll attempt to cover (but not limit ourselves to) the following topics:

▶ Your audience and the music you have to offer
▶ The realities of "professional" studios
▶ Differences between analog recording and digital recording
▶ Developing a home studio equipment list

Giving the Audience What You Have

There's an old saying that goes something like this: "The man is just as hitched to that plow as the mule." Though at first glance you may not think this has much to do with the process of recording your music, the fact is—unless your goal is to create music in a vacuum—you are producing art that is tied to other people—other people's expectations and other people's entertainment. In other words, your audience is almost as important to your music as, well, the music.

Who Is Your Audience?

Who listens to your stuff? Or, who *will* listen to your stuff? Put on your marketing cap for just a moment: Is there a market for your music? Who are they, and what do they expect?

In order to answer these questions, you'll need to do one of two things:

1. Hire a market research firm or ad agency to conduct focus groups and telephone surveys for you and about you and your music. Cost: around $100,000 for a good firm and a handful of focus groups.

2. Identify ten other artists who are most like you, principally in terms of their music, but also their vibe, image, and lyrical style. Cost: the price of each artist's CD, unless you already own it.

If you can afford (1) above, then you probably don't need this book. Give it to one of your musician friends who can really use it.

Choice (2) is where it's at: One of the best ways to understand what your audience wants or will want is to get a feel for who they really are. Though it's not a hard-and-fast rule, generally, people tend to like a particular genre of music and/or a certain vibe or lyrical style best. If your music is similar to Moby's, then you should be listening closely to Moby's records and registering the quality of his recordings (as well as how the CD is packaged). If your singing and lyrical style are a lot like Adam Duritz of Counting Crows, then you should examine the recording style and quality of the Crows' CDs. The bottom line is, you can get a feel for what kind of quality and the types of songs people expect from popular artists who are selling lots of records.

For example, you don't have to listen to an entire Crows' album to know that people who like their music are a little less concerned with pristine recording quality and a little more concerned with melody and lyric. It's not a stretch to figure that out. On the other hand, the production on a Queen album is completely different, and people who like Queen expect Queen to sound like Queen: lush production quality, bright tones, and ironic lyrics. If your music sounds a lot like Queen's, your recording requirements and values are going to be different than if you write songs like those of Adam Duritz.

What's the Point?

Maybe it's simpler just to "do what you do" and not worry about the audience. After all, you're an artist at your core and, ultimately, it's whatever you have to say and/or your tunes that define your artistry. Right?

Don't believe it. There's lots more to the story.

When you make the jump to becoming your own engineer, producer, manager, and marketer, you've got to ante up and do the work required of those jobs. If you don't, chances are good that no one is ever going to hear your music, because it's not going to get recorded, mixed, distributed, or marketed. Music in this day and age has taken on a serious dichotomy—on one hand, it's ultimately the performance and material that provide something valuable to listeners; on the other hand, it's a business full of details. As a home recording artist, you're going to have to manage the details, wear the hats, and make it happen.

That means creating an end product that lives up to the expectations of your audience. Can you do it with home studio equipment? Ten years ago, the answer to the question would have been damn close to "No." Today, it's "Yes," but that doesn't mean it's effortless.

Got Milk? Go Professional!

One of the things you have going for you is the ability to create what your audience expects, keeping in mind there is no shortage of professional engineers and producers whose primary audience is other professional engineers and producers—not your listeners. This is not said to suggest that there aren't a number of highly competent, well-run studios who truly understand their clients. There are, and they do. And they will, rightly, charge you a small fortune to do it. If you've got the milk, they'll dip cookies for you all day long. If you *don't* got the milk—or if your tastes are running a little more toward no-fat than latte these days—then that's what this book is for!

Over the past decade, the cost of recording gear has fallen, while better, relatively inexpensive new technology has gone gang-busters. This has enabled nearly anyone to equip a personal studio for a few hundred to a few thousand dollars and to record their tunes with all the comforts of home.

As more and more home recording artists are born, there has been a great deal of discussion and dialog between the "amateurs" and the "professionals." Devote an evening to reading newsgroups like **rec.audio.pro** and **rec.music.makers.songwriting**. Aside from gaining some wonderful and helpful tips from some very knowledgeable folks, you'll also enjoy some great—and sometimes petty—debate over the merits of home recording vs. commercial recording studios.

Without doubt, both home studios and commercial studios each has its place in recording-dom. High-end recording gear, experienced engineers, and acoustically marvelous spaces are the main advantages of commercial studios—and they are big advantages.

Conversely, in addition to the cost, commercial studios are businesses that operate on strict schedules, and even if you do have a little money to burn, you're going to feel some pressure to get in and out of the studio. You're forced to do your best with a short time window and you cannot play around and experiment with the songs, instruments, arrangements, and tracks. In a few situations, this can be an advantage—we all need a little forced discipline sometimes to get things accomplished. The other 95 percent of the time, we need the ability to play whenever we want, without a time clock, free to create, explore, discover—and screw up—then start all over again. Sound a little like the creative process in general? Sometimes it can be a nightmare, but most of the time, it's the intuitive glue that keeps us married to our creations.

In short, if you want to spend money in a commercial studio, go for it, but that's not what this book is about. This book is about helping you to achieve semi-professional to professional results and still retain the creative freedom that fuels your music.

Analog vs. Digital Audio

A fundamental question you'll have to answer is what kind of home studio you want. There are two choices, really: analog or digital (or some combination of the two). Which is better? The answer has been hotly debated for some time, particularly among professional engineers, and both will get you where you want to go. For the home studio, however, digital is a better choice, for three key reasons: money, space, and quality.

Unless you just inherited all of Uncle George's cool studio equipment—his 64-track vintage mixing board, all his effects racks, and his $20,000, 2-inch reel-to-reel—you are not going to produce the sound quality you can get with digital equipment for the same money using analog. A four-track tape recorder won't cut it; neither will a 4-track quarter-inch reel without superior mixing and effects capabilities.

Even if you do have your hands on vintage, high-quality analog equipment, you've got to have three to five times the space to house it and keep it in running order. Contrast that to a typical digital setup, which you can set up in a space the size of your half-bath.

NOTE

There are several "home studio" books on the market that are actually books which show you how to spend all that money you don't have on studio equipment. Many of these books have excellent sections on mixing and recording, since they're typically written by engineers and producers who run large, expensive studios. There's nothing wrong with these books; however, most of them are not written with the economy or reality of a home studio in mind.

Why Is Digital So Hot?

On the surface, recording sound as digital audio is not unlike recording sound using an analog tape recorder—in fact, you'd be hard pressed, on first glance, to tell the difference—but in reality, it's much different. Recording audio digitally means you are recording numbers on a computer, not a pattern on analog, magnetic tape. The difference is profound; the numbers are usually far more accurate than the tape, unless you can afford very high-quality, expensive tape, the equipment it takes to use it, the cost of maintaining it, and a space to put it in.

NOTE

DAT, or digital audio tape, is a medium that can store digital audio in its digital form, much like a computer's hard drive. There are a number of DAT machines and components on the market, including some that use the popular ADAT standard, which allows you to store multiple tracks (usually eight per tape).

The numbers that are recorded digitally are called *samples*, and, depending on how many samples you record and how large the numbers are, you can have different levels of audio quality. For example, CD-quality digital recordings are based on a standard which always means that 44,100 samples are generated for each second of sound recorded. Put it another way: the *sampling rate* for CD-quality audio is 44,100 samples per second.

Likewise, the *bit depth* for CD-quality audio is 16 bits. This means simply that each one of those 44,100 samples represents a number 16 bits in length, which, in the computer programming world, is a common (and relatively small) number.

NOTE

The idea of a *bit* is simple: a bit represents either 0 or 1. By combining bits, computers produce much larger numbers. For example, 8 bits is nothing more than 2^8, which yields a range of numbers from 0 to 255 (256 numbers), while a range of 0 to 4,294,967,295 (or –2,147,483,648 to 2,147,483,647) is 32 bits.

A 16-bit number has a range of 65,536 different values, from 0 to 65,535, or, in some cases, –32,768 to 32,767. It's a pretty good-sized number, about the same as the salary of a junior-level second engineer in LA at the time of this writing.

Since sound is analog by nature, an audio wave pattern must first be converted to numbers before a computer or other digital recording device can record those numbers as a representation of your music. The piece of hardware that does this is called an analog to digital converter—or ADC for short.

NOTE

In many cases, the computer chip that does the digitizing also handles the analogizing. Hence, you'll see DAC/ADC or ADC/DAC or DA/AD or even AD/DA. You'll also see both types of converters referred to as simply an "A/D converter."

Similarly, there is a DAC, or digital to analog converter, which converts the numbers back to an analog audio signal you can hear during playback. Why? Because, so far, no human has gained the ability to hear numbers! In addition, digital recorders often employ filters in order to cut off unwanted sound data above or below frequencies that are of interest to human ears. For example, white noise or radio frequencies are often discarded during the ADC process to produce cleaner results.

A digital recorder stores all the samples—and the timing of each sample—that it receives. If the digital recorder is on a computer motherboard or a sound card, the amount of data it can store is limited only by the size of the hard disk(s) on the computer. If it's on a digital audio workstation (DAW), then it's limited by the fixed hard disk in the DAW and its on-board memory.

To recap, here's the process, as shown in Figure 1.1:

1. The digital recorder uses an ADC to convert an electronic signal from an audio device (such as a microphone or your guitar).
2. The ADC process converts the signal into numbers called samples, which are stored on a hard disk.
3. The recorded samples are then sent to the DAC part of the digital recorder, which converts them back into an electronic signal.
4. The electronic signal is routed to your amplifier, which boosts the signal to audible levels.
5. The signal is sent to your speakers, so you can hear all the mistakes you're making on this take.

Figure 1.1
The ADC/DAC process is actually quite simple.

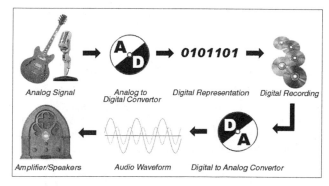

Analog Signal   Analog to Digital Convertor   Digital Representation   Digital Recording

Amplifier/Speakers   Audio Waveform   Digital to Analog Convertor

Yeah, But Analog Is Cool

But isn't analog the warmest, sweetest sound around? Digital sounds cold, doesn't it? Maybe. Maybe not. There was a time when digital recording wasn't up to the accuracy of analog tape recording, but things have changed. Processors have gotten much faster—and cheaper—and dozens of professional-quality sound cards, as well as DAWs, are on the market today that didn't exist a few years ago.

That doesn't mean analog doesn't have its merits, in any case. Let's take a look under the hood.

The most simplistic explanation of sound is that it is a series of vibrations. A guitar string produces vibrations, as does a human voice. Your eardrum vibrates in response, which is the reason you can hear sound at all.

Because of this, it makes sense to record sound by capturing vibrations, in a fashion not that dissimilar from the way your ears do it. Early attempts at capturing sound had to do with recording the movement of a needle that vibrated at the frequencies of sound waves in its vicinity; tracing the needle back across the path it recorded would cause the needle to vibrate just as it did when the original sound was present. That's where the word "analog" comes from: the recording of the needle created a sound analogous to the original sound.

Today, analog is chiefly a reproduction of sound on magnetic tape, facilitated through the routing of an electrical signal received from a source sound, such as a microphone or your keyboard. At some point, amplifier circuitry adds energy to the source signal and boosts it enough that it can be filtered, effected, equalized, and so on, so that the result is a recording that is, typically, clean and warm at its core. To record this signal, the electrical signal must be saved in some manner. Recording to magnetic tape, the electrical signals are turned into magnetic pulses, and as the magnetic tape passes over a recording magnet (head), the tape is magnetized.

This approach has some limits. First, the amplified signal-turned-magnetic energy is never transferred in a smooth, wavelike fashion to the tape, but in pulses, and so the resulting recording is not a completely accurate representation of the source sound. Second, the tape itself is physically limited to just how much magnetic energy it can store.

Even with these limits, for mastering, you can record sound between 5 Hz and about 45 kHz with high accuracy (with good equipment). However, every time you run the stored signal through electronics in order to listen to it, or re-record the signal, some of the signal is lost due to imperfections in electronic circuits, the tape, and electrical loss in wires and cables. To make matters worse (much worse), when you record a track and use that recording as part of another recording, the result is a second-generation recording of the original track. Continued re-recording of a track accumulates loss at a rapid rate, and your original pristine recording eagerly begins its journey to the Ninth Circle of tape-noise Hell.

Is this cool? Yes, actually, if you can afford the equipment to keep you in the lower circles of overdubbing. Otherwise, it makes a strong case for going digital.

More Power Means More Responsibility

In analog recording, there is some overhead for missing audio information yet still obtaining a fairly accurate recording. The process overall isn't as accurate as it is in the digital domain, but it's very reliable. In the world of digital recording, there is less room for error: The cost of doing digital business means understanding that you're dealing with purer electronics, and so that means you have to get right with the idea that, though errors are few and far between, when they happen, they usually ain't small.

Data will become lost. Hard drives will crash. Unexpected, mysterious strange happenings will sometimes occur without notice. You need to accept this as a given. One remarkable aspect of digital equipment is that it ultimately requires less maintenance than analog circuitry, but it can be temperamental—especially when dealing with computer sound cards and their associated hardware drivers.

At a micro-level, most digital architecture does some interesting things to avoid problems. For example, when writing digital data, it's possible to write an extra bit of information to allow the circuitry to know if the number being read should be an even number or an odd number. This is known as a parity check. If the number is even, and the parity bit designates odd, there is an error, and the data is either re-read or deleted as an error.

Another type of error check, meant to handle larger errors where entire chunks of information are missing, is known as a CRC error (cyclical redundancy check). This is the same type of error handling done by computer modems when sending and receiving data over a phone line. A mathematical check is done on the data being transferred and periodically matched to an expected result. Any result other than the expected result is a CRC error. To limit the amount of data that might "drop out," data is written in an unsequential pattern. If three blocks are lost, they are not necessarily in order, and the cyclical redundancy check can try to replace the missing data with the data it expected to receive. Sometimes, correct approximations can be inferred from the previous and next bits of data and a reasonable approximation put in place of missed data.

Digital recorders do a multitude of other interesting things behind the scenes to keep their activities reliable, and you're probably thanking the author of this book right now for not going into them. The point is this: Don't buy the cheapest thing you can get your hands on, and be ready for the occasional out-of-the-blue crash (which invariably happens at the most inopportune time). Take that attitude, and you're on your way to producing home studio recordings that sound damn good.

Getting Ready for Your Home Studio

This book focuses on a digital home studio setup. Here and there, you'll see a note or tip which is directed at external components other than a mixing board, but for the most part, the emphasis is on a PC-based, digital home studio setup with an external mixer. That said, this section is a quick rundown on the hardware, software, space, and external gear options that make the most sense at the time of this writing. These recommendations are made with value in mind—the most equipment you can get for your money. Your mileage, either prior to picking up this book or if you're just starting out, will vary. Most of these options are covered elsewhere in the book in more detail.

As a minimum, depending on the kind of music you do, the following are must-haves for a successful home studio:

▶ **Space**—A quiet, comfortable space in which to record is essential. Chapter 2 covers this in detail, and you'll find out that a bad space can make even the best equipment sound bad.

▶ **A good microphone**—There are almost as many microphones to choose from as there are singers (and instrumentalists) to use them. One of the best values on the market today is the Rode NT1 (around $200) or its slightly more expensive cousin, the NT2. If you're on the slimmest of budgets, a Shure SM58 ($100) will do in a pinch. For instrument miking, you just about can't beat the Shure SM57 ($100). Do not underestimate the importance of a good-sounding mic—it's one of the major advantages commercial studios have had in the past, since they can afford to pay thousands of dollars for high-quality large condenser mics like Neumann's U 87 and U 89 series. These days, you can buy a large condenser mic (like the NT1) that will come very close to the expensive Neumanns.

▶ **Mass storage for your master recordings**—This book focuses on using CD-ROM and CD audio as a primary means of storage (see Chapter 16), but you can also use a DAT or an external hard drive to great effect. Any way you look at it, you have to have a reliable, lossless way to keep track of your tracks.

▶ **Mixers**—Behringer or Mackie, Alesis in a penny-pinching pinch.

▶ **Computer systems**—Compaq, Dell, and Gateway are all reliable pre-built PCs.

▶ **Sound cards**—A SoundBlaster Live! will do as a bare minimum; however, you'll want to purchase a professional-quality board with higher bit depth and true full duplex capabilities, as well as multiple inputs and outputs. See Chapter 11 for more detail on the right sound cards to use.

▶ **Processors**—Pentium III-, Celeron-, and Pentium II-class machines are currently abundant, cheap, and have plenty of processor for multi-track digital recording. Pentium IIIs and Celerons are the best choices and are widely compatible with sound cards and other peripherals for use with PCs. The AMD Athlon is also a good choice and reasonably priced. Avoid IBM/Cyrix 6x86, MII, and MIII chips.

▶ **Motherboards**—If you're rolling your own (building your own computer), motherboard manufacturers to look for are Intel, ASUS, Gigabyte, Soyo, FIC, and A-Bit. Look for the Intel i440BX chipset—just ask for a "bx chipset." Avoid the i810 chipset if possible; it works well—when it works.

▶ **Memory**—Use a minimum of PC100 RAM and buy RAM with a lifetime warranty. Don't skimp on RAM quality unless you're already a hardware geek and you know what you're doing. The extra $10 or $15 savings is not worth the potential headaches.

▶ **Hard Drives**—Maxtor, IBM, and Western Digital are the best choices for hard drives, hands down. Get 7200 RPM platter speed, ATA-66 or higher, and make sure your motherboard supports it.

▶ **Operating System**—Windows 98 Second Edition, Windows Me, or Windows 2000.

▶ **Digital recording software**—This book focuses on SONAR and uses SONAR in all its examples; it's currently by far the most bang for your buck. Sound Forge, Cool Edit Pro, Steinberg WaveLab, and Emagic Logic Audio are also proven choices.

2

Choosing Your Space

On the seventh day, while God was resting, he was approached by the spirit of the Buddha himself:

God: "What's up, B?"

Buddha: "I could really use some help. I'm getting complaints about meditating too loudly. I need to build a perfectly soundproofed studio for chanting."

God: "Well, it's my day off, and there is no such thing as 'perfect sound.' How much money do you have?"

While everyone has an opinion about what constitutes a bad mixer, a bad microphone, or a bad set of speakers, most people agree about how a bad-sounding room sounds. In all likelihood, both your home studio space and your savings account are less than optimal for creating near-perfect sound, so this chapter will show you how to find a compromise you can live with, including topics on:

▶ Choosing your space
▶ Evaluating your room's unique sound
▶ Making your space sound better
▶ Using soundproofing techniques
▶ Locating your equipment
▶ Monitoring it all
▶ Cabling and connectors

Choosing Your Space

You've pretty much got two choices when it comes to where your home studio will be: either commandeer an existing room in the house (or use the garage) or build a new room.

In terms of space, what would a home studio cost to build? At the time of this writing, basic partitions (studs with sheet rock and no insulation), cheap carpeting, and suspended acoustic ceilings in an existing shell total somewhere near $50 per square foot. Not cheap—but much cheaper than, for example, the cost to build a standalone room, which ranges these days anywhere from $125 to $250 per square foot, depending on where you live. In fact, commercial recording studios average about 30 percent more than that!

Do the math: As a bare minimum, a full conversion of your 400-square-foot garage to a real studio space is going to cost you a minimum of $20,000, and probably at least a year out of your life to manage the project. If you've got the money, the time, and the dream, it's one alternative. If you don't have the money and the time, but you do have the dream, you'll have to compromise a bit, by appropriating an existing room and making targeted changes to that space to achieve a level of audio fidelity you can live with.

Common-Sense Considerations

First, there are some fundamental pieces to the home studio space puzzle that you'll have to keep in mind. The most important considerations are:

▶ **Isolation**—From the outside of your studio by anyone else and from the inside to your neighbors' ears. If possible, choose the room that's the most isolated from neighbors and external noise. Also remember that *isolating* sound is an entirely different topic from *getting* a good sound. It's soundproofing vs. sound acoustics (more on that later).

▶ **Doors and windows**—These are almost always problems in any type of studio. Check for acoustical "leaks" behind door casings and window jambs; it's not uncommon for the shims that are used to square doors and windows to leave gaps behind the moldings. These types of sound leaks are deceptive and can make your other sound-absorption methods doubly hard.

▶ **Acoustic treatments**—For walls, floors, and ceilings this is perhaps the most critical part of your studio space.

The degree to which you focus on these core aspects of setting up your studio has to do with the kind of music you'll be recording as well. For example, if your primary need is to have a place to play your drums, then your soundproofing needs will probably take precedence over equipment layout and, to some extent, sound quality. Conversely, if your music is mostly soft acoustic ballads, less soundproofing is fine, as is more natural ambience in the room, which may actually be an advantage, since atmosphere, as well as equipment placement, will probably be critical.

In any case, you're going to have to deal with the room's acoustics at some level, so it helps to know something about spatial acoustics.

The Complexities of Room Acoustics

Though there is no perfect-sounding room, sound waves travel and strike the walls in a room in predictable ways. What's not quite as predictable is the way sound is reflected back into a room once it hits the walls.

To put it another way, reflected sound is the most inaccurate aspect of room acoustics, and controlling it is the key to making your studio space sound good to you. Of course, there is control and there is control. *Real* control is *real* expensive and involves spending a lot of money and finding the right people to build your studio for you; with real *money*, and real *time*, you could turn a high school gym or dormitory showers into a world-class studio. The other kind of control involves educating yourself a little bit and making a few key decisions about your recording space. With a lot less money and time, you can significantly improve the quality of your space. You won't get as near to perfection as you might if you had Bill Gates' money, but the goal of this chapter is to put you on the path to enlightenment, not make your home studio space perfect.

Absorption and Diffusion

Controlling the amount and kinds of sounds that are reflected from the walls of your home studio allows sound that is truer to that of the instrument or voice (or monitor speaker) to come through. Controlling reflection is done by adding materials to your space that either absorb or diffuse sound. Material which absorbs sound attempts to quickly stop the sound waves from vibrating—effectively making the sound go away. Diffusing materials work a bit differently, by scattering the sound waves to reduce reflections.

In order to understand how best to absorb and diffuse a room's sound, you should know a thing or two about reflection itself. There are three basic kinds, or modes, of reflection: axial, tangential, and oblique (and there are frighteningly complex physics equations to boot, from which you are, most happily, spared). They sound all high-falutin', but the basic idea is pretty simple:

> ▶ Axial mode means reflection from two surfaces of a room.

> ▶ Tangential mode means reflection from four surfaces of a room.

> ▶ Oblique mode means reflection from six surfaces of a room.

The worst of these is axial mode; sound that is being reflected from floor-to-ceiling or wall-to-wall usually produces the most obvious, often unwanted, reverberation and mangling of sound frequencies.

NOTE

A room's corners can be a trouble spot, too. Corners create "pseudo-bass," by deceptively boosting bass frequencies in a room by as much as three to four times their actual levels. "Smoothing out the corners" is an important part of improving a room's sound.

On the Surface

The degree to which any of the modes of reflection manifests itself is mainly dependent on the kinds of surfaces in the room. If you've ever been to a basketball game or have sung in the shower, you already know that the hardest room surfaces, such as paneling, concrete, vinyl, and hardwood, are to blame for the worst reflections. Generally, the smoother, harder, and less porous the surface, the better (and more unpredictably) it reflects sound waves.

It's a mistake to think that making a room's surfaces completely absorbent is the only way to make a room sound best, though. While it's true that covering the walls and/or ceiling with 2-inch or thicker foam and carpeting the floor might create a better sounding space, you can do a more effective job by strategically placing materials that diffuse sound in addition to materials that absorb sound.

In fact, some of the best-sounding spaces tend to be ones with a proper blend and placement of good absorption and diffusion, and a little natural ambience is often preferable. The trick is to work with the room's dimensions and space, along with your equipment, rather than blindly spreading out absorbing material around the room. That's not to say that installing a base layer of acoustical foam evenly around the room, for example, is a bad idea, but in some cases you'll get better results by putting most of your absorbing material on one or two walls (or focusing on the ceiling and floors) while placing diffusing materials where it makes sense—for example, in the corners of the room.

For example, if your music is heavy on electric guitars or any other live, amplified instruments, then facing the amps toward one wall that is covered with a diffusion/absorption combination (such as eggshell-type acoustical foam) is a far more effective method for getting a good sound— and volume levels you can deal with—than trying to deaden the room by installing thick foam or carpet on all of the walls.

Eggshell Mania

Acoustical foam products from companies such as Sonex and Technifoam are the most common commercial means of getting good sound absorption and noise reduction over a fairly wide range of frequencies. These "eggshell" foam sheets are sold in a variety of sizes and styles and typically range in thickness from 2 to 6 inches.

Acoustical foam has been a popular way to achieve good sound for a number of years, and there have been as many different eggshell and placement configurations as there have been recording studios. An average installation covers anywhere from 40 percent to 60 percent of wall space, in addition to carpeted floors and randomly spaced eggshell treatments attached to different areas of a drop ceiling.

Eggshell-type patterns absorb echoes bouncing back into the room to control reverberation, while diffusing some frequencies to prevent over-deadening. The standard, cheaper types of foam usually have fewer color choices and don't line up all nice and pretty at the seams, while the more expensive lines come in a huge range of designs and colors.

Acoustical foam, when used in moderation, can give you better sound by helping you to control unwanted reflections; however, treating the entire room can sometimes make the room sound *worse*. While foam does an effective job on midrange and, to a greater extent, upper frequencies, it takes an impractical amount of it to control reflections in the low and lower-mid ranges. This means that if you cover the entire room with 2-inch or 4-inch acoustical foam, you're losing the highs but leaving the lows, effectively deadening your mixes. A totally dead room usually means a totally dead mix.

A great Web site for getting the specifics on pricing and styles is **www.acousticfoam.com**.

TIP

A cheap way to get noticeable absorption and diffusion is to use bookcases along the wall with randomly stacked books. It's an effective way to get rid of harsh reflections without killing your overall sound.

Speaker Placement

If you're able, using decent speakers and placing them properly can make all the difference. If you don't already know why, here are the reasons:

▶ **Bass response**—You cannot get accurate bass response from a set of headphones. Though high frequencies are heard primarily through your ears, bass is heard through your ears and just about every other part of your body (yeah, that, too).

▶ **Flat response**—If you do not have particularly flat speakers, at least learn where they are not flat and figure out a way to compensate during mixdown. Ideally, flat response should lie between 40 Hz and 16-18 kHz.

▶ **Imaging**—Live stereo sound has to deliver the left and right sides of the mix to both your left and right ears, while headphones only go L-L and R-R. The result is that it's hard to get the same mix in air that you can get on headphones, and vice-versa.

▶ **Phase**—All stereo signals contain frequencies that are out of phase, as well as phase cancellation. Since sound coming out of speakers mixes in the air before reaching your ears, these sounds will diminish before they reach you. With headphones, there is no phase degradation. This can, again, deceive you into thinking you have a better, or worse, mix than you really do.

NOTE

"Multimedia" speakers might be okay for playing a round of Unreal Tournament, but for music recording, you really need a clean power amp and a pair of good reference speakers.

If your music uses a lot of deep bass, then you'll definitely want to focus on a subwoofer (preferably matched to your other two monitors). If your space is limited, look at Bose's satellite systems, with one big woofer that sits on the floor and two or more tiny tweeters. A better choice is a pair of "nearfield" reference monitors. Nearfield monitors are typically small cabinets with very good fidelity designed to be listened to in smaller, lower-volume situations and at close range. Yamaha NS-10s are hands down the most popular nearfields (they're very flat above 100 Hz), but Tannoy and Event are also very good. As for a power amp, get the cleanest-sounding amp you can afford.

An important aspect of achieving a balanced sound when placing speakers is symmetry. A pair of speakers, for example, should be the same distance from you as they are from themselves, and they should also be equidistant from the walls to either side of them. Picture an equilateral triangle. Speakers should also be at ear level and at least four feet from you to avoid phase problems. In addition, putting speakers too close to corners tends to emphasize bass frequencies (often in unpredictable ways), so, if you can, keep the speakers out from the corners, not cattycornered.

CHAPTER 2

Size Matters

Room dimensions play a big role in how a room behaves acoustically. Depending upon the size of the room, certain frequencies can sound louder than others, because some frequencies will resonate at louder levels as *standing waves*.

A fundamental idea in physics is that "two objects cannot occupy the same space at the same time." However, sound waves seem to violate this idea, since they can pass through each other and continue on. This is known as *superposition*. When two sound waves of identical amplitude and wavelength are going in opposite directions, they can create a superposition of a standing wave. Figure 2.1 shows three waves: Wave 1 is traveling to the left, while Wave 2 is traveling to the right. Together, they produce a standing wave. The standing wave is the result of adding the amplitude of Wave 1 with Wave 2; it is called "standing" because it, in a sense, does not move; it's constantly being recreated by the other two sound waves.

Figure 2.1
Standing waves can fool you into thinking you've got more—or less—going on than what's really there.

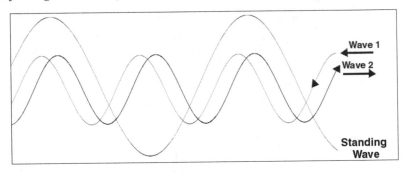

The size of your room will tell you at what frequencies you will tend to get standing waves. There's actually a little math here, in the form of an equation:

$$S = 1{,}130 \,/\, 2L$$

where 1,130 is the speed of sound in feet per second, and L equals the length of the room. For example, if your room is 15 feet long, you will get a standing wave at around 38 Hz (1,130 / 30). Also, multiples of your room's standing wave frequency will result in more standing waves, though they diminish in volume and are less pronounced the higher they get. In the example above, the next standing wave will be around 76 Hz, then 114 Hz, then 152 Hz, and so on.

If you calculate where your room's standing waves exist, then you can make adjustments by using equalization, speaker placement, or acoustical materials which will increase how accurately you perceive your audio mixes. In the case of a standing wave at a low 38 Hz, for instance, an effective solution might be a simple as a strategically placed, four-foot bookshelf in one of the room's corners.

Frequencies Flying All Over the Phase

Low-frequency signals have very long waves and seem to exist just about anywhere. In other words, they're omnidirectional. As a result, depending on the size of your room, the low frequencies may not be fully developed when they hit a wall, and they could cancel out or boost a portion of a subsequent or other diminishing sound wave.

As frequencies climb, things change. Mid- to high-range frequencies, for example, tend to have very short wavelengths, and so they are usually fully developed by the time they strike a surface and start reflecting. The result is that fully developed waves can reflect back to your ears and into the mix along with the sound coming from your speakers. This is called "early reflection," and you cannot tell the difference between most early reflections and the sound coming from your speakers. This can affect tone, as well as cause more inaccuracy in your perception of the stereo image.

> **TIP**
>
> Get your speakers' dispersion angle. It's in the manual or, likely, in the documentation on the manufacturer's Web site. You can then measure sound wave impact points by stretching string from the center of your speaker at the correct dispersion angle. Where the string touches the wall directly in front of it is where your room's sound will benefit from acoustical foam.

Soundproofing

A good sound is not the same thing as a "noiseless" sound. In other words, getting a good sound is altogether different from soundproofing. Acoustical foam will not keep your neighbor's new riding lawn mower from making its way into your new song's intro anymore than it will it keep your neighbor from calling the police in response to your 30-minute Keith Moon altar-call. Even if you lined the room with 6-inch solid foam, you wouldn't hear a significant effect on the transmission of sound into or out of the studio.

To properly soundproof, you've got to cover a different set of bases:

▶ **Space in your space**—If you add a layer of drywall, for example, to the existing walls, you'll gain virtually nothing. On the other hand, if you build a new wall even a couple of inches out from the existing wall, the air pocket between the new wall and the old wall will dramatically decrease amplitude.

▶ **Tiny leaks cause big problems**—Even small holes, such as the gap between a doorjamb and the door, will do serious damage to your sound-blocking efforts. Airtight seals are critical.

▶ **The denser the better**—Dense materials have more mass and, hence, don't vibrate as much as less dense or springy materials. Particleboard is a tad better than plywood, which is a bit better than drywall, which is better than acoustical foam for soundproofing.

Unfortunately, properly soundproofing can potentially be one of the most expensive aspects of putting your space together, since the most effective way to attenuate sound is to put a solid wall in its way. That usually means construction of some kind. Unless you're an experienced carpenter, it's going to take time and money.

One tip is to use multiple walls, rather than one wall or partition. Two or more walls with an air gap in between them will always give better results than a single wall of double or even triple the thickness, and the wider the gap, the better the sound isolation, particularly at low frequencies.

CHAPTER 2

Cabling Basics

An oft-overlooked aspect of most home studios is proper cabling. Learn here from the mistakes of tens of thousands of home studio engineers before you: Don't use cheap cable or connectors.

Good connectors will have low contact resistance and hold up for years. Brands like Switchcraft and Neutrik have been industry standards for some time, and you generally can't go wrong with either one of these brands. In general, stay away from Radio Shack, though their gold-plated connector types will do in a pinch.

Cables play an even bigger role in the quality of your audio signal. Even if the diameter, gauge, and construction are similar, two cables may have significantly different electrical properties—such as their respective resistances, capacitances, inductances, shielding density, tensile strength, jacket friction, and so on. This means you should look at your cable's specifications and keep them as consistent as possible.

Perhaps the most critical part of good cable is shielding. The best kind of shielding is foil shielding, but there is a downside: Foil-shielded cables are not the strongest, and they don't flex very well. Use foil shielding where cable movement is minimal—with racks and effects boxes, for example.

Braided and wrapped cables are a better choice for mic and instrument cables. Use cables with good-quality and stable insulation, with a tightly braided shield that is held firm by the outer jacket so the shield itself doesn't become loose when the cable is flexed.

TIP

In any recording environment, balanced connections are, absolutely, the only way to go. Balanced connections are far less likely to pick up interference from other cables, and the redundancy of two signal conductors in a balanced connection usually yields better quality audio. Balanced connections use two conductors carrying the same signal but with the polarity of one of them reversed.

TIP

Audio cables can be particularly susceptible to interference from power cables. It's *very good* practice to keep the cables carrying your signal away from the cables carrying the electricity! One of the ways to accomplish this is by using a *snake*, which is a bundled set of audio cables inside additional insulation. Snakes are a bit more expensive than buying separate cables, but they will save you interference—and organizational—headaches down the road.

NOTE

The *impedance*, *resistance*, and *capacitance* of your cables and your equipment are probably the most important, and most confusing, part of a strong audio signal.

When you connect headphones to an amplifier, for example, the load (headphones) will draw some current from the source (amp). How much current is drawn depends on the impedance of the load in ohms. An ohm is a unit of resistance, reactance, or impedance, depending on the type of load; some loads are resistive and some are reactive, while impedance is a combination of both resistance and reactance.

Look for cable that has the least resistance and the lowest capacitance; resistance is usually measured per thousand feet, and good cable will be under 100 ohms per 1,000 feet.

With gear, the closer the impedance (the ohms) of the equipment being driven is to the source impedance of the device that's driving it, the more powerful the signal. It doesn't have to be perfect (and never is), but the closer the better.

In the Garage: A Dream Setup

This section briefly describes an example of a home studio space that requires some money, time, and careful planning. The idea behind this "dream studio" is to give you a glimpse of what you're getting into. The following list comprises just the fundamentals for a sound-isolated, pristine-sounding home studio space in the garage to be used as a music studio. Measurements of garage: $20 \times 20 \times 12$, approximately 400 square feet.

- ▶ Professional, acoustically treated walls, ceiling, and floor so that maximum sound frequencies will be contained inside the studio and not disturb family members in the house, persons outside, or in nearby houses.

- ▶ Separate air conditioning/heating unit for the studio. Use silencers, filters, and so on, so that incoming/return air ducts do not leak sound out of the studio. Incoming air should be silenced enough to enable recording without ventilation noise.

- ▶ Quiet, well-lit track lighting, with quiet, non-fluorescent bulbs.

- ▶ Acoustically sound doors and windows: one door going into the house and one going outside to driveway. The doors should have appropriate acoustical seals in order to contain as much sound as possible inside the studio.

- ▶ Dedicated electrical circuits and several sets of duplex (grounded) electrical outlets along each wall. Outlets must handle electric current fluctuations and noise caused by home appliances, air conditioning, and lighting, as well as radio, TV, and cordless/cell phone frequencies.

- ▶ Telephone outlet, cable TV outlet, thermostat control panel, and light switches.

- ▶ Acoustic wall around appliances like furnaces or water heaters, with acoustically treated pipe inserts into the wall so that sound will not leak through.

- ▶ Custom control room for mixer, computer, amp, and other control gear.

CHAPTER 2

Total cost and time: Your mileage will vary, but figure at least $20,000 and around one year of project management.

In the Garage: A Practical Example

Another way to look at a garage studio is to figure out how to make small improvements that will increase sound quality while doing some minimal soundproofing. This example looks at the same garage as the one in the last section: a typical garage with measurements $20 \times 20 \times 12$, approximately 400 square feet.

▶ $10-per-square-yard carpet over a thick pad on the floor, covering the main studio area, about 12×12.

▶ Gaskets added to the doors so that isolation from the rest of the house is much improved. Noise from the street coming through the garage window is an occasional problem helped through the judicious use of extra-thick drapes purchased at the local thrift store.

▶ Speakers located to each side of the window, since speakers tend to move drywall as well as air. Because they are nearfield monitors, they're not right up against the wall. Hang them about 4 feet from the floor, equidistant from a 4×8 card table that will do as the main control table for the studio.

▶ Speakers about 8 feet apart, putting the sweet spot 8 feet from the wall along the center line of the room. Once the equipment is set in place, a check for reflections and phase interference is conducted with a mirror and a flashlight. The mirror is set on the mixing table and the flashlight aimed at the mirror; if the light beam falls near the speakers, there is a potential reflection problem.

▶ To combat reverb and standing wave problems, 2×6 R-19 fiberglass placed on the walls near the monitors to clean up short reflections and drastically improve the sound quality between the monitors. Adding a couple of panels along one of the side walls practically eliminates any standing waves; this also cuts down some of the low-frequency reflection coming from the corner.

▶ Two 4×8 particleboard bookshelves on the facing wall to the R-19. With a few strategically placed books, the bookshelves dramatically improve sound quality by diffusing and absorbing sound, while also adding some additional sound isolation benefits.

Total cost and time: About $300; a weekend.

3

Assembling Your Digital Studio

Make no bones about it: The only way in this day and age that you're going to affordably achieve anything resembling a good sound is to use digital, computer-based home studio equipment. There are a few other places in this book that (hopefully) do an effective job of convincing you of this, but this chapter is not one of them. This chapter presumes that you are on board. It presumes you're sold on digital recording, and you need a little advice on how to pick and choose your equipment and get it all set up. To that end, you'll learn:

▶ Which parts of a digital recording setup you'll use the most

▶ How much the hardware costs

▶ What constitutes a good system configuration

▶ How to choose a sound card

▶ How audio software applications work

▶ How to connect the studio components, do cabling, and plan for wiring

Computing Audio

This is a curious time in the history of home recording. Thanks to market forces, improvements in manufacturing and distribution, and the proliferation of the Internet, the barrier of high costs has been all but eliminated for digital home studio recording. Digital recording for the home recording artist has never been more powerful or affordable.

What are the features? You can work much faster, easily edit waveforms, cut and paste to your heart's content with all the ease of a word processor, and keep all of your work in the pristine fidelity of the digital domain.

What are the benefits? You save time, money, and achieve audio quality that ten years ago was possible with only the most expensive equipment available. Your guitar sound will be better, your vocal performances cleaner, your composition a lot closer to what was in your head when you wrote the piece. In short, you're a lot closer to the vibe—to the "right on"—today than you've ever been. Here's a quick list of the some of the most "right on" aspects of your digital recording studio:

CHAPTER 3

▶ Most upgrades to your "equipment" will be newer versions of existing software or new software products, and software is almost always less expensive than new, expensive outboard gear.

▶ You can cut-and-paste audio data in the same way that you can cut-and-paste text in a word processor. This is called non-linear editing, and it significantly decreases the amount of time you must spend doing routine and mundane tasks. This also means you can easily play with multiple arrangements and tracks, and the only limit to the number of tracks you can record is the capacity of your hard drive and the speed of your processor.

▶ Software effects and audio enhancements are almost always cheaper—and easier to use—than their standalone counterparts.

▶ Your audio stays in the digital domain all the time, meaning that you will rarely—if ever—experience a degradation in audio quality.

▶ The amount of space a computer-based system takes up, including an outboard mixer, is miniscule compared to using all external, analog equipment.

▶ Though noise can still be an issue, depending upon the type and quality of the system you use, it has become less and less of a concern due to advances in component cases and power supplies.

Sound too good to be true? Well, it's not! Order now for *rush delivery*! Seriously, there is another aspect of your digital studio that you're going to have to deal with—the learning curve. Unless you're already computer-audio savvy, there is really no way around it. Here are some of the most important points:

▶ If you're using a Windows-based system and other musicians you write or exchange jams with are using a Mac, you may experience some incompatibility problems. This is less of a problems these days, since many Mac programs can now utilize the Windows Wave file (.WAV) format, but it is a potential problem to be aware of.

▶ Using the mouse and coordinating data on the computer screen will take some getting used to. If most of your experience has been with analog gear, you'll find using a mouse to be awkward and it will feel limiting to you. Audio software has traditionally tried to mimic hardware, so you'll encounter virtual mixers which rely on virtual knobs and sliders for the grunt-work. Interfaces are getting better, though; for example, SONAR provides you the ability to design custom console layouts to use for interfacing with real-world equivalents; and monitor resolutions, colors, and mouse technology provide you with a lot of options. In general, though, using a mouse will never be as intuitive as turning a real knob— you will acclimate to it with some practice.

▶ As you become more and more computer savvy, you are going to gradually become aware of the basic components of a PC. Motherboards, RAM, and hard drives will invariably become a part of your audio vocabulary, because, as newer versions of software are produced (or conceived), you'll want to upgrade and take advantages of future technology and features. Don't be afraid of these components. There is nothing magical about them, and learning how to upgrade any of the parts in your computer requires only a little patience and time. This ain't rocket science!

Real-World Costs

Though component costs are currently at an all-time low, you're going to have to spend some of your cash. In other words, it may be cheap, but it ain't free.

The average costs for computer hardware, a mixing console, software, a CD-R or CD-RW drive to archive your music, and monitors, are shown in Table 3.1 This table also shows comparable costs for a standalone digital audio workstation, or DAW.

NOTE

The acronym "DAW" is also used, with more and more frequency, to describe any general digital audio setup, including a computer-based setup. In this book, you will always see it used to refer to a standalone, separate component (such as the Yamaha AW4416 (see **www.yamaha.com**)), which typically includes a mixer, built-in effects, and a hard drive on board.

Table 3.1
The Basic Costs of Doing Digital.

Component	Computer	DAW
Computer	$750-1,800	-
Mixer	$500	-
Software	$300-500	-
Recording Hardware/Sound Card	$100-1,000	$1,000-3,000
Monitors	$250-1,000	$250-1,000
Mastering/Archiving	$200	$500-1,000
Total	**$2,100-5,000**	**$1,750-5,000**

Perhaps the most interesting thing about Table 3.1 is just how close the total price is to that of a DAW—yet the storage capacity of a computer hard drive vs. a DAW is typically much, much bigger (ten to twenty times bigger).

Add to that the ability to use your computer for other tasks, such as word processing, e-mail, and the Internet to distribute and advertise your work, and there really is little contest.

TIP

A few years ago, a dedicated computer for PC audio recording would have been practically your only option, due to slow processors and hard drives and expensive RAM. Today, it's not all necessary, though it is still ideal. Having a dedicated machine for your studio will still minimize potential hardware conflicts. If you can't even think about the extra money for a separate system right now, having a separate hard drive dedicated to recording has some speed advantages as well.

CHAPTER 3

In addition, a computer is almost infinitely expandable compared to a standalone system, which means you won't have to worry much about needing to add on hard drives. You can buy large, fast hard drives these days for under $200. For example, a Maxtor 7,200 RPM ATA-66, 60 GB (that's right—60 GB) is well under $200 at the time of this writing. The bottom line is that the issue of storage, or of simply having enough disk space to get through your latest project, is no longer an issue!

The Software, Uh, Really Works Now!

Audio recording software has grown in leaps and bounds just in the last five years. This book focuses on SONAR (see Figure 3.1), as well as Sound Forge (see Figure 3.2) for some additional mastering and final mixdown tasks, but there are a number of other excellent programs available to do the same thing. Cool Edit Pro and Pro-Logic are two fine examples. All of these software applications handle both audio recording and MIDI sequencing to various degrees (SONAR actually has the best mix of both worlds).

Figure 3.1
SONAR is the most full-featured value for PC-based home studio recording today.

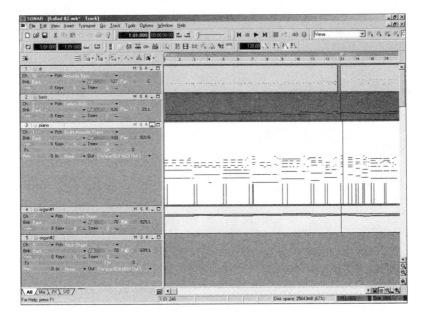

Figure 3.2
Sonic Foundry's
Sound Forge 5.0 is
an excellent audio
editing application for
mastering stereo tracks.

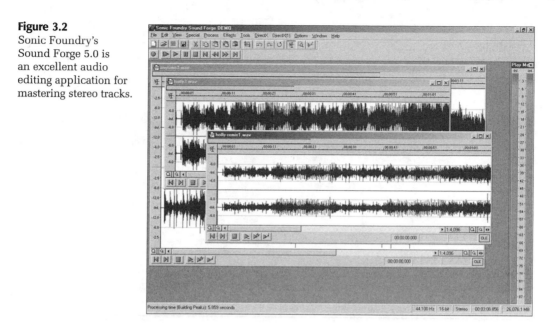

Go Direct With DirectX

With the advent of DirectX plug-ins, there is at least something of a standard by which software companies can deliver the latest and greatest effects and audio enhancement tools without redesigning the wheel.

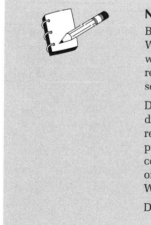

NOTE

Before DirectX, developers creating audio (and video) applications for Windows machines had to customize their software so that they would work well on a large number of different hardware devices and configurations. The result was instability (and often frustration) because of equipment and software driver incompatibilities.

DirectX created a "hardware abstraction layer" (HAL) which uses software drivers to communicate between game software and computer hardware. As a result, software developers can use DirectX to write a single version of their product without worrying about the wide range of hardware devices and configurations out there. This essentially means that you can generally count on the audio hardware and software you buy to work well together on the Windows platform.

DirectX is currently in version 8 and is pretty stable.

CHAPTER 3

DirectX plug-ins can save you time and money and rival results you can achieve from an entire rack of hardware. Figures 3.3, 3.4, and 3.5 are examples of popular plug-ins. Think of just about any effect—from any reverb type you can think of to a lush chorus to multi-tap delay to pitch correction—and it's most likely available as plug-in.

Figure 3.3
TC Works' Native DeX is the Swiss Army knife of single band dynamics processing.

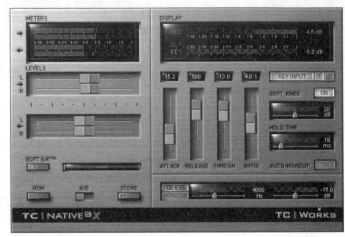

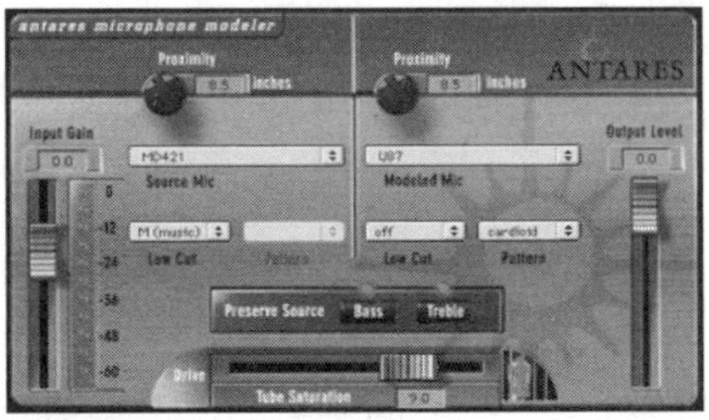

Figure 3.4
Antare's Microphone Modeler lets you get some killer vintage mic sounds.

Figure 3.5
You could be the king of karaoke with AnalogX's free Vocal Remover plug-in.

In a nutshell, DirectX can:

▶ Literally replace any number of hardware racks, generally costing thousands of dollars, at a fraction of the cost.

▶ Work with any DirectX-compatible, host-supported audio software you choose.

▶ Save you development time by giving you the ability to preview effects in real time before you commit them to your audio files.

▶ Save processing time. With DirectX plug-ins, you can process effects more quickly, about 15 percent faster than those typically built into typical audio software.

Let's look at that first bullet point in a little more detail, briefly. Plug-ins are very flexible when combined with your audio software; in terms of cost, there is no comparison. If you buy a good hardware reverb, for example, you will spend at least $200 for one box. With a plug-in, you're going to spend more like half that amount, but when you need a different reverb mix for eight different tracks, all you need to do is load up additional instances of the plug-in into memory. It's like having eight reverbs for the price of one.

But Shouldn't I Be Using a Mac?

The Macintosh (Apple) platform is a wonderful operating system for home studio recording. If you use a Mac or intend to, more power to you. However, this is not the platform this chapter—or this book—focuses on. Why? There are several reasons, and management thought you might like to know:

▶ **Value**—With recent advances in microprocessor speed, a PC represents the best *value* for a home studio setup today.

▶ **Power and flexibility**—There is enough horsepower available for PCs these days that you can use your PC for a few other things, not just as a dedicated audio recording box. You can do this with a Mac, too, but your software choices are much more limited.

CHAPTER 3

▶ **Software**—SONAR is the recommended recording software used in this book because it is the best *value* on the market today for a digital home studio. SONAR is not available for the Mac platform.

▶ **DirectX plug-ins**—DirectX audio plug-ins, unfortunately, don't work on Macs, though it should be noted that several of the companies that produce plug-ins for DirectX do, in some cases, produce their Mac equivalents.

So, if you have a Mac or intend to use one, you will still find this book very useful. However, you will find some of the tutorial material and step-by-steps less helpful, since they deal with specific features in SONAR.

Windows and the Wide World of Computer Geekdom

The first thing to be aware in the PC domain is the relationship between the computer itself and the sound card. This is an important relationship, because these two pieces are the heart of your system.

Briefly, The Computer

Obviously, no computer, no audio. The PC you use for digital audio recording needs to be relatively powerful, and the three most important components—processor, RAM, and hard drive—can vary widely in power and cost.

For example, as this book goes to press, the most powerful processors are the Pentium 4 1.4-1.5 GHz chips. These processors are much more expensive than, say, Pentium 3 chips up to about the 750 MHz range.

If the question is, "Do I need 1.5 GHz of speed?" then the answer really is "No." This is different than the question, "Can I use 1.5 GHz of speed?" where the answer is probably "Yes."

The reason has everything to do with the way audio is processed on a computer, or any electronic device, for that matter. The faster the processor, the more quickly algorithms for effects and audio processing can occur. This is important for things like adding real-time reverb to your tracks as you record them, for example. The reality is that today's general, non-audio, bare minimum (and cheap) processor standard is around a Pentium 3, 500 MHz, and that's more than capable of recording and playing back a large number of simultaneous tracks. However, if you can afford more, get more. It will only decrease your processing overhead and allow you to more comfortably take advantage of new effects algorithms and plug-ins as they become available, as well as decrease the amount of time it takes for audio processing to occur. This means you could, for example, apply a larger number of effects at the same time.

RAM, or random access memory, also plays an important role, but it has a lot less to do with effects processing. Instead, RAM is most important for recording and playing back lots of tracks simultaneously. Generally, the more you have of it, the better. A minimum of 128 MB will work wonderfully, and 256 MB will make your day.

Hard drive speed is even more critical—because of the way in which Windows manages loading programs into memory from a hard drive and because of the rate at which audio accesses that memory. Recording audio onto your hard drive takes roughly 5 MB per track per minute, and at that rate, space gets used up in a hurry. In addition, the more hard drive space you have, the more room you have to store tracks as well as mastered songs after they're mixed.

At a minimum, here is a system configuration that will give you lots of pleasure for years to come:

▶ Pentium Class III 500 MHz processor or higher

▶ 30 GB, ATA-66 or higher hard drive

▶ 128 MB RAM or higher

▶ CD-R or CD-RW for archiving finished projects

▶ Full duplex sound card, 16 bit or higher

The Sound Card

So what about your sound card? A full duplex sound card allows you to listen to previously recorded tracks and record new tracks at the same time, and this is absolutely essential for overdubbing. In addition, you've got to decide which features in a sound card are most important to you. These include:

▶ **Inputs and outputs**—The number of inputs and outputs you'll need depends a lot on how many instruments you'll typically be recording at once. If your studio is mainly a solo endeavor (just you), then you'll probably never need more than four ins/outs, since you'll rarely, if ever, need to record more than four mono or two stereo instruments simultaneously (let alone one). An exception to this is if you're a drummer and you want to isolate several pieces of the kit to its own track in the mix; in that case, having at least eight inputs and outputs is critical. Of course, if you're going to be recording more than a couple of musicians at one time, focus on eight ins/outs. The type of inputs and outputs is important, too: generally speaking, go with quarter-inch jacks.

▶ **Bit-depth**—Go with a minimum of 16 bits. Period. More than 16 is even better, and there are a number of cards that do 20-bit and 24-bit resolution these days. Though you'll end up downsampling to 16 bits when you cut your CD audio, just starting out in 24 bits will almost always give you a more accurate recording.

▶ **Interfaces**—Different sound cards have different types of additional interfaces, such as MIDI or S/PDIF. MIDI is important if you do MIDI (see chapters 9 and 10); SP/DIF is useful only if you have a mixing board or instruments (this would be unusual) that can take advantage of it. S/PDIF inputs for most sound cards use coaxial-based RCA connections that use an electrical digital signal—instead of optical signal—to transmit audio data. The KORG 1212 I/O, Digidesign AudioMedia III, E-MU Audio Production Studio, Ensoniq PARIS, Emagic Audiowerk, and Event Electronics' Layla (just to name a few) all have coax S/PDIF interfaces.

CHAPTER 3

▶ **Software support**—Stable software drivers for your sound card are very important. The rule is simple: Buy known brands, check the manufacturer's Web site, and read up on the brand name using Google.com. If the support area of the manufacturer's Web site completely sucks, or if every newsgroup posting about the card has something bad to say, then just stay away.

The section "Choosing and Installing a Sound Card," in Chapter 11, goes into a lot of detail about choosing and setting up your sound card. Suffice it to say, a cheap sound card is something you should try very hard to avoid.

If the Computer's the Heart, the Mixer's the Brain

There are actually *two* brains—the mixing capabilities of your software and an external mixer, if you use one. Should you use an external mixer? There are two schools of thought on this one.

The first route is that if you buy a sound card that has enough inputs and outputs (8/8 as a minimum), you may not need an external mixer at all. You can use the inputs and outputs on the sound card and do your mixing right within SONAR, for example. On first glance, this approach seems fairly straightforward. But there is, as they say, more to the story.

The first problem with this is an ease-of-use problem. Depending on the sound card you use, you will either have a breakout box (a separate box hooked up to the sound card, with quarter-inch jacks, and usually rack-mountable), or you will be dealing with cables coming directly from the card. If you don't have a breakout box, you will find it difficult to manage the different cables, keep track of which instrument is plugged into which input, and easily manage switching cables around when the need arises.

If your sound card does utilize a breakout box, then you're in much better shape. However, depending solely on the inputs and outputs of the box means that you have no pre-fader control over the input signal, and you'll lose at least one of your outputs, because you'll need a pair of outputs for monitoring left and right channels. That brings you to three stereo channels or eight mono channels on a 8/8 sound card! In addition, you lose the ability to mixdown a piece of stereo equipment, such as the stereo outputs of a keyboard, to a mono input pre-fader, which can be frustrating if you don't want to lose both signals in the original sound or instrument.

The second solution makes a bit more sense: Use an external mixer in addition to your sound card. You can then use the software mixer to submix tracks, if you have more audio tracks than mixer outs, and take advantage of pre-fader adjustments to volume as well as some basic analog equalization, via the mixer, if needed.

In addition, you can use the mixer as your monitoring system and take advantage of features such as XLR connections for your microphones and onboard phantom power for mic(s). If you can afford a digital mixer, then you can even keep everything in the digital realm, too, but a digital mixer is not critical. The amount of signal loss you will experience by using a good Mackie or Behringer mixer is minimal compared to the ease of use and flexibility of the board.

You've Got to Have *Connections*

Properly connecting your equipment is, frankly, mostly common sense. You need to know the kinds of connectors and the lengths of the cables you'll be needing, because at some point you'll need to power it all up.

Cables

In order to keep cable lengths as short as possible, lay out your equipment beforehand, measure the distances between the needed connections, then plan and buy accordingly. This isn't just a cosmetic thing: Cables that are too long may eventually cause additional hum in the signal path, while cables that are too short are too easy to accidentally pull out or trip over.

TIP

Choosing appropriate lengths will also ensure that you aren't coloring the tone of the signal running through the cable any more than necessary. Cable *inductance*—how much the cable signal changes and when—often varies depending on how the cable is lying; usually, the more bunched-up it is, the higher the inductance. This is not good, since the higher the inductance, the more likely it will alter the tone of the audio signal.

Buy decent-quality cables. Don't scrimp unless you're on the slimmest of budgets and you have no choice. Most music stores, even ones catering to professional musicians and audiophiles, will sell an assortment of everything—from the low-end junk cables to the very high-end, expensive wires. The best route is to take a look somewhere in the middle. You'll be hard-pressed to find a lot of real sonic differences between the midrange-priced cables and the high-end stuff.

If you can, go with stock wire and buy your connectors separately. It's a bit more of a pain to solder connectors in, but in the long run, it's less expensive and easier for you to maintain consistent quality.

Cable prices will vary, depending mostly on capacitance and resistance, and the rule is the lower the better. Low resistance means a stronger signal, and low capacitance means better frequency response. Cable with good resistance will be under 100 ohms per 1,000 feet, while capacitance is typically under 100 pf (picofarads) per foot.

NOTE

Most, but not all, semi-pro and professional microphones (the Rode NT-1, for example) are "low impedance," which means the mic is designed to connect to a pre-amp with an impedance of under 1,000 ohms. Conversely, there is "high impedance," which runs from 20,000 ohms on up and covers just about all guitars and electronic instruments.

Make sure you match impedances. Low impedance connections are quieter and can use fairly long runs of cable of 50 feet or more, while high impedance connections should use the shortest cable possible—usually less than 25 feet.

http://www.muskalipman.com

For cables with built-on connectors, look closely at the connectors. The area of the cable which connects to the connector and the connector itself are responsible for about 95 percent of all cable failures—it's rarely a short or a break in the middle of the cable somewhere—so this step is critical. Look for:

▶ **Metal casings**—Forget about the cable if the connectors do not use metal covers.

▶ **Heat-shrink tubing surrounding the wire underneath the connector**—You can check for this by unscrewing the connector.

▶ **Connectors that appear to be solid and heavy duty**—not flimsy.

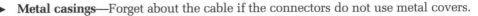

NOTE

Generally speaking, cables with pre-molded connectors are a bad idea. Plugs that have tight, plastic molded ends may look pretty but will fail, and fail fast, at the junction of the wire and connector. Many pre-molded cables also use poor shielding and are very high capacitance.

Cables that are spiral wound are also a no-no (most of them, anyway: There are some high-end cables that are self-retracting, but they are very, very expensive).

The cable itself should be fairly heavy, up to a quarter-inch thick for high impedance cables, and almost as thick for low impedance XLR cables. Check for a manufacturer's warranty as well—it can come in very handy, and a number of midrange cables offer lifetime warranties.

Figures 3.6, 3.7, and 3.8 show low impedance, high impedance, and speaker cable, respectively. Note that speaker cable differs most from the other two types in that it is not shielded. This is typically the case, and it is fine for the speaker cables connecting to your monitors. All other audio cables should always be shielded—either low impedance or high impedance, depending on the piece of equipment. No exceptions to this: Never use unshielded cable for anything other than speakers.

Figure 3.6
A low impedance cable is a balanced connection with two main wires and shielding.

Plastic or rubber cover

Shielding

Wire 1

Wire 2

Figure 3.7
A high impedance cable
has only one main wire
and a ground wire.

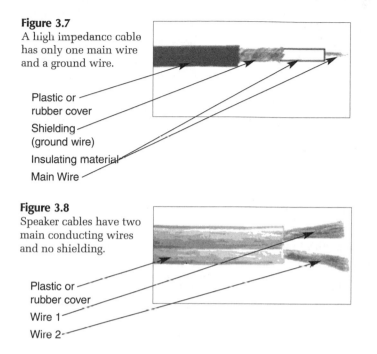

Plastic or
rubber cover

Shielding
(ground wire)

Insulating material

Main Wire

Figure 3.8
Speaker cables have two
main conducting wires
and no shielding.

Plastic or
rubber cover

Wire 1

Wire 2

You will also need to determines the types of connectors you'll need; most likely, they will fall into one of three categories: quarter-inch phono plugs, XLR, or RCA:

▶ **Quarter-inch plugs**—These are the most common in any home studio, and you'll use them to connect up most of your gear. Switchcraft (**www.switchcraft.com**) is pretty much the industry standard, but they aren't cheap. They are, however, far superior to connectors purchased from the likes of Radio Shack and other hardware retailers. This is not to knock Radio Shack: They are the only game in town on a Sunday at 4:30 in the afternoon, and thank Buddha for 'em, but you do get what you pay for. A quarter-inch plug will have a ring tip, which is the main signal wire, while the rest of the plug is the ground.

▶ **XLR connectors**—These rugged plugs are used in mics as well as in some PA systems. Mic cables that use XLR connections at both ends typically have a male connector at one end and a female connector at the other and, with low impedance gear, can be easily strung together for increased distance. XLRs have three pins—two for the main signal wires and the third (along with the rest of the plug) for the ground. Make sure when you wire an XLR cable that you mark which pins go to what, to avoid wiring it backwards.

▶ **RCA plugs**—RCA connectors are the least common type of connector in most studio gear, but you will invariably have to deal with them. If you have to move RCA-based cables around too much, they will quickly become, for the most part, unpredictable and noisy. If you use gear with RCA plugs, it's not a bad first place to check if line noise suddenly pops up out of nowhere.

CHAPTER 3

The Joy of Soldering

To do all this cabling and connecting stuff right, you're going to have to splurge for a soldering kit and learn how to use it (hint: read the kit's manual). Don't just jump right into it—you want to *avoid* damaging connectors and wire when you work on your cables.

One tip: To keep the frequency of explicatives down, don't forget to put connector covers on *before* you solder the connector to the cable. That way, you won't have to un-solder what you just soldered. Make sure you put the cover on facing the right direction, too.

In addition to solder, use electrical tape liberally—for instance, around the wires you solder to the connector and any potential stress areas in the cable itself.

Actually, the most difficult part of soldering is probably not the soldering: It's stripping the wire and dealing with braided shielding. But over the long haul, you'll save money and get consistently better sounding recordings, hands down.

The only downside to becoming the soldering expert Mother always wanted you to be is that the activity itself spews out poisonous chemicals such as pinene. Breathing in these fumes has been known to cause headaches, nausea, eye diseases, and worse. Proceed with caution.

Electric Studioland

In addition to cabling and connectors, don't forget about the electrical outlets you'll be plugging everything into. The physical location of your gear should be as close as possible to an outlet, and you should use outlets—a dedicated circuit, if possible—that are not being used for other appliances or electrical sources in the house.

In fact, one of the most common causes of electrical fires is the improper use of extension cords. If you're using a typical-quality household extension cord and running from an outlet to all of your studio equipment, say, ten to twenty devices or more, spend a few bucks on a halogen fire extinguisher, which is specially designed to put out electrical fires.

In addition, if you're the kind of person who makes performance art with power strips, then make sure you buy strips with built-in circuit breakers or surge protection—the kind that will shut down in the case of a short. And if any of your gear has internal fuses (power amplifiers, older synthesizers, speakers), use only the fuses recommended by the manufacturer. A spare fuse or two ain't a bad idea, either.

In short, use the best surge protection, electrical-related components, and extension cords you can afford.

If you don't have relatively easy access to an outlet or your recording space is in need of power or re-wiring, do yourself a favor: Hire an electrician to do whatever needs to be done. Unless you are totally comfortable with electrical wiring or have significant experience with wiring, don't mess with it. You probably wouldn't defend yourself in court, nor would you perform open heart surgery on yourself. Fooling around with anything electrical without knowing precisely what you are doing is just as serious, if not more so.

Finally, if you can hook up all of your gear so that you can power it all up with one switch, you'll find the process of getting started with any session (especially those spur-of-the-moment creative impulses) much easier than if you have to power up every single piece of equipment while the bell tolls. This goes for your cable connections, too. All this is facilitated through the use of a good patch bay, which is discussed in detail in Chapter 13.

4

Listen to You

If you plan on recording vocals, this chapter is for you. Heck, even if you have a master plan to conquer the classical music world, this chapter is for you. Why? Because the human voice is just about one of the hardest things on earth to record well, so knowing a thing or two about vocal recording techniques will spill over into any recording you do.

This chapter covers the following topics:

► Evaluating your own vocals

► Selecting a vocal microphone

► Group vocal recordings and background vocals

► Vocal mixes and effects

Your Voice

Let's start by taking a quick look at the physical mechanics of a singing voice. If you "don't sing" (kind of like the way some musicians "don't dance"), you may feel the need to skip over this section and go on to "Selecting a Microphone." But stick with this one for a bit, because understanding a little about how a singing voice works will go a long way toward helping you to understand how to record it.

That said, it should be noted that the human voice is a complex topic unto itself and is the subject of countless books, university courses, and, these days, Web sites. This chapter, let alone this book, can in no way cover the subject in detail. In fact, there are a number of techniques for learning to sing well and some of them are quite different in their approaches. Most of them start with the same fundamental concepts, though, so we'll cover them briefly here and try to interpret them in a way that makes sense.

Posture

Good posture is a big deal for an opera singer and probably a bit less of a big deal for a rock singer, but it winds up being important in either case. The bottom line is that you'll generally sing better if you're relaxed and don't feel tension in your upper body. Try not to slump your shoulders too much or stick your chin up (or out), but stay relaxed.

Breathing

Breathing properly when singing is always critical, but unless you practice your breathing for a long time, it's difficult to understand just how it helps. After all, it's an involuntary gig to begin with, as we all remember from our sixth-grade health class. At a minimum, the more easily and comfortably you breathe, the better your singing will be. This means not singing when you have a lung infection or after your second pack of Marlboro Lights. Keeping your sternum lifted up so that your diaphragm moves more easily is the general rule of thumb.

Support

"Support" refers to how you control the air pressure in your lungs in order to hold the note or maintain accurate pitch. It's also how loudly or softly you're singing and, to some extent, your tone. All this relates to how much air you're pumping in and out of your lungs; the key is to stay relaxed and consistent to keep from producing sudden bursts of air.

Registers

The idea of a "register" varies widely, but what most vocal coaches (and listeners!) will agree on is that breaks, or noticeable transitions between notes, in a singer's register are not pretty. For example, if your voice cracks, you are "breaking up" and it generally doesn't sound good. The idea (or ideal—both work in this case) is to maintain a consistent sound, which, practically speaking, often means simply singing within your range and knowing how far you can push yourself during a performance.

Resonance

Resonance often has more to do with what happens as the air is on its way out of your mouth and into the microphone. How you move your jaw and tongue, a nasal inflection, the movement of the soft palate, and even the larynx itself—all have a great deal to do with resonance. Doing your Bob Dylan impersonation is an example of changing how your vocal sound resonates.

Expressing Yourself

Expression is the most subjective part of singing and also the most critical. The "dynamics" of your voice, its unique tone, the speed with which you sing, how clearly you sing the words, the interplay of the lyrics with the notes—these are the things that ultimately have the most impact on your singing. This has as much to do with the material itself as it does your emotional state when you sing.

No one can tell you how to express yourself, because that's your unique vibe, what you bring to the table as a singer (and sometimes, as a recording engineer, to recording the singer). At the moment of expression, you aren't typically thinking about your posture, or breathing, or resonance—or any of the other physical elements that are helping you to express yourself in song.

In fact, that's the whole point of this section—that your expression should be *your* expression, not something else. What's "something else?" Well, it could be your impersonation of Bob Dylan, which, unless you're a standup comic or a singer in a cover band, is *Bad* with a capital "B."

Above all, you should strive to be yourself, to sing how you sing (whatever that is) and not imitate someone else. This is one of the biggest problems with singers and has been the cause of many a band's demise; often singers who keep trying to emulate their favorite rock stars end up being unable to get in touch with the material they're singing. Though imitation might be the sincerest form of flattery, it is also a sure-fire way to sing off-key, out-of-range, and in a completely different emotional direction than the song itself demands. This makes for mediocre performances and, in most cases, mixdown nightmares.

Don't fudge on the one thing you've got that nobody else has—you. Even if you're covering a song, it's your interpretation of the song and your own expression of it that matter, not your attempt to try to sound like the singer who has already brought his or her own unique vibe to the song.

End of soapbox. High horse dismounted. Let's move on to something you *should* imitate as much as your wallet will allow—the intelligent selection and acquisition of a damn good microphone.

Selecting a Microphone

Recording vocals—more so than any other instrument—is *almost* as subjective for the home recording artist as it is for professional studio engineers. I say "almost," for two reasons. First, in a home recording setup, you are less likely to use a microphone for anything other than vocals (with the possible exception of guitars and live drums—see chapters 6 and 7, respectively). Second, as a home recording artist, you may not be able to afford the space, instruments, or multiple microphones necessary to make a lot of live recording very worthwhile.

One thing's for sure: The growth of home recording over the last several years has brought with it an explosion in the number of cheap microphones available as well as cheap microphone preamps. Manufacturers have responded to budding musicians and home recording artists everywhere by creating lots of low-end models which, when you get down to the nitty-gritty, all sound about the same and will give you the same horrible results.

NOTE

A microphone preamp is an amplifier that takes the microphone output signal (sometimes with the aid of a small DC 48-volt voltage circuit) and amplifies that signal from around –60 to –50 dbV to an acceptable recording level of either –10 dbV or +4 dbU. This is necessary because most microphones don't have enough signal amplification built in. The term "preamp" rather than just "amp" is used because the level of amplification is not typically enough to be heard clearly, but it is enough for an external preamp or mixer to amplify further. Yeah, you guessed it: "preamp" stands for "pre-amplification."

TIP
Never record your vocals by plugging a mic directly into the eighth-inch jack
on your sound card. Use the mic inputs in your external mixer or a separate
external mic preamp. The frequency response of a typical sound card's
microphone input is not hot enough to give anything resembling a good
performance.

Microphone Types

There are two fundamental types of microphones (there are a few others, such as ribbon
microphones, but we won't cover them here): dynamic and condenser. While you'll find
dynamic microphones are cheaper, they don't pack anywhere near the punch of (usually more
expensive) condenser mics for vocal recording.

Dynamic Microphones

Dynamic mics use a wire coil suspended over a magnet to pick up sound waves (see Figure 4.1).
The coil moves in response to sound over the magnet and produces voltage that is the electronic
equivalent of the sound. Dynamic mics output a reasonably accurate reproduction of sound, but
their accuracy is determined more by fluctuations in voltage rather than in the source sound,
e.g. your singing.

Figure 4.1
A dynamic microphone operates like a speaker "in reverse." The "diaphragm" is moved by the air waves from sound.

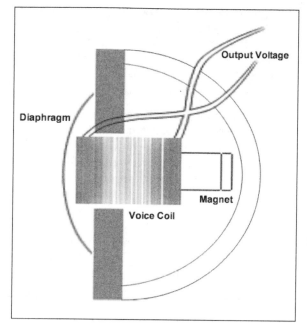

Small diaphragm dynamic microphones are far and away the most popular mics used for live recording and live performance. Because of their simple design, they can withstand a lot of abuse and they don't require a voltage source to work properly. Two of the most commonly used dynamic mics are the Shure SM-58 and SM-57 models, but there are many other, similar dynamic mics from companies like Audio-Technica, Sennheiser, AKG, and Sony. At the time of this writing, most of them can be bought for less than $100.

TIP

Those cheap Radio Shack mics you can buy for $10 or the generic computer mics you've seen at the check-out stand are dynamic, small diaphragm mics, too. Unless you are on the slimmest of all possible budgets, don't touch them. No matter how good your voice or your singer's voice sounds, these mics will never give you a good sound.

CHAPTER 4

There are also large diaphragm dynamic mics. Though less common, they are used for very loud, bass-heavy instruments such as kick drums, bass amp speakers, brass instruments, and, in some cases, guitar amps (no pun intended!). They are not best for recording vocals, however (unless all your vocals are spoken-word only). A very popular large diaphragm dynamic microphone is the ElectroVoice RE-20, which has been a favorite among broadcasters and engineers (for drums) for many years, as has the Shure SM-7.

The bottom line with dynamic microphones and vocal recording in the home studio is that, while you will get a fairly accurate general vocal reproduction, you will rarely achieve a warm, rich sound while accurately conveying the mid-range and high-range frequencies—and the mids and highs are typically the most important part of a vocal performance. For truly killer vocal recording, you've got to consider a condenser mic—there's just no way around it.

Condenser Microphones

Condenser (or capacitor) mics capture sound a bit differently than dynamic mics. As shown in Figure 4.2, a condenser mic uses a stretched diaphragm running parallel to a thin, charged plate. Electrical current is sent through both the diaphragm and the plate, and fluctuations in the diaphragm create slight changes in current, producing an output signal. The charge itself typically comes from a DC voltage source—either a battery or, in the case of a mic preamp or mixer, 48-volt "phantom power."

Figure 4.2
Air pressure from
sounds against a thin
diaphragm causes a
condenser microphone
to pick up detailed
frequencies.

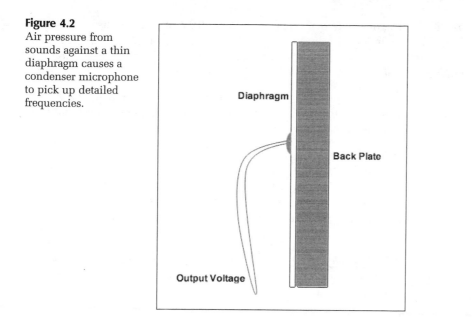

The key to the condenser mic is its two-piece design and its plate, which is always charged. The diaphragm can also be made quite thin, so condenser mics tend to be much more accurate than dynamic mics, particularly in the mid and high frequencies. These are exactly the places you want accuracy when recording vocals.

The flip side is that condenser microphones are not usually as rugged as dynamic mics, which makes them difficult to maintain for stage use. However, with a minimal amount of care, they are perfectly suited to a studio environment.

Of course, just like dynamic mics, there are both small and large diaphragm condenser microphones. Small diaphragm condenser mics have great high-frequency response and are excellent for drums and cymbals, acoustic guitars, or just about any other stringed instrument where high frequencies are critical.

For vocals, however, large diaphragm condenser mics are as good as it gets. With a large diaphragm, you achieve a fuller, warm sound, but you have all the advantages of a condenser mic's design—meaning the mids and highs are accurate and rich.

A number of condenser mics are worth mentioning. German-made Neumann condenser microphones are highly popular, from the vintage sound of a U 87 or U 89 to Neumann's recent tube mics, the M 147 and M 149. These are very good choices. AKG is another company that produces sterling-quality large-diaphragm condenser mics. Their fairly recent C 12 VR model and the C 414 series are excellent condenser microphones and are popular in professional studios (as are the Neumanns).

Of course, the Neumanns and the AKGs of the world share one thing in common: They are not only expensive new (well into the thousands of dollars) but, in many cases, more expensive used (particularly the original, vintage U 87s and U 89s).

Thankfully, there are a few good, low-end choices that are, remarkably, very close in sound quality to the expensive mics. These economical large-diaphragm condensers have become quite popular just in the last few years. The Rode NT1 and NT2 are excellent examples of very high, yet affordable, quality. At the time of this writing, for example, an NT1 can be found for less than $200. The mic lacks some of the frills of expensive large diaphragm condenser mics—such as multiple response patterns, a pad, a roll-off filter—but that's just fine, because you don't need these accessories to get a stellar vocal sound with the NT1. (That, incidentally, is why we're not covering these kinds of features in any depth.) Other good choices on the low end of the condenser cost spectrum include the AKG C3000B and the Shure SM87.

Response Patterns, AKA "Pickup Patterns"

Every microphone possesses a particular response, or "pickup," pattern—meaning the ability of the mic to capture all or some of the sound in the space surrounding it. (Note: Many large diaphragm mics feature dual diaphragms that can be switched between different patterns.) Although there are actually several different kinds of pickup patterns, most of them are based on three fundamental patterns.

Omnidirectional

A good omnidirectional mic is great for capturing sound in open spaces, making it ideal for acoustic instruments or live background vocals. An omnidirectional pickup pattern, as shown in Figure 4.3, is able to pick up sounds coming from all sides of the microphone.

Figure 4.3
An omnidirectional pattern is ideal for capturing ambience and sound in open spaces.

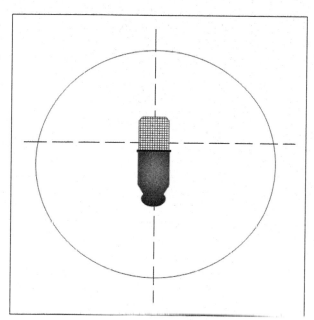

Cardioid (Unidirectional)

A cardioid mic pattern (see Figure 4.4) detects sound coming from directly in front of the mic, while sounds to either side are barely detected, and sounds behind the mic are ignored.

The cardioid mic pattern is an excellent pickup pattern for vocal recording in the home studio. Since sound from the back and sides of the mic come close to being ignored altogether, you'll pick up less unnecessary noise in a studio that isn't fully soundproof, while the front of the mic will be dedicated to outputting your vocal performance. Cardioid mics are useful for live stage sound for the same reasons.

Figure 4.4
The cardioid pattern is
heart-shaped (hence its
name). Its pattern of
response makes it the
all-around best choice
for multipurpose
recording in the home
studio.

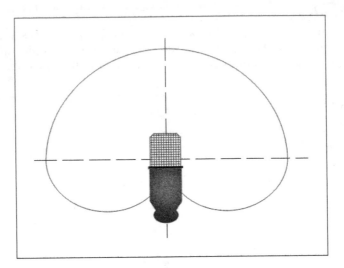

Figure-8 (Bidirectional)

Figure-eight mics have a pickup pattern shaped like—yes, you guessed it—a figure-8, and they pick up sound equally well from both the front and rear of the mic, while ignoring sounds from either side. Figure-8s work particularly well in small rooms, for live classical music, and for generating a stereo mic field.

Figure 4.5
A figure-8 pattern is
useful for setting up
a stereo mic field.

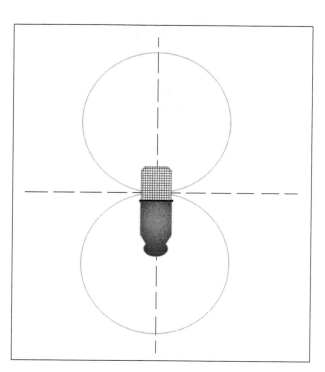

NOTE
A stereo mic field is probably something you won't be dealing with in the
home studio, since you can achieve all of your stereo effects in the mixdown.
It's most useful in a live recording situation where you want to create a live
stereo mix.

Vocal Microphone Placement

With a condenser mic, you're already one up on much of the home recording competition,
because you've opened the door to capturing a vocal performance with a very high degree of
accuracy, thanks to the high sensitivity of the condenser's design.

This does, however, bring up one small problem—a problem that exists in any case but is most
certainly a problem with a condenser microphone: placement of the microphone in your home
studio setup.

In chapters 2 and 3, you learned about the important parts of putting together space and equipment that work with your budget, musical goals, and recording style. You learned that how you set up every piece of the equipment in the studio can greatly affect your performance and mixdown process. This is especially important when recording vocals.

This is a good place to put on your finicky, particular, anal-retentive hat; stressing over mic placement is actually going to be healthy for you in the long run, because the results will be worth it. Ask yourself the following questions:

1. What's my singing style (or the singing style of the vocalist(s) I'll be recording)?
2. How close to the mic do I like to get?
3. How much soundproofing do I have in the studio?
4. Am I using headphones or monitors?

Singing Style

How do you move when you sing? Do you plant yourself in one spot and croon like Sinatra (rest his soul) or do you feel the need to do gymnastics like Mick Jagger?

If you're a mover and a shaker—and you can't seem to keep it from happening—you're going to have a few problems in the home studio, and those will affect the kind of mic(s) you choose.

You'll probably want an omnidirectional mic so that you can hear all of the performance. The downside to this is that because of its wide pickup field, an omnidirectional will be noisier than a cardioid or figure 8. Which means you need a quieter room, and that means more expense (see Chapter 2 again!).

While there are no set rules, ideally you want to sing directly into the diaphragm of the microphone, which is called singing "on-axis." Singing on-axis is going to give you the most faithful reproduction of the performance, but it may not be the most intuitive way for you to sing or "work the mic."

Working the Mic

"Working the mic" is what many experienced vocalists do. It's different for every singer, of course, but it comes down to manipulating distance and position from the mic in order to accentuate the good areas of a singer's voice and play down the bad areas.

In addition, moving closer or further away from the mic can also have a big effect on how intimate or distant the vocal line is. An experienced singer will often use slight changes in position to make parts of the vocal more or less dramatic. Of course, a singer isn't thinking about these things during the performance, and a singer isn't typically going to calculate or script the performance beforehand to ensure that the vocal line follows the material emotionally. It's a completely intuitive thing, as it should be.

CHAPTER 4

Pattern Selection and Microphone Placement

As a home recording artist, you may have to dissect the process a little bit for your own vocal style (or the style of the singer you're recording). This is not far off from what a professional studio engineer must do. A full-time professional engineer gets to see and hear it all—from the mumbling, wobbly grunge singer to a stuttering choir to the vocalist who eats the mic as much as she sings into it.

But a professional studio has the luxury of employing different types of microphones in a fully soundproofed, controlled environment. This is probably not what you've got to work with, so you'll need to select a mic that, to a large degree, is based on how you work the mic. Here are some tips:

▶ For most any large diaphragm condenser mic, the ideal place to position it is slightly higher than the vocalist's mouth, with the mic pointed downward toward the singer. This arrangement is almost directly on the diaphragm and has the added advantage of providing a bit more breathing room and a more "open" feeling for the singer.

▶ How "dead" the room is can be critical to vocal recording. On a limited budget, you want the room as soundproofed as it can possibly be. The "natural" reverb in the room is something that, for a home studio setup, will ultimately be more of a hindrance than a help when it comes to mixdown time. You can (and will, in many cases, depending on your vocal sound preferences) add reverb or other effects during recording for monitoring only (that is, you don't actually record the effects, just the singing), but you should always record vocals completely dry.

NOTE

Suggesting that you circumvent the natural sound of your recording space for the driest possible vocal sound is not exactly a commandment on the professional engineer's wall. In fact, in a professional environment, it can practically be bad advice. Again, this is because a professional studio simply has the resources (such as a few dozen expensive microphones and $500-a-sheet soundproofing material) that you don't have. If your aim is to get the vocal as close to authentic as possible, while preserving the performance for maximum flexibility during mixdown, always record the vocals without any effects whatsoever.

▶ You'll want to use a "pop filter" (also called a "windscreen") to keep the "p's" and "b's" (and a few other consonants) from ruining an otherwise good performance. A pop filter prevents unwanted air blasts generated by the pronunciation of certain words and consonants from making their way into the recording.

TIP

Pop filters can be had for as little as $20 up to well over $100. Here is the $2 alternative method which, incidentally, works quite well:

1. Obtain a pair of pantyhose from your local department store. Size and quality do not matter (unless you plan on wearing them first!), so the $2 pair or the 99 cent special will do just fine.

2. Procure a metal coat hanger from your closet or from the closet of someone you love.

3. Stretch the pantyhose (just the hose part, not the cotton crotch) over the hanger and fasten with a good tape such as clear packing tape.

4. Secure the top part of the hanger to your mic stand, just below the microphone itself, using a pair of pliers and/or additional tape. Alternatively, you can attach the hanger to a separate mic stand.

5. Bend your new apparatus so that the triangular part of the hanger (the part with the pantyhose attached) is positioned about 6 inches directly in front of the microphone's diaphragm.

6. Test your new invention by singing "Peter Piper picked a peck of pickled peppers" to the tune of McCartney's "Yesterday" and record the results.

Getting the Right Kind of Feedback

Headphones should almost always be used when recording vocals—unless you can afford a small, completely dead room with high-quality monitors just for singing. Even then, headphones are the surest way to hear the singing and the music as clearly and flexibly as possible. And it goes without saying that you do not want to deal with feedback from monitor speakers during vocal recording. With sensitive condenser mics in particular, this is exactly what you will be dealing with.

The Headphone Mix

Getting a good headphone mix is critical, for good reason: You want the headphone mix to sound as much like the finished product as possible, since the mix of the other instruments may have a huge effect on how the vocal line is performed.

This shouldn't stop you from experimenting with changing the headphone mix as the vocal takes wear on, though. In fact, this can be crucial. When you're singing, the most important part of your performance tends to be the volume of your voice in the mix relative to the volume of the other instruments. For some singers, hearing themselves loudly and clearly is important; for others, inspiration comes more easily if the music shares equal billing or is louder.

TIP

Adding a little reverb for warmth to a vocal headphone mix—while still recording the track dry—can often extract a slightly more passionate performance. The reverb will tend to smooth out your voice so that you sound a little better than you, well, sound!

But as time wears on, changing up the volume levels of the other instruments in the mix can go a long way toward keeping a singer inspired and "into" the song. Be willing to change the volume levels to keep the inspiration high.

Headphone Mix for Multiple Vocals

Picking one's voice out of the music mix is one thing, while picking out the lead vocal among other human voices is quite another.

A tried-and-true technique for singing the lead vocal over backing vocals (or vice versa) is to listen with only one ear to the headphone while singing. It seems pretty obvious and works quite well—kind of like that old bend-your-ears trick you may have experimented with in third grade—but you'll want to be careful not to record audible leakage from the unused side of the headphones. Make sure the unused headphone is held tightly against your head to keep the leakage to a minimum.

That brings us to the subject of multiple vocals in general. The next section is a closer look at some techniques for recording both multiple vocal lines and backing vocals.

A Multiple Vocal Primer

As a home recording artist, adding additional vocals can be some of the hardest work you'll do—next to mixing all those vocals down (see Chapter 13 for more details).

Unless you're doing post-Laurie Anderson, experimental crowd-noise ambient music, if you intend to record more than one vocal track into the song, it's usually for one of three reasons:

1. To add vocal harmony or a countermelody to the song.
2. To reinforce the vocal line by doubling (or tripling, or quadrupling) the line.
3. Both 1. and 2.

Okay, so technically it could be for three of three reasons, but you get the point: You can reinforce any sung line by re-recording it or duplicating it as many times as you want (commonly known as "stacking" vocals), or you can simply add different parts.

As you'll see, which direction you head ultimately has less to do with how the song is written and more to do with the dynamic of the song as it unfolds during both arranging and recording: Do you want big and glossy vocals or stripped-down, natural harmonies? Let's briefly look at both approaches.

Stacking Vocals

Stacking vocals—recording the same lines over and over or duplicating those lines in your audio recording software—is a common technique (think Brian Wilson). It produces a fat, somewhat glossy sound that tends to hide flat notes and pitch problems.

An important aspect of stacking vocals is re-recording the same performance rather than simply copying one track over and over using your digital recording software. Why? Because of the subtle differences in the performances, which creates bits of dissonance that give each

CHAPTER 4

performance a slightly different vibe. This produces that full, "wall of sound" sound. Though you may be tempted to fire up SONAR and start layering vocal tracks by copying performances to new tracks, predictable results are hard to achieve.

It follows that in the home studio you can stack effectively by singing and recording the line over and over, but you can also achieve a very similar effect by employing a vocal "harmonizer"—an external device that works in real time or during mixdown—or by using a software effect that can transpose a vocal line to whatever pitch or part you desire. There are advantages and disadvantages to each.

Vocal Harmonizers

Vocal harmonizers work by adding on the harmony parts you specify in real time. At the time of this writing, these pieces of hardware (from small box devices to rack-mount units with more features) range in price from about $300 upwards to $2,000 or more.

A vocal harmonizer is a rather sophisticated piece of effects gear. It works by employing algorithms that transpose your voice in real time to any number of steps above or below each note you're singing.

The least expensive units typically have less capability, but they are still remarkably good. Digitech's Vocalist Performer, for example, is less than 7 inches square and weighs about a pound, and although it doesn't support MIDI, it can provide up to two harmony vocals to accompany your vocal performance. It even offers three reverb presets for different room ambiances. With only six possible harmonic variations, you can combine and create hundreds of different stacks.

It also has doubling capability, which is just enough pitch transposition to create dissonance.

More expensive models are MIDI-equipped and provide almost unlimited combinations of harmonies at every half-step along the scale (they also do straight-up pitch shifting in a number of other scales and some remarkable things with dissonance). The bottom line is that a vocal harmonizer can be a very useful addition to your vocal performances if stacking the vocals suits the dynamic of the song you're recording.

NOTE

For excessive detail on MIDI, start with Chapter 9.

Software Harmony

Another option is mixing the harmonies during mixdown through the use of software or DirectX plug-ins that alter pitch. There are numerous applications available these days that do just that, so it shouldn't come as too much of a surprise that the most significant aspect of pitch-shifting software is just how widely the quality varies.

For example, the standard pitch-shifting algorithms which come with SONAR (see Figure 4.6)—while they work easily in real time—are not going to produce a realistic wall of harmonic sound. The pitch-shifter in Sonic Foundry's XFX1 DirectX pack is slightly better, but there are also a number of other DirectX plug-ins on the market which will give you a higher-quality shift in pitch. PurePitch, from WaveMechanics, is quite good (but currently PurePitch is available only for the Macintosh platform), though a bit on the expensive side at around $500 at the time of this writing.

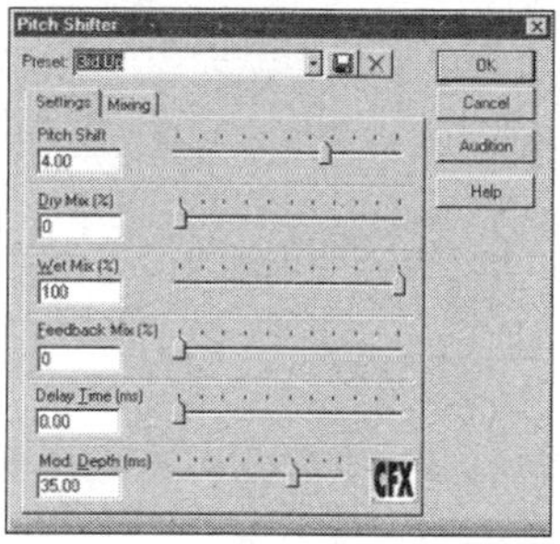

Figure 4.6
The standard pitch-shifter in SONAR is great for playing around with, but it doesn't give a very realistic sound.

How About Pitch-Shifting That Pitch-Corrects?

If you've ever put everything you've got into a lead vocal, only to discover that you've missed the pitch-mark a few times, you know the frustration that comes with trying to "fix" a vocal performance. It seems that the more you punch-in, edit, copy, and paste, the more the emotional vibe of the performance degrades. Even if you do finally get the flat spots edited out, you always seem to lose that original "special something" that was in the performance.

The Antares Auto-Tune DirectX plug-in (it's also available in a single rack-mount piece of hardware) is a great example of a solution to this problem. Auto-Tune is a set of very well-written algorithms that correct pitch deficiencies with great precision, in real time, at a speed as fast as 4 milliseconds (which is faster, by the way, than MIDI, which runs at around 7 milliseconds).

Auto-Tune has an automatic mode for quick and easy use and a graphical mode for more anal-retentive tweaking. The graphical mode is useful for things like clearing up small, unwanted inflections, removing vibrato, or employing unusual scales.

Toward a More Perfect Harmony

If you're going for a more natural, stripped-down harmonic sound, you usually start by limiting the harmonies to one or two parts, and you rarely, if ever, double the vocal lines. The result is a more realistic harmony, something you can't achieve very easily through stacking. If you want to evoke a sense of intimacy, for example, this technique works best (think The Eagles).

In terms of backing vocals, there is another layer of reality to this approach, however. The reality is that to achieve an intimate, more natural-sounding backing vocal track, you'll need to plan on doing a minimum of effecting and/or compression to the track. This is because, rather than doubling your vocal takes for that thick, "wall of sound" vibe, you'll most likely be piecing together the best parts in the final mixdown.

This also means re-evaluating the kind of mic you need as well as the sound of your recording space. In order to successfully pull together a number of recordings of the same parts and use them in different places, you want the most consistent sound you can get in the first place—otherwise, you'll have a devil of a time getting the different takes to match up, not to mention normalizing the volume of the different tracks.

By default or design, achieving a more perfect harmony is more difficult than stacking vocal tracks, and you're simply limited in how far you can go with the subject of the next section: vocal mixing.

Vocal Mixing

The reality of home studio recording is how involved you are in every aspect of a project. If you write the music, play the instruments, sing the vocals, record the tracks, and then mix it yourself, your objectivity almost vanishes. And if you have to spend hour upon hour getting the mixdown just right, you no longer have anything approaching objectivity: You have become so close to the project that an objective set of ears is impossible.

Such is life, and there's not a lot you can do about it. You don't have $300 an hour to hire a professional engineer to provide that objectivity for you, so you have no choice but to reach for it yourself.

It follows then that you want to do as little mixdown as possible, while still acknowledging that you needed all that room you gave yourself when you were tracking. This is especially true with vocals.

TIP
The word "tracking" is just another way of saying "recording a track." If you crash a party at a professional studio, use the word "tracking" and they'll think you're one of them.

Troubleshooting Vocal Mixes

Each mix is different, but you'll notice that with almost every mix, several common problems can crop up again and again. Being as close to the music as you are, you may not always notice them, though, so this section is little bit about what to look for and remember during vocal mixdown.

The Problem Could Be Noise

Most people easily recognize distortion or unwanted noise, but knowing what causes it and how to avoid it is not always so easy.

The easiest distortion to understand and fix is the ugly crackling noise that happens when you overload an AD/DA converter during digital recording or when you've cranked up the mic's input gain way too high. The solution is obvious: Lower the mic gain until you're consistently normalizing the mic's signal path. The trick is not to lower the gain so much that you introduce other kinds of noise, such as humming or RF noise.

There are two ways to approach getting the gain just right, and both of them should be utilized:

1. Check the mic's maximum SPL (sound pressure rating) and don't exceed it. For example, the Rode NT2 has a maximum SPL of 135 dB, which means that anything louder than 135 dB is going to distort, period.

2. Experiment with the microphone! Get to know the mic before doing any "real" recording by putting it through several test runs, recording the tests, and playing them back to compare notes. Write it all down, and do it again. Once you get to know the mic and how far you can push it with your gear, you won't need to write anything down. But until then, do the math.

There are also all kinds of other noises that make their way into your vocal mix that are not so obvious, and of course it's usually your other gear that's causing the distortion. Determining exactly which piece of gear is causing the problem is the difficult part. Other mics, a mic preamp, every mixer bus you use (and sometimes the ones you're not using), the computer or DAW (digital audio workstation), your other instruments—any of these can add distortion whenever their electro-mechanical limitations are exceeded. The only way to get a handle on all this is to understand what those limitations are, and that means experimenting with levels and cracking open a few manuals.

Since almost all manuals for any kind of recording or musical gear categorically suck, this is not an idea that will get you up in the morning, so look at it this way: If you test your gear once and take a few notes, you may never have to reach for a manual again (yeah, right).

The Problem Could Be Space

One of the easiest mistakes to make in the home studio is to overcompensate for the room's sound (and lack of soundproofing) by adding too many effects to the vocals. Reverb, delay, chorus, and all those other cool, exotic DirectX effects you just installed are great tools, and they go a long way toward adding ambience and realism to your vocal mix, but overusing them will take the life out of your performance before you know it.

Different effects have different values for you to control to manipulate the output of the effect; covering them all could turn out to be a very large book. The effect you'll use the most—and the one that can give you the biggest headaches—is reverb.

Reverb falls into three main areas: plate reverb, room reverb, and hall reverb. Plate reverbs usually offer shorter decay and, therefore, are best for vocals, while room and hall reverbs are generally best for your other instruments.

NOTE
Decay is the amount of time it takes for a reverb to fade. Short decay times will put a little edge back into your vocals when the lines start to bunch together in the mix, while long decay times create a kind of sustain effect that can be useful for dramatic transitions, like build-up between a chorus and a bridge.

The clever way to apply reverb is to use it according to the individual need of each vocal part—not applying it to everything at once. If you over-apply reverb to the entire vocal mix, you will be pushing the vocal sound further and further away from the rest of the mix, until the sound is too distant to be understood. And what you want is depth—not a misunderstanding.

Another way to compensate for a less-than-optimal recording space is to make judicious use of panning. The concept of panning is really simple: Every signal of every track you record can be placed at any point on the surface of the "stereo plane" (the audio landscape that represents your music being outputted to two or more speakers) to create variable sound positions, or a "three-dimensional" vibe to your vocals.

Experimenting with different pan settings can be quite revealing. For example, say you've recorded four similar vocal tracks, each with about the same volume and effects level. Table 4.1 suggests the kinds of variation in the mix you can generally expect by trying different pan settings:

Table 4.1
Panning Variations

Pan Settings	Result
All Centered	Maximum possible "closeness" or blend of all vocals.
1Left, 2&3&4 Centered	Vocal 1 will be much more present in the mix than the other vocals.
1Left, 2Left, 3Right, 4Right	Vocals 1 and 2 will blend together, as will vocals 3 and 4, but the distance between the two pairs will be very wide.
1Left, 2Left, 3Left, 4Right	Vocal 4 will be somewhat distant from the other three vocals, and even more distant from the music.
1Left, 2Right, 3&4 Centered	Vocals 3 and 4 will tend to blend with the music, and vocals 1 and 2 tend to compete with each other for room.

Table 4.1 is a generalization—your own mileage will undoubtedly vary according to the kind of vocals you're recording and your own style of music. But you get the idea: Panning is a very effective way of accentuating vocals when they're out of control and you're pulling back on them when necessary.

The Problem Could Be the Level

As we touched on earlier in the chapter, the human voice is highly prone to wide (some might say extravagant) dynamic fluctuations. Couple this with the way you or the singer works the mic, and you've got the potential for a lot of hard-to-handle level adjustments to make in the mixdown.

When this happens, compression is worth every penny you'll pay for it. A compressor can level out peaks in a vocal performance (or any other performance—bass, for example, is very commonly compressed during mixdown) by attenuating levels that go where you don't want them to. This applies to both boosting levels as well as quieting them, and smart use of compression is almost miraculous in its ability to make a molehill out of a mountain (or vice versa!).

Compressors vary widely in price. You can purchase anything from a small guitar-pedal compressor for around $50 to a sophisticated, knob-ridden rack-mount unit for thousands of dollars. There are also a number of good DirectX software-based compressors on the market.

In general, a good place to start compressing is with a compression ratio of about 2 to 1, with a small release, and with the gain at around 5-7 dB.

It should be noted that although using a compressor is an easy answer, it's not always the best answer. If you are working with audio recording software or a DAW, for example, the quickest and most effective technique is usually just to select the offending area of the vocal track and lower or raise the level.

The Problem Could Be the Frequency

EQ can be your friend or it can be your enemy—but most of time it's going to be your friend. Though Chapter 13 covers equalization in some detail, it's worth a mention here specifically with regard to vocals.

EQ is one of the more subjective aspects of listening to music. That's why even the cheapest of today's boom boxes has some form of EQ, because everyone likes to hear the music just a little bit differently. But there are a few guidelines useful for getting the most out of your vocal performances as they relate to the rest of the mix.

For example, in a typical pop song, the biggest concern is usually the relationship between vocals and drums. A good general tip here is to try and match the EQ levels of the lead vocal with the kick and snare drums so that they tend to dominate the song together—so that they occupy the same musical cubby-hole, if you will. Another way to even out your "wall of sound" backing vocals a little is to drop back on the 1K to 3K frequencies.

Table 4.2 shows the general effects of boosting vocal frequencies in some of the most common ranges:

Table 4.2
EQ Treatments.

Frequency	Result
200-500 Hz	Warm, thick, smooth
1K	Hollow, edgy, banging
3K	Punchy, excited, hot
5K	Bright, poppy, clear
7K	Slightly brighter
10K and above	Breathy, airy, sparkle

Of the above frequencies, 5K is the one you'll end up being concerned with the most when it comes to mixing vocals. 250K or so will add more warmth to your vocal performance, and 500K is sometimes very helpful when smoothing out harmonies or adding body to a lead vocal. If you're mixing backing vocals and you've already tweaked the levels to where you want them, try easing back or forward in the 5K to 7K range to get the most out of your EQ. If you're equalizing multiple lead vocal lines, you may also want to play with the 10K and higher ranges to add a little spark and realism back into the performances.

Phase Cancellation

If you're using more than one microphone for vocal recording, you run the risk of encountering problems with phase cancellation. Phase cancellation is when frequencies in one vocal performance cancel out frequencies in another, and vice versa. The amount of cancellation can vary widely. In general, the only way to prevent phase cancellation is to alter mic positions or attempt to reverse the phase by using an external adapter or your mixing console (or DAW), if it supports reversing phase.

The Zen of Microphones: Guidelines for Vocal Satori

Okay, so maybe the title of this section is a bit strong, but, hey, you want to end on a high note don't you? The following are some quick and dirty, yet highly useful, tips to remember for recording and mixing vocals:

▶ Always use your best mic for vocals (for some people this is a no-brainer, because you have only one mic!).

▶ Monitor your vocal performances with all the effects you want, but record them dry.

▶ Don't overdo reverb unless you just can't sing!

▶ If you are using a DAW or software recording, use a high-pass filter during mixdown—it can keep the vocal from becoming too muddy.

▶ Use headphones when recording vocals. Sealed headphones (the Sennheiser HD25 is a good example) are much better than open designs.

▶ Boosting frequencies between 200-300 Hz will make almost any vocal thicker.

▶ A short delay of up to 50 ms (milliseconds) can boost the "size" of your lead vocals and make them sound a bit "fatter."

5

Keyboards & Synths

For the home studio, a synthesizer is almost a requirement. Don't have the dough to hire a horn or string section? You can do an awfully good job of it with a decent synth. Need marimbas, a killer piano sound, and a drum kit, but wouldn't have the space for them even if you did have the money? A synth will, in all but the most demanding cases, do just fine. Synthesizers come in many forms and use a number of technologies, and knowing what works best for your musical style and skill may save you a bit of time, money, and a few headaches. This chapter will show you:

▶ How synthesizers work

▶ The differences in synth technology

▶ What kinds of synths are available

▶ The alternatives to traditional synthesizers

▶ How to select the right synth

▶ How different genres of music use synthesizers

Key Choices

There are lots of synthesizer choices—from sampling modules to digital stage pianos to full-fledged workstations to simple wave files in a DLS (DownLoadable Sounds) file on your computer. The main thing—other than General MIDI—that they typically share in common is expense: Unless you're rich, you'll probably be able to afford only one, at best a handful, of these instruments or modules.

To get to the heart of the kind of synthesizer you'll really use—the kind that will make you want to play it every time you see it—there are a few things you should know. Think of them as the Three Commandments of buying a synth. If Moses had been a musician, here's what he would have brought down from the studio with him:

▶ Thou shalt know a thing or two about the technology of the synthesizer.

▶ Thou shalt know what's available, what to look for, and the common similarities and differences between synthesizers.

▶ Thou shalt not get so caught up playing the ultra-cool sounds in the music store that thou forgetest that most of those sounds will never make their way into your recordings.

If you keep these commandments, you may just find yourself in synth heaven. The rest of this chapter is a roadmap for showing you how to reach that longed-for spot.

The Technology of Synthesizers

In the strictest sense of the word, a synthesizer is an electronic device that produces sound. In the common sense of the word, a synth is an electronic musical instrument.

Various synthesizers produce their sounds in different ways, and most are equipped with a piano keyboard. Though a keyboard is the most popular type of input device, a synth can use just about anything, really, like mouthpieces, guitar strings, drum pads, or even your computer's mouse or keyboard to control sounds. Whatever you use, the reality of what you're doing is simple: You operate a series of switches that turn sound circuits on and off.

Hence, synthesizers "synthesize" sound that can be used on stage or recorded along with natural instruments or other synthesized sounds. Some synths are used to mimic acoustic instruments such as flutes, brass, drums, or guitar, while others are used as electronic sound canvasses, capable of creating unique sounds that could never be created with acoustic instruments.

Historically, one of the first known electronic synthesizers—perhaps *the first*—was the "Cahill Telharmonium" built by Thaddeus Cahill in 1902. This "instrument" used a 200-ton array of 145 Edison dynamos that produced different pitched hums according to their speed; each of these coils was about the size of a refrigerator and, together, they filled an entire floor of a building in New York City. This made the whole setup a bit hard to gig with, so the output of the Telharmonium was "broadcast" over telephone lines.

NOTE

At the time of this writing, you'll find a complete write-up on the Telharmonium online at **www.obsolete.com/120_years/machines/ telharmonium/index.html**.

The earliest *portable* synthesizer was a device invented in the 1920s by Leon Theremin. The theremin consists of two antennae that create an audio circuit that can be modulated by moving a hand in between the antennae—one for controlling volume and other for pitch. Brian Wilson used a theremin to create those otherworldly sounds in the song, "Good Vibrations."

Other early synthesizers that attempted to build complex sounds from scratch with individual analog components were too big and expensive for anything other than strictly academic purposes. They were very unstable, often drifting out of tune, but in time engineers made them more reliable and practical to use. Most notably, Robert Moog's Minimoog synthesizer (Figure 5.1) captured the imagination of the music world in the late 1960s.

Figure 5.1
In its time, the
Minimoog was
revolutionary for its
compact size. (Photo
courtesy of Brandon
Daniel).

Oscillators

In the land of synthesizers, the primary source for generating sounds is the oscillator. An oscillator is a circuit that produces waveforms, which are types of audio waves. Early synths employed voltage-controlled oscillation, meaning they were operated by analog circuitry.

Each waveform has its own recognizable audio thumbprint; there are three basic waveforms—the sine, square, and sawtooth waves—from which almost all synthesizer sounds are produced. These are shown in Figures 5.2, 5.3, and 5.4 respectively.

Figure 5.2
Sine waves produce
sounds that are pure
and flute- or bell-like.

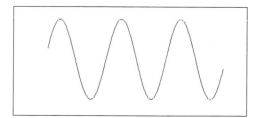

Figure 5.3
Square waves typically
sound bright and
hollow.

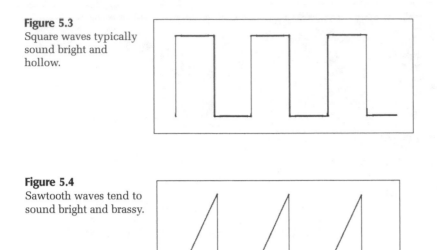

Figure 5.4
Sawtooth waves tend to
sound bright and brassy.

Of course, there are other types of waveforms, most notably rectangular, trapezoidal, and trigger waves. These, however, are essentially derivatives of the three fundamental waveforms.

NOTE
Some synthesizers feature a special source component called the white noise (or pink noise, in the case of early Moog modular synthesizers) generator. White noise is a waveform that would resemble a snow blizzard if measured on an oscilloscope. It is sometimes used to create special effects such as wind sounds or percussion instruments that are atonal in nature.

One of the most interesting facts about waveforms is that they will maintain their basic shape irrespective of changes in frequency (pitch) or amplitude (loudness). In fact, this leads to one of the most distinguishing abilities of the synthesizer as an instrument: It can generate a perfect sine wave.

Filters

One of the most powerful modulators available on a synthesizer is the filter. By removing different ranges in a waveform's frequencies, filters can alter the quality of that waveform. In fact, a sawtooth waveform can be reshaped into a mellower sine wave with proper filtration. This approach to synthesis is called subtractive synthesis (as opposed to additive synthesis, which combines simple waves into more complex waveforms) and represents the basis of sound generation on many synths, old and new. In essence, the tone control(s) on your home stereo are just simple filters.

The way in which a filter acts upon a source waveform depends upon the type of filter employed and its "cutoff" setting. For instance, a low-pass filter will "subtract" all harmonic overtones above 1000 Hz with a cutoff at 1 kHz. Unfortunately, filters don't do their job perfectly due to extraneous frequencies, known as "rolloff," which pass through as the filter closes in on a signal.

Some of the most common filters are:

▶ A Low-Pass filter, which rejects frequencies above a cutoff setting

▶ A High-Pass filter, which rejects frequencies below a cutoff setting

▶ A Band-Pass Filter, which rejects all frequencies outside a pre-determined band of frequencies

▶ A Band-Reject Filter, which rejects only the frequencies within a pre-determined band of frequencies

Filters can also have resonance, which refers to the slope of the filter's cutoff level. For example, when resonance is set high—meaning frequencies closest to the cutoff level are emphasized—a sort of vibrational effect occurs when any object comes in contact with the waveforms initiated by the sound source.

In general, the amount and kind of resonance is dependent on the makeup of the object. For example, the soft trailing tone of a piano after its hammer has struck has a completely different kind of resonance than what is created by your pick on a guitar string. However, on a synthesizer, the resonance created by a filter occurs at bands of frequencies usually either below or just above the cutoff level, and most synths are capable of some far-out resonances.

Envelopes

The purpose of an envelope generator is to add dynamics and flexibility to synthesized sounds, something that occurs naturally in the acoustic world but has to be made to happen in the synthesized world.

The envelope generator model evolved out of the standard low frequency oscillators that were voltage-controlled on early synths. There are four stages in the process of envelope generation: attack, decay, sustain, and release (ADSR). An envelope generator is a single ADSR oscillation that produces a dynamic contour each time a note is played or a key is struck.

NOTE

Technically speaking, envelopes were created to provide variable voltages set off by a single trigger as opposed to the continuously variable voltages provided by LFOs (low frequency oscillators).

Attack and Decay

Consider a banjo and a cello (not two instruments you'd likely hear playing together!). The picking style of a banjo player is very different from the bowing of a cello in many ways, but one important difference is the time it takes to produce the actual source sound and bring it to full volume. A pick does so quickly, but a bow is quite slow by comparison.

In a synthesizer, this is called the attack time, and it's the first variable piece of the process of envelope generation. The next piece is the decay time, which is how the harmonic content of a sound behaves just after it has begun. Envelope generators control the amplitude (volume) of the sound during both attack and decay, as well as the cutoff of the filter. Most often, both the volume and the filter are controlled by the same envelope generator; however, they can be controlled by separate envelopes.

Exactly how does it work? Consider an acoustic guitar: When a string is plucked, a waveform with lots of harmonic overtones is quickly produced. Then, the string is held and many of the harmonics begin to trail off. An envelope generator can replicate this event by rapidly amplifying the source signal and opening the filter connected to it (a short attack). This produces a loud signal with many frequency overtones. Thereafter, the envelope generator begins closing the filter, rejecting more and more upper harmonics (decay stage).

Sustain and Release

The point at which a guitar player holds the vibrating string with his finger corresponds to the sustain level of an envelope. During sustain, the filter will stay partially open, shaping the source waveform into a desired timbre. The volume may also be affected at this point, because the level is often less than the peak level of the attack stage.

The final stage is the release. This defines how a sound behaves once the key is "released" and source waveforms stop being generated. Amplification will begin to go toward zero and the filter completely closes. On an acoustic guitar, the release time is moderately fast, but this can vary depending on the resonant properties of the guitar body.

The envelope generator itself falls under the more general category of synthesis controllers. A controller is any component, analog or digital, that is applied to one or more of the primary sound generating elements: source, modulator, or amplifier. Controllers give you great flexibility by extending a keyboard's dynamic and sound shaping potential. In addition, a controller can also be the electronic keyboard or other input device itself. It "controls" the source waveform's frequency.

NOTE

Here is where things can get a little confusing. In the three-pronged model for sound generation, the oscillator is the chief sound-producing element. But an oscillator can also serve as a controller. For instance, a low-frequency oscillator (LFO) can be applied to a signal to create a vibrato effect. The oscillator creating the waveform and the oscillator causing the vibrato effect are two separate components. In fact, the frequency required to make a waveform is much higher than the one needed to produce vibrato.

The same LFO can be applied to amplification, causing dramatic changes in volume, as if you were repeatedly turning the volume knob on your stereo up and down. In addition, some LFOs can actually be inserted into frequency range, effectively making them HFO (high frequency oscillators!), though the results tend to be very distorted.

The key is to keep the different components as separate entities in your head. In fact, the very early experimental synths were made up of distinct pieces of hardware ("modular synths"). These massive components had to be reconfigured with patch chords to achieve the same results we enjoy today with a few simple buttons.

TIP

You'll sometimes hear an instrument sound—particularly by some equipment manufacturers—referred to as "patch." This actually comes from the days when patch cords had to be used to reconfigure components on early synths.

CHAPTER 5

Digital Synthesis

Early on, Moog and others dealt in the world of analog synthesis, through direct involvement with hardwired oscillators, filters, and waveforms. Very quickly, though, a computer chip found its way into synthesizer architecture, and a whole new type of synth was born. Today, MIDI-based digital synths offer a ton of benefits, like on-board effects, user-definable patch banks and extended polyphony (the ability to produce lots of instrument sounds, or multiple voices, simultaneously), and they stay in tune! Ironically, a number of digital synths these days are even used to emulate the old analog sounds.

Digital synthesis comes in two flavors—FM (frequency modulation) and sampling, or wavetable synthesis.

FM Synthesis

FM synthesis uses a signal to modulate the frequency of another signal, and the result is a sound much more like that of an arcade game from the 1970s than it is a Steinway grand piano. Each FM voice needs at least two signal generators (called operators), and the more sophisticated FM synthesizers use several operators per voice.

Operators are the digital equivalent of oscillators, but more powerful. Operators create sine waves but can be set to a particular pitch, volume, envelope, and so forth for each key that is struck, effectively making each operator a kind of micro-synthesizer in its own right. In addition, operators can either carry waves or modulate waves, depending on a number of factors, including their relationship with other operators. The relationship is based on an algorithm—a piece of computer code that sets the rules up for how the operators interact.

The Yamaha DX-7

The digital circuitry available to manufacturers was so powerful that it began to change the look and feel of synthesizer interfaces. On earlier analog units, for example, dials or knobs were used to control one single function each, but digital interfaces could assign multiple functions to a single button. Eventually, programming and editing features were organized into layer upon layer of digital menus, which opened up wonderful new ways of creating synthesized sound.

First appearing in 1983, Yamaha's DX7 was one of the first all-digital synths, and it is still well known today for many of its sounds. The DX7 was quite different from any other synth of its time, both in its interface and its sounds. The DX7 was the first popular synth to introduce the idea of buttons instead of knobs and sported the first (very small, non-lit) LCD panel. It offered thirty-two preset algorithms for creating instrument sounds, and the results were complex and unpredictable, in many cases never-before-heard.

Other popular, groundbreaking synths in the early '80s were the Wave PPG (predecessor to the Waldorf), the Fairlight digital sampler, the E-MU Emulator, and Sequential Circuits' Prophet 5 (the first fully programmable polyphonic analog/digital hybrid).

Though FM synthesis has produced some way-cool sounds and added an entire new sound category to music, it does have a number of limitations. Chiefly, if you're aiming to re-create the sound of an existing instrument or other sound using a synthesizer, FM just will not do it for you. The best way is to record the sound, convert it to a digital sample, then change the pitch according to the notes you play. This is the essence of a far more powerful form of sound synthesis: wavetable.

Wavetable Synthesis and Sampling

Wavetable synthesis, also known as sample-based synthesis or sometimes simply "sampling," is the most popular form of synthesis these days and for good reason: The instrument sounds can be frighteningly realistic.

Instead of synthetically manufactured oscillators creating source waveforms, wavetable makes it possible to digitize a waveform from the natural world directly into memory or storage device. This "sampled" waveform can then be modulated and amplified in a regular synthesizer-like fashion.

The diversity and vastness of sample-based sounds available to the home recording artist is nothing short of astounding, making it possible to play a virtual orchestra in your small studio or to sample your own live instruments and then play them back however you want them, using an electronic keyboard or other input device.

NOTE

Strictly speaking, wavetable synthesis means two different things: First, it can refer to the technology behind a sound card's MIDI-based, sample playback capabilities, where samples are stored in a RAM (random access memory) "table." Or there is the classical definition, which is to produce a sound by sequencing through a "table" of ROM (read-only memory) for different waveforms in response to a playing a note. For all practical purposes, though, these definitions are interchangeable.

So how does it all work? Sample-based synthesizers and sound cards use a type of subtractive synthesis that you'll see referred to primarily as PCM (pulse code modulation), though you'll also see AWM (advanced wave memory), AWM2 (advanced wave memory version 2), and even AI Synthesis (by Korg). These terms pretty much mean the same thing: An acoustic audio signal—for example, your voice through the microphone or the sound of your Steinway grand—is sampled, or digitized, and the recording is stored in RAM or ROM. The sound can then be played back at will, using a controller device (such as an electronic keyboard), along with traditional controller functions of modulation and volume, pitch, and so on.

If a synthesizer can sample sound and store the result in RAM or to disk, it is called a sampler; if it can play back samples at different pitches, it is usually called simply a synthesizer or a sample playback synthesizer. Most samplers and sample-based synths use subtractive synthesis, although some instruments are very limited as to how much processing they can perform.

PCM has become the coding technique used in almost all digital musical instruments and sound cards. Wave files also use PCM as the core technique for storing audio "buffer" data, as do a number of other common audio file formats. With most digital recording software, too, the core standard for sampling audio data is PCM.

NOTE

See chapters 11 and 12, "Fun-Da-Mental Audio," and "Serious Audio," respectively, for the gory details about audio file formats and digital audio.

The only drawback to digitally sampled instruments is that they offer fewer options for expressive playing. For example, you might have a killer alto saxophone sound, but playing it like a saxophonist does, using a keyboard with a limited amount of control over the final sound, isn't easy. Sampled audio is difficult to shape because of its fundamental nature—a "digital waveform" cannot so much be changed through modulation as it can be affected through a limited set of effects filters.

This isn't to say that the actual playback parameters themselves can't be modulated with interesting results; however, you won't typically find this kind of advanced control on most commercial synthesizers.

CHAPTER 5

Sample Looping—Heaven on ACID

One of the most interesting developments over the last several years has been the emergence of software applications like Sonic Foundry's ACID Pro. ACID Pro is essentially a wave-based, loop-based music production tool that allows you to actually pull together samples of wave files and combine them to create songs. It takes sampling to a whole new level.

Although it can function as a basic multi-track recorder, ACID Pro serves as a "loop sequencer" of sorts. It allows you to insert pre-made loops of wave data, either from professionally recorded libraries or sounds you record yourself, and takes care of time stretching, automatic looping, and pitch shifting for you. You can sample anything, from a single note on a guitar, to a guitar chord, to eight bars of backing vocals (or any number of bars you want), or the full drum kit. This model is quite different from traditional recording. Instead of playing all of your instruments "from scratch," you play whatever you need and then loop, loop, loop. If you're a hip-hop artist or DJ, this approach works quite well; however, if you're a more "traditional" musician, it takes a bit of getting used to. It's incredibly powerful.

ACID Pro currently supports 24-bit, 96 kHz audio and provides powerful, multi-channel audio for many sound cards, including the low-end as well as the more professional-level sound cards. ACID Pro also allows you to insert up to two DirectX effects at once through the use of envelopes which you can draw graphically on the computer screen. Volume and pan envelopes are handled in pretty much the same way, and ACID Pro also includes support for generating MIDI clock sync and generating/chasing MTC or SMPTE. This makes syncing with your other gear and/or software fairly simple.

The interface, shown in Figure 5.5, is easy to master, and you'll have it figured out by the time the coffee is brewed. The interface revolves around working with tracks, events, and loops. On the left-hand side, you load up the tracks either by double-clicking on them from the bottom explorer window, or simply draging and dropping. For each track, you can control the volume, pan, mute, and solo. One audio file (typically a wave file) takes up one track.

ACID Pro is not a multi-track in the sense that you can put any audio regions you want on a single track. ACID Pro is designed so that a track is a timeline for single events, and events are individual instances of a track. In Figure 5.5, for example, the track "Fonky" contains one event.

How you loop the tracks is achieved through the main window, which is where you set loop and event lengths. Right-clicking or using the + and – keys will allow you to change pitch quickly as well. In fact, the quality of the algorithm that controls pitch changes is one of the major strengths of ACID Pro—in addition to its simple and no-frills interface.

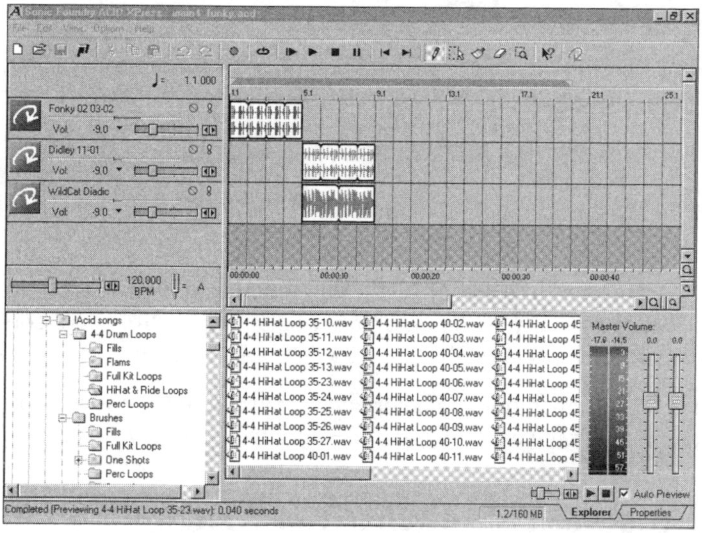

Figure 5.5
ACID Xpress—the
"light" version of ACID
Pro—is well known for
its intuitive and easy-to-
follow interface.

ACID Pro also allows you to burn your own audio CDs, though beware—the CD burning feature has very basic features and will, in most cases, not be suitable for CD or CD-ROM mastering. For instance, you can't add lead-ins, such as cross-fades and fade-ins, and you can burn only one song at a time, meaning master disc recording to CD-R rather than CD-RW is not possible.

The software also allows you to export your work to a number of other audio file formats, including RealMedia (.rm) and Windows Media format (.wma and .asf). You can also import MP3 files.

ACID Pro ships with a full complement of loops and demo songs to get you started, including full sample songs and a number of useful loops and riffs: bases, drums, guitars, keyboards, and many others. This content is enough to get you started using ACID Pro; however, if you really like the software, it won't be long before you'll be shopping for add-on CDs with more loops. Don't worry—there are plenty available in most popular music genres.

NOTE
ACID Pro 3.0 also includes Sound Forge XP Studio, worth about $80 as a standalone product at the time of this writing. Sound Forge XP studio is a stripped-down version of Sound Forge 5.0 and is excellent for basic audio editing of your ACID loops and audio files.

CHAPTER 5

Making a Sound Decision

So what kind of synth do you get? If you already own a synth, does it work for what you want it to? And what are your options?

Armed with a little knowledge about wavetable, PCM, RAM and ROM, MIDI (see Chapter 9), voicing, and polyphony, you already have a step up by knowing a bit about what synthesizers are and what they are capable of. You shouldn't be confused when the salesperson at the music store starts batting terminology around like air molecules.

You might, however, discover a little newfound emotional confusion when he starts playing on a keyboard or two, especially when he produces some incredibly cool sounds in and around some masterful playing. It's enough to make you want to just buy the whole synth department.

This calls for a little preparation, so before you head out to the music store, it helps to think about what you really want and what you'll really use—not just what sounds awesome.

Get What You Need—Not What You Want

What you need for your home studio and what your emotions tell you while you're in the music store can be two different things. It's like buying a car—you can't get that Corvette convertible out of your mind but all you really need is reliable transportation to the next gig—plus you don't exactly need to go bankrupt any time soon.

What do you want to achieve in your home studio? What sounds do you use most? Make a list. If you're a keyboard player who does jazz pieces, your needs will be radically different than if your main instrument is guitar and you do thrash metal. List the sounds that are most important to you. Are they solid drum sounds? If so, you may want to focus on a good drum machine. Realistic piano? If so, focus on digital pianos instead of regular synths or workstations. Synthetic noises? Some cheaper-quality synths and vintage models will have lots of these sounds.

Do you need a full seven octaves of weighted keys to tickle or do you need drum pads to tap? Or is a basic MIDI controller the best bet, in which case you may want to look at getting a controller, along with a rack-mounted module for your sounds, and/or software such as GigaStudio (see Chapter 8) for your computer. If studio space is at a premium, modules can be the golden ticket—and in many instances modules cost less than their keyboard-ready equivalents.

The most important thing is to listen. Either bring a pair of headphones to the music store with you or ask for a pair when you get there—with everyone else in the store playing, it will be hard to really hear the sounds without them, and you won't feel self-conscious in front of a new audience of other musicians. Plug the headphones into the headphone jack of the synth and spend some time with it. When you feel as though you've heard all the sounds you want to hear on a particular synth, go try another, and another. Try out synths that are way out of your price range and the cheaper home keyboard models. Listen for the differences.

TIP

When you're auditioning synthesizers, turn off the onboard effects, since reverb and other effects are notorious for disguising weak samples and low-quality loops! If you can't figure out how to do it, ask the salesperson. If he or she can't figure it out, you may want to seriously consider going to another music store.

When you're done sampling everything that looks interesting to you, go home. I repeat: Go home and think about it. Even if the salesperson gives you the deal of the century and you're 90 percent sure it's the synth you've always wanted, politely say, "I think we've got a deal, but can you hold it for me for one day? I need to think it over." Give yourself some time to think about what you learn in the store—unless you've got money to burn, you're going to have to live with your purchase for a long time.

Chasing Down the Right Synth

Music has been stuffed into almost every genre imaginable (Math Rock, anyone?), so while it's impossible to narrow the field of synthesizers down to a few categories, this section aims to focus on the most common genres, what's available in those genres, and what generally works for most musicians.

These are general guidelines, based to some extent on some of the most popular synths as well as some of the best values. Some of the synths in this section aren't even manufactured anymore, and the prices can vary widely. Wherever possible, the super expensive stuff is left out. The assumption here is that you don't have an extra $5,000 in the cookie jar earmarked for a new synth, so most of these synths will generally be in the $500 to $2,000 range.

NOTE

A wonderful resource for checking out other musicians' experiences with synthesizers (and lots of other instruments as well) is HarmonyCentral (**www.harmonycentral.com**). Check out the Synth Database for reviews on literally thousands of different models.

Rock/Pop

Most rock and pop songs will use a synthesizer primarily for warm string pads, basses, pianos, electric pianos, percussion, and string and brass ensembles. Workstations—synthesizers that offer enormous numbers of different sounds and usually include a sequencer—are probably the most common type of instrument for rock and pop artists, particularly for gigging, since one good workstation can often do the trick. Korg, Roland, and Yamaha are the most popular brands for full-featured workstations, which also typically include on-board sequencing capabilities.

Though the warmest classic synth sounds come from analog synthesizers, sample-based synths are usually far more useful in the studio for rock/pop. Most likely, you'll need realism over expressiveness. For the times when you need a killer keyboard solo or some really bright pads, you might want to consider a used analog in addition to a sample-based synth. A Yamaha DX-7 or Korg PolySix are both good choices and aren't too difficult to find used at reasonable prices.

In addition, without liquidating your bank account, you can afford to look at some of the synths that have sampled some classic sounds—for example, E-MU's Vintage Keys synth, the E-MU Proteus series, or the Roland JV-1080.

Techno

Techno is a wide genre, but it tends to gravitate toward the analog and FM-synthesis-based sounds. A lot of techno also involves controlling filter cutoff and, in particular, resonance during a performance, so using a synth that has lots of controls (typically knobs and dials) will probably be important to you.

Some of the most popular techno synths are the x0x series from Roland; most of them are vintage units, and some of them, like the TR-808 and TB-303, can get expensive.

Fortunately, there are plenty of other ways to get a similar, although not identical, sound. The TB-303, for example, has been emulated by the Syntechno TBS-303. A number of other monophonic bass synthesizers will give you a TB-303 sound, such as Novation's Bassstation, but also give you the ability to create a number of other deep bass sounds. Novation also makes the Drumstation, which does an effective job of emulating the TR-808/909.

Lots of other analog synthesizers have been used and are popular in techno, from most of the Roland Juno series to the Korg M1 to the E-MU Extreme Lead. Samplers are important, too, but you'll find some of the sample-based techno synths these days far less expressive than the analog or analog-modeled units.

Ambient

Ambient is a subtle genre of music, but it can have demanding requirements when it comes to a synthesizer. Reverb, delay, chorus, and other effects are often critical in an ambient piece, and much of ambient uses sampling as well as analog synthesis.

A sampler is probably more important than analog synthesis for ambient music, since ambient is a genre that rests on producing new and unique sounds. Analog synthesizers are also popular because of their warmth, but samplers are much more useful from a creative perspective. Make sure you look for real samplers, not just sample playback synthesizers. You'll want the flexibility of programming and really experimenting with the sounds.

That said, Brian Eno composed many songs with nothing more than a Yamaha DX-7 and a lot of reverb and delay. It's the expressiveness of analog that makes it important to the ambient genre. Look at samplers first, though. In the home studio, you have more opportunities for experimenting with new sounds than you do new ways to express old sounds. For new synthesizers, look at samplers from E-MU, Akai, and Kurzweil, as well as analog-emulators like the Nord Lead and the Prophecy. The Oberheim Matrix 1000 is also a cheap, rack-mounted warm analog synth, and it works very well for ambient music.

New Age

Korg has consistently been good at making New Age sounding synths. For example, the entire 01/W and X series are excellent for all kinds of New Age music, as well as the Trinity (and TR-Rack). The Kurzweil K2000, for example, produces some excellent swirly pads as well as solid realistic instruments—though it's on the expensive side.

On the used side, an Emulator II, Prophet 5, or Roland Jupiter 8 are also very good choices for New Age sounds.

Jazz/Blues

For traditional jazz and blues music, organ sounds are the most common, and the Hammond B3 sound is the most revered. The B3 is not really a synth, and it is rare and very expensive these days. Fortunately, many companies, including Hammond, with its XB series, have produced remarkably good synths that sound a lot like a B3 and range around the $1,000 to $1,500 mark. In addition to the B3, realistic instruments and warm pads are popular in jazz and blues, so sample-based synthesizers and sampling synthesizers will work fine as well. Semi-weighted keyboards may also be important to you if you're used to either an organ or piano feel.

Rap/Hip Hop

Loops and more loops—that's what fuels rap and hip-hop these days. Look for samplers and a good turntable, obviously. Rap also relies heavily on drums, so focusing on a good drum machine is critical—for example, the TR-808, TR-909, or more likely a high-quality sampler. Some rap artists use old analog synthesizers, too (Snoop Doggy Dogg, for instance), but on a home studio budget, focus on the sampler and turntables first.

Film Scoring

If you score films or aspire to do so, you should be on the lookout for synthesizers that are highly programmable, versatile, and as expressive as possible. Synthesizers made by Korg, Kurzweil, and Waldorf, just to name three, have been the most popular among film composers for this purpose.

Weighted keys may be very important to you for expression as well as for comfortable controller options. For example, Kurzweil is well known, and Korg is becoming known, for touch pad controllers instead of the traditional modulation and pitch wheels.

Building a home studio for film scoring can be quite expensive, with costs ranging from $1,500 for a used Trinity to well over $5,000 for a high-end Kurzweil.

CHAPTER 5

6

Getting the Guitar Sound

The guitar is where it's at if you're doing anything approaching rock music, and it plays a part in virtually every other popular musical genre, too. This chapter will help you turn otherwise amateur-ish sounding guitar tracks into recordings you can be proud of, by showing you how to get the most out of your setup. We'll cover:

▶ Evaluating your playing style

▶ Recording acoustic guitars

▶ Miking vs. pick-ups

▶ Acoustic-electric choices

▶ Electric guitars and amps

▶ Recording guitars direct

First Things First: Do You Like Your Guitar?

It almost goes without saying that you must have a fundamental affection for the instrument you're playing if you're going to get a good sound, a good performance, and a good recording. At the very least—if your budget prevents you from buying the guitar sound you're in love with—you should know your guitar's strengths and weaknesses and its limitations, in addition to your own.

The best way to find out what features and feel you really like is to play as many guitars as you can. If your friends have guitars, check them out, and spend a Saturday or two camping out at a music store with a wide selection. In general, ignore brand names and focus on the sound; just because a guitar has a name you've heard of on it doesn't necessarily mean it's right for you or your level of playing or playing style. For example, a Gibson Les Paul is well known for its rich upper-end tones and sustain, but there are many guitarists who simply don't care for the sound of a Les Paul (that's why there are Fenders!). In addition, the same models don't always sound the same and, in some cases, may sometimes sound strikingly different. In fact, every manufacturer (even Gibson) turns out an occasional dud, and every manufacturer (including no-name brands) turns out the occasional must-have.

Evaluating Quality: Basic Tips

What a guitar is made of has a lot to do with its sound. A cheap acoustic guitar, for instance, will probably have a top made of plywood, which over the years will pull itself apart. It won't sound too good, either, since plywood doesn't resonate well at all. A spruce or cedar top will sound much better and will last for a very long time, with care. The back, sides, and neck of an acoustic can be just about any type of solid wood; maple and mahogany are the two most popular.

Electric guitars can be made of almost anything, but the hardest woods, like maple, ash, or walnut, are best. These types of woods are durable and provide a fair amount of sustain for a solid-body construction.

Fretboards are usually either ebony, rosewood, or maple. Ebony, the most expensive, is extremely hard and durable, but rosewood runs a close second.

NOTE

If a fretboard has been varnished, painted or stained, it runs a greater risk of cracking, chipping, shrinking and swelling, making the guitar difficult to play and even more difficult to keep in tune. A notable exception is Fender's popular lacquered maple fretboards, which hold up quite well.

Fretboards should contain level, even frets across the board and none of them should stick out more than the others. A binded neck will usually ensure this, but binding is not necessary for the frets to be level, and a warped binded neck is not unheard of. Perhaps the most important aspect of the neck is that it is straight, which is critical for intonation but also important for the frets to have the right "feel." If you hold the guitar up and sight down the neck, the fretboard may be either flat or slightly curved, but if the fretboard doesn't look level, the neck may be twisted or warped, in which case you should stay away. The machine heads should also work smoothly, though this is less of a concern, because you can replace them easily on most models. On an electric guitar, all the switches and knobs should work smoothly.

How Does It Feel?

The feel of the guitar is just as important as the sound. Make sure the neck is a comfortable width for your hands. For example, Gibson and Epiphone acoustic guitars tend to have much wider necks than Fenders or Martins, so they're usually a better choice for thick fingers or big hands.

Check out the action—this is critical. Low action, meaning the strings are close to the frets, means an easy-playing guitar. However, especially in the case of acoustics, low action can often mean less resonance, less-complex tone, and, in some cases, string buzzing that can be difficult to get rid of.

Make sure the body and weight are comfortable. If the body is too big or too heavy, you won't last a week with it. On the other hand, if it's too light or doesn't have the right "balance" for your playing style and body size, you'll find it difficult to wring a good performance out of the guitar. If the guitar is even slightly uncomfortable, it will affect your playing in an adverse way; you'll play best when the instrument feels comfortable and balanced.

If it's an electric or acoustic/electric guitar, make sure the controls are easy to reach and use. Some manufacturers put controls in places where you can quite easily move them accidentally while you are playing. This will annoy you to no end.

Recording Guitars

Recording guitars can often be a frustrating experience, because there are so many variables. For electric guitars, duplicating the warmth and tone of different guitar amplifiers in the home studio environment is tough; for acoustic guitars, it's a bit easier, but harder still to get a simultaneously noiseless and accurately reproduced sound.

The Basics

If you're reading this chapter, then you have recorded or want to record guitar parts in your music. If you haven't already discovered it, you'll be pleased to know, first, that most songs that use guitar contain several guitar parts mixed together, and this can really give a recording a unique guitar sound. A common technique used to beef up guitar parts, especially in rock and pop, is layering.

Layering is achieved by recording several identical guitar parts to separate tracks, and then bouncing them down to two stereo tracks. This can create a virtual guitar chorus, or "wall of sound," which can work wonders for everything from thin-sounding distortion to acoustic second-strumming rhythms.

If you do layering, usually two to four separate layers are plenty, since any more than that starts straying into the "extreme lack of clarity and definition" category. For lead parts, more than two layers can present a problem, and even then it's most common to record the main solo line and then add a second countermelody or harmony part with the same guitar tone.

You also don't have to mix down to stereo. For example, if you do more-or-less standard guitar/bass rock music, mono, rather than stereo tracks, usually works just fine if you have other instruments to fill out your sound, such as synthesizers, horns, and vocal harmonies. In general, however, by mixing down to two stereo tracks, you'll achieve a richer sound and provide more flexibility for tweaking that sound during mixdown.

Stereo Separation

How you handle stereo separation and levels is important and will take a little experimentation. Here are the basic concepts:

▶ Pan closer to the center for more thickness, and farther left/right to hear them separately.

▶ Panning hard left and hard right respectively can sometimes be highly unnatural sounding and distracting to other frequencies in the mix, especially vocals; on the other hand, hard-panning for a bridge or another break in the song can exude a lot of harmonic complexity and add texture to the overall composition. In short: Judicious use of hard-panning can be very cool, and overuse can be a mess!

▶ Be careful when mixing together two guitar harmonies or counter-melodies to either side of the stereo mix. You'll want to fold the harmony part toward the background for touching up and fullness, not blend the tones as you would your vocals. Too much blending, and you will lose the lasting impact of the melody, as well as its "punch," or the natural attack and decay of the instrument itself.

▶ When taking the best parts of multiple takes and combining them into one track, use short to moderate pans for transitions between the spliced tracks, essentially performing a crossfade on the two separated tracks. This makes a doubled lead, for example, more natural—as if you'd played the whole thing yourself in one shot. You'll also want to join the different tracks, either on a beat or in the middle of a long note, to more effectively mask the edit.

TIP
If you know you're going to be splicing guitar parts, it's always good practice to play along well before and after the part. Give yourself plenty of room to figure out the best place to make the edits.

The Acoustic Guitar Sound

Recording an acoustic guitar starts with the instrument. Either it's an acoustic that you'll need to mic, or an acoustic/electric with a pick-up built in. There are advantages and disadvantages to both.

The biggest benefit to using an acoustic/electric is the clarity of the sound. You'll get a clean, noiseless recording if the electronics in the acoustic/electric are of good quality. The downside is that you'll be harder pressed to reproduce the sound of the guitar accurately. This makes complete sense when you think about it: The whole point of an acoustic guitar's design is to create sound in a natural space for human ears—not to process sound directly from the strings by way of electronics. That's why a dreadnaught is four inches thick and hollow.

If a song uses a simple acoustic guitar intro that winds up rocking after eight bars, this isn't a big concern. You'll get a sound you can live with comfortably using a built-in pick-up. If, however, you're doing folk music, new age guitars, bluegrass—anything that really depends on the character of the acoustic sound—you'll need to use a microphone.

The tried-and-true standard is the Shure SM57, which sells for around $100 new (at the time of this writing), and it will give you a good tone with enough experimenting. A good condenser mic, however, is much better. The Rode NT1 and NT2 are both good choices and are in the few-hundred-dollar range.

A good condenser mic should be able to nicely reproduce all the nuances of an acoustic. Here are the guidelines:

▶ For a full sound, place the mic 6 to 12 inches away from the sound hole of the guitar. Generally speaking, to avoid getting a muddy sound, don't put the mic directly in front of the sound hole; put the mic either ahead of or behind the hole, yet aimed towards it.

▶ For a warmer, mellower tone, aim the mic toward the twelfth fret or so, at least 3 but no more than 9 inches away.

▶ For a really bright sound, mic closely and near the bridge.

▶ For capturing the sound of your space along with the guitar, move back 1 to 2 feet, or use two mics, one close to the hole and one at least 2 feet back.

Another option is to record in stereo, by placing two microphones in criss-cross ("X") pattern, with one aimed at the sound hole and the other pointing toward the bridge or neck. Be warned, though: Creating this kind of variation in the tone will take a good deal more patience than usual to master.

> **NOTE**
> The Rode NT1 is discussed in more detail for vocal microphone techniques in Chapter 4.

The Electric Guitar Sound

Once you're into a recording session, the last thing you want to worry about is your electric guitar sound. Ideally, you'll want to have already decided upon the amp sound you'll use, starting with the guitar tone itself, and, having worked your way down the EQ, gains, and effects, you have a pretty good idea of how the guitar should—and will—sound.

Recording *is* the time to fine-tune how the guitar sounds fits with the other instruments and the feel of the song. The delay or chorus effect you used when practicing without the other instruments may have sounded just right, but it may not work in the final recording or it may muddle other parts or sound too muddled itself in the mix.

Amplitude can also be one of the hardest pieces to get right. The most common mistake is cranking gain up so much that the guitar tracks behave more like phase cancellation effects than actual instruments. In addition, using massive amounts of distortion, though it may work quite well live or during a practice jam, produces so many harmonics in your tone that it can make one note indistinguishable from the next.

In particular, if your guitar parts are intricate, a little less gain will add enough clarity to allow the notes to come through in the mix. Couple this with paying closer attention to your use of midrange frequencies on the amplifier. Though opting for little or no midrange during a live performance will head you in the direction of that "scooped" sound every time, in the studio you'll need to pump the midrange just a bit to keep the guitar from being buried by the other instruments—particularly drums.

Miking Your Amp

The SM57 is, hands down, the most popular mic for a guitar cabinet; in fact, it's pretty much the industry standard. Condenser mics are not generally useful for getting a sound you can live with from your guitar amp, though there are a few exceptions, chiefly Audio Technica's AT4050 multi-pattern large condenser.

The most important aspect of miking an amp is, well, the amp—and the speakers. Amplifier tone is one of the most subjective things on earth, and trying to corral it into a comprehensive discussion could easily take up the entire book, so it qualifies as one of those "beyond the scope of this book" topics. Here are some general tips, though:

CHAPTER 6

▶ With most amps, the volume should be as high as you can get it (or as high as the neighbors will allow). Generally speaking, the hotter the amp, the more consistent and warmer its output, and you can add a bit of compression to smooth things out during recording.

▶ In a multiple speaker cabinet (2×12, 4×10, and so on), check each of the speakers thoroughly to find the sweet spots—the spots which produce the most consistent modulation and tone that you like. Most likely, one or two of the speakers will sound better than the others.

▶ Keep the mic angled at an acute angle to the grill cloth—not perpendicular—and generally about 1 to 3 inches away. Direct the mic into the cone but not right on the center.

▶ As a general rule, plan on recording the guitar dry and add your effects during mixdown.

▶ If you want to add some natural reverb, stereo miking in a large room—by using a distant mic as well as one right on the grill cloth—can be quite effective. You'll have to play around with the exact distances according to the room size and natural sound, and watch out for phase cancellation—this technique can produce quite a bit of it. The solution is to keep changing the distances between the two mics. Of course, it just about goes without saying that if the room itself doesn't sound good, your amplifier isn't going to sound too good, either.

Direct Signal

Recording electric guitar without using a microphone is another option for the home studio, and, with the right setup, you can achieve some interesting and desirable guitar sounds. With all but the most expensive hardware (and even then it's no walk in the park), you need healthy doses of both patience and practice to get a good recording.

The first method is to use the preamp output from the back of your amp, routed through a direct box to match impedances and, to some extent, eliminate hum.

NOTE

Don't disconnect your speakers when using the preamp output. You can potentially damage the amp, your mixer, or yourself—especially with a tube amp.

Using the preamp output usually produces fairly harsh sounds, so this technique will have you doing some heavy equalization to counter the lack of warm frequencies. The tone control on the guitar itself can be quite useful when fine-tuning preamp output as well—don't ignore it.

Another approach, which, thanks to newer technologies, has gained quite a bit of popularity in the last several years is using a speaker simulator to simulate the power amp and speaker of your amp. The best units use physical modeling techniques to handle the simulation. With a fair amount of tweaking, you can achieve some highly realistic sounds.

The Pod, from Line 6 (**www.line6.com**), is one of the best values available at the time of this writing, selling for around $300. Using physical modeling techniques that Line 6 calls "Tube-Tone Modeling," the company has painstakingly analyzed the characteristics of various amps, different types of tubes, and how the sound is colored and shaped to design a software-based model of some of the most popular amps in the world. The Pod is not a sampler, but a chip/software-based device for recreating tones. It features sixteen different models from a "Small Tweed" vintage Fender amp, to "Rectified," the Mesa Boogie Dual Rectifier. The back panel features stereo inputs and outputs along with MIDI in and out. The Pod also provides some good, basic functions, including output level, EQ, reverb, and gain.

The unit also has a built-in tuner, a noise gate, and a tap tempo button that allows you to change the speed of flanges or delay times by just tapping the button for the desired effect. The tap tempo button also lets you access additional features like drive and presence boost. There are even some basic effects on board, including delays, choruses, tremolo, flange, and a killer rotary sound.

Tricky-Dicky EQ

Probably the most important factor in creating your guitar sound is how it is equalized. Electric guitar frequencies range from around 100 Hz to about 10 K, and equalization can be added at any point during recording, from initial tracking to the final mixdown. If you have to bounce tracks, or if you have a limited number of EQ bands, it's a good idea to make changes as needed and save most of equalization for the mixdown. Here are the guidelines:

► Boosting distortion in the 100 Hz range will get you closer to those ballsy power chords you get out of your cousin's Marshall stack.

► You can regain some clarity by making a cut at around 200 Hz.

► 400 to 600 Hz is where most of the tone exists, so tweak this area carefully.

► 3 kHz is critical, because this is where the guitar's edge typically exists. Boosting this frequency will certainly make the guitar cut through the mix, but too much will give you a serious headache.

► A boost between 5 and 7 K will add some air and sparkle to the guitar.

► Up over 10 kHz, you can experiment with small boosts to get a little more flavor and blend with vocal harmonies and cymbals.

> **NOTE**
> For acoustic guitars, the following frequencies are most important:
> ► Boosting 500 Hz or so will typically give you a fuller sound.
> ► Cutting at around 300 Hz can take some of that fullness back out.
> ► You'll get a little more pluck in the 1-3 kHz range, and a little more pick from 5-7 kHz.
> ► For more sparkle, boost above 10 kHz.

CHAPTER 6

Finally, don't overlook the simple things. Make sure the guitar is in tune and the intonation is spot on (as much as it can be!). Also, use new strings when recording, and stay loose: You can almost promise yourself that the fiftieth take isn't really going to sound much better than the forty-ninth!

7

No More Drummer Jokes, Please!

This chapter is not about "percussion" in the traditional sense; it's about working with a standard drum kit (hi-hat, kick drum, snare, cymbals, and toms) in its various incarnations. The focus is on getting a good drum sound and on how to best integrate drum kit pieces into your sound. Acoustic, MIDI, and sample-based drums are discussed, including:

▶ MIDI drums

▶ Looping and drum samples

▶ Setting up your kit

▶ Working with MIDI drum kits

▶ Rolling your own MIDI kit

▶ Quantization and Groove editing

▶ Event-based MIDI editing

▶ Live skins

▶ Getting a good sound from acoustic drums

Drums for Non-Drummers (Or, "Dig Those MIDI Drums!")

If you're not already a drummer with your own trap set, the ideal way to get authentic-sounding drum tracks into your recordings is to bring in a drummer and mic his kit. The "ideal way," you should note, has a few caveats:

▶ You need to know exactly what you want the drum parts to be, otherwise you will waste an enormous amount of the drummer's time, and his ability to do exactly what you want will diminish accordingly.

▶ It almost goes without saying that you need a really good drummer—one who can catch the groove of your music, who "gets it" and cannot only do exactly what you ask of him, but make it better.

▶ You need money to buy enough high-quality mics to get a good sound. The best drummer in the world is worthless to you if you can't mic him properly.

▶ You need more money to create the space in which to record the drums (see Chapter 2), one that captures the performance but is hot enough to work within your mix.

▶ You need even more money to soundproof the space—otherwise your drum session will last about as long as it takes the police to arrive.

We'll deal with some of these points later in this chapter, but for now, consider some less-than-ideal ways to integrate drums into your recordings:

▶ **MIDI**—Though MIDI is the cheapest route, it may well be the most difficult and time-consuming.

▶ **Looping Samples**—Using sampled drum loops, thanks to better collections of loops these days (mostly due to the popularity of Sonic Foundry's ACID software), is far easier than it once was.

MIDI (Musical Instrument Drumming Interface)

If you're not a drummer, it's hard to think like one. Yet this is exactly what you must try to do to get something approaching realism out of MIDI drums. This is not, repeat, *this is not* an easy thing to do. You don't have to download more than a handful of MIDI "covers" of popular music from the Web, for example, to instantly understand just how difficult it is.

But it is possible. If you can think a little like a drummer, you can get authentic, live-sounding drum tracks using a keyboard, module, or drum machine that sounds deceptively like a real drummer.

So how does one think like a drummer? Well, you could switch your drink of choice to a White Russian, be unreachable for days on end, and always be late for rehearsals, but this won't make your MIDI drum sounds groove any better.

All kidding aside, thinking like a drummer means trying to understand drums like a drummer. This is the real difficulty, since the techniques drummers use to sound like, er, real drummers are precisely the things that are hard or time-consuming to do with MIDI. For example:

▶ Snare rolls with strategically placed, random rim shots

▶ Flams insides of rolls

▶ Random volume, attack, and decay with cymbals

▶ Random volume variation with the snare, toms, and kick

▶ Switching between sticks, soft mallets for cymbals, and brushes

▶ Playing the snare behind or ahead on beats differently for each bar

▶ Cymbal chokes

▶ Hitting the snare with both sticks, one just off from the other

▶ Slight variations in tempo and volume on any given fill

▶ Following the music for certain parts of the song and leading on others

Drummers use these techniques anywhere, any time, with varying degrees of subtlety and dynamics, often without even thinking about it too much. Your task is to learn to fake these kinds of techniques using MIDI, and that involves gaining an understanding of what MIDI can do for percussion instruments.

Dynamics

A drum kit is an extremely dynamic instrument, and there isn't a MIDI drum module or keyboard in existence that will give you the dynamic range of a set of drums.

But you can get close. A relatively quick, easy way to increase the dynamics of your MIDI drumming is to edit velocity. Velocity is mostly amplitude, but it often includes some filtering to make a hard hit brighter as well as louder. You can control the dynamics of a MIDI instrument by using the event editor of your sequencer or, in the case of SONAR, you can introduce variation in velocity by using the Controller Pane in its Piano Roll View. Figure 7.1 shows the Controller Pane with the velocity controller changes highlighted.

Figure 7.1
SONAR's controller editing capabilities make it easy for you to add dynamics to your MIDI drums.

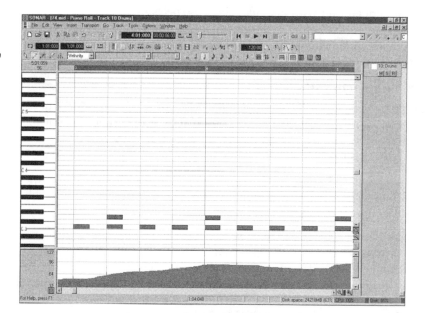

TIP

An even better way to increase the dynamics of your MIDI drums is to set up variable key mappings of the same drum sounds you're using for a particular composition. Set up a soft kit, a medium kit, and a very loud kit. Then alter the kits when you play back the sequence at places in the song where it makes the most sense. It's time-consuming as all get-out but works wonders for dynamics.

Octopus Syndrome

A real drummer does not have eight arms to hold you; he has only two hands and two feet, while you've got a practically unlimited palette of percussion instruments to work with in MIDI. While it's tempting to just let the individual instruments "double up," that is, playing a fill on top of a backbeat that's already using four sounds on every beat, it does not sound realistic.

Since a drummer can only actually produce four different percussion sounds at a time, so should you. For example, when a drummer does a fill, he switches from hi-hat to pedal hat because he needs his sticks for the other skins. No drummer plays the same hi-hat pattern from the beginning to the end of a song. Neither should you, if your goal is to produce realistic drums.

Vary the Snare

Different drum patterns have different feels, from "tight" to "digging" to "laid back" and so on. The feel almost always originates from where the drummer alters snare beats relative to either beats 2 and 4 or 1 and 3.

You can fool around with moving your snare beats up or back just a tad in your sequencer's note event editor. It's incredibly time-consuming, but it's a highly effective way to add some feel to your drum mixes. This technique all but eliminates that "robotic" or zombie-like precision that can occur with MIDI drums.

Be a Smart Quantizer

Contrary to popular belief, quantization is almost always your friend. In fact, it's one of the most important tools you've got for doing drum sequencing. Nobody has the ability to lay down a spot-on drum groove using a keyboard, and the lack of air space and interplay between the instruments that a real drummer has at her disposal only increases the need for effective quantizing.

Be smart about it, though: never quantize an entire drum kit together; quantize only the individual sequences, then work with each sequence by itself to add velocity changes and adjust the timing of individual beats.

Features like Groove Quantize in SONAR, as shown in Figure 7.2, also allow you to add an offset to individual sequences at regular intervals. This is excellent for tweaking your hi-hat, kick drum and toms. Use it to quickly do basic adjustments to your drum sequences, then go under the covers and do some tinkering around with the notes and velocity.

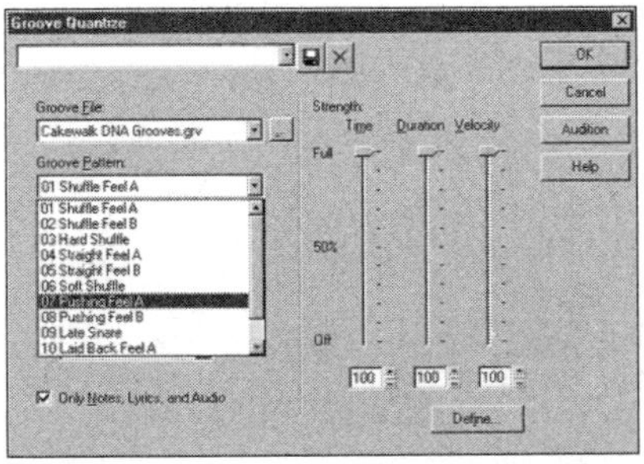

Figure 7.2
The Groove Quantize feature in SONAR can greatly speed up quantize editing, with far more interesting results than straight-up quantizing.

Using MIDI Triggers

If you've got the money, a MIDI-based trap set can be a big advantage. You get the opportunity to play like a real drummer, but you don't have to be an experienced drummer to hear some immediate benefits, since you can control "feel" and amplitude much like a real drummer, then quantize away your errors at the end of a session.

Yamaha (**www.yamaha.com**) and Alesis (**www.alesis.com**) make some of the most popular pre-built MIDI drum kits on the market.

Roll Your Own MIDI Kit

A much less expensive option is to create your own MIDI trap set by using sensors to trigger MIDI notes, either adding them to a cheap acoustic set of drums or creating your own surfaces to beat on. There are almost as many ways to do this as there are types of surfaces and sensors to build it with.

One of the most inexpensive setups can be had by using PVC pipe, Remo practice pads, Radio Shack piezo audio transducers, and a drum module with trigger inputs.

There are a number of drum modules on the market, but the Alesis DM5 is one of the most popular drum modules available, has respectable sounds, and, most importantly, has twelve trigger inputs with five programmable parameters for each one, twenty-one programmable drum sets, four audio outputs, and a hi-hat switch. The unit also features an 18-bit sample rate, 540 different sounds, and random sampling capability.

You can buy Remo practice pads at just about any music or drum retailer; they run around $10 a pop. The piezo transducers are ultra-cheap (a buck and a half apiece, Radio Shack part number #273-073) and work quite well.

To build a frame out of PVC pipe, you'll spend around $25 or a little more, depending on how elaborate (and how big) you make the kit. One quarter-inch PVC with enough T-fittings and L-fittings to fill out your kit's design is stable, though you could buy a larger diameter PVC for a more rigid setup. A handsaw will work just fine for cutting the PVC, while the Remo pads can be attached by drilling holes through the tubes and running bolts into the pads.

You'll also need to construct footswitches for the kick drum and the hi-hat; a cheap on/off switch can be had from Radio Shack for about $5, but a little actual drum hardware is better, such as inexpensive kick drum and hi-hat pedals which you can mount onto wood brackets.

The piezo transducers install as follows:

1. The piezo should be soldered to decent quality, shielded cable; check the polarity and the instructions to wire it correctly. The module-end of the cable will need to be soldered to a quarter-inch plug or whatever your module is expecting.

2. After you do the soldering, make sure to plug everything into your module first and test to ensure the piezos all work. They're fairly reliable, but since they're so cheap, buy a couple of extras just in case.

CHAPTER 7

3. Next, you'll need to unscrew each Remo pad and cut a space in the foam for the piezo. Make sure you don't place the piezo directly against the surface of the pad, or you will get a sharp rebound sound on contact. An exception to this is if you remove the main sensor element of the piezo from its frame and install it flush with Remo pad surface.

4. Drill a small hole into the bottom of the Remo pad to run the cable from the piezo.

5. Once you get all of your Remo pads equipped, you'll want to play around a bit with the trigger settings, primarily gain and velocity.

Drum Loops & Samples

Another option is to forego MIDI altogether and use pre-sampled loops for your drums. Thanks to the large number of sound libraries available these days, this is now a reasonably effective option. It is a completely different method, though, since you'll be doing a lot of auditioning of drum sounds, then cutting and pasting these sounds (or bits and pieces of them) into your audio recording software.

The ease with which you can do looped samples depends a lot on the quality of the samples you buy, as well as your own level of patience for selecting and editing the sounds. The advantage is that, with pre-recorded drum kit loops, you get a highly accurate sound. You also get the airplay between the original instruments that were recorded to create the sample.

Sonic Foundry's ACID software (see Figure 7.3) is one of the best applications available for auditioning and putting together your drum patches.

Figure 7.3
ACID is very well known for its simple, intuitive design.

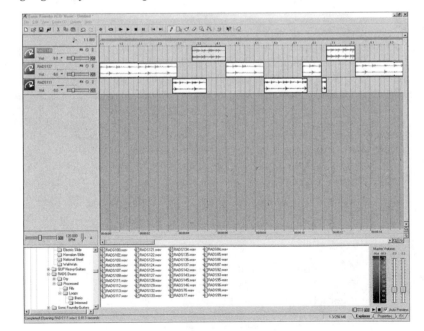

At the time of this writing, ACID Pro comes in a few different flavors, ranging in price from around $40 for ACID Hip-Hop, Latin, DJ, Rock, and Techno, to $80 for ACID Music, to about $400 street price for ACID Pro.

The most significant difference between ACID Pro and the rest of the ACID family is that Pro allows you to use up to eight DirectX effects per project, while ACID Music supports only one, and the others have no DirectX support at all. In addition, Pro also supports a bit depth of 24 bits, whereas the others are 16-bit only. Pro also has multiple sound card support, as well as multiple audio outputs.

Is this enough to justify the price difference? If you're going to use ACID primarily for assembling drum tracks, probably not. If, on the other hand, ACID looks like a tool you might use as your central piece of recording software, the extra investment is probably a good idea.

Recording Acoustic Drums

If you own a set of acoustic drums or have recorded them before, you probably know just how tricky the process can be. The variation in tone, frequency, and volume can be a challenge (or a nightmare, depending on how you look at it).

There are two basic ways of recording real, live drums.

Close Miking

Miking each individual drum, known as *close miking*, while placing a couple of additional mics overhead for the cymbals, gives you the most control over each piece during mixdown, particularly the amplitude and stereo placement of each instrument.

You have a great deal of flexibility with this method, too. You can use different types of microphones, for example, to emphasize or de-emphasize each instrument's unique tone and timbre. You can mic both sides of a drum, change the relative positioning of mic in infinite ways, and alter the input gain of the mic for a load of different effects and sounds.

Good microphone values for close miking are the ever-reliable Shure SM57, AKG DA20, Senheiser 421 (for kick and/or floor tom), and Shure SM81. There are many other, more expensive mics, as well as specialty mics that are made for certain percussion instruments, like a hi-hat microphone.

Having all of this freedom has its drawbacks, too: it's expensive, it's time-consuming, and it's not hard to make a career out of looking for the perfect trap sound. In addition, some engineers dislike this method, because you lose much of the soundfield interplay created by the interaction of the different drums. Still, close miking probably remains the most popular way to record acoustic drums. The next few sections offer some tips for using close miking effectively.

Kick-Butt Kick

A good kick drum mic, such as the Senheiser 421, should be placed roughly halfway into the kick and should be pointed at the beater. If you bring the mic in from either side of the drum and angle it at the beater, you stand a better chance of avoiding leakage from the snare drum mic; you can experiment with the depth of the mic's pickup by trying different angles, but you'll want to keep the mic lined up with the beater as much as possible.

Use a pillow or sandbag in the kick drum angled toward the drum head that the beater kicks to dampen out unwanted frequencies.

Trapping the Snare

The Shure SM57 is a tried-and-true mic for capturing a snare sound; you'll want to angle it at about 45 degrees, while varying the height depending on how much space you want in the sound. Be careful, though: The farther away you place the mic, the more potential you've got for phase cancellation.

Tommy Guns

Miking a tom is similar to miking a snare, except you'll want to place mics farther from the drum head, usually at least 2 inches past the rim. The distance of the mic from the head has a little more range—you can go as far as 6 inches or more, but, again, watch out for dreaded phase problems.

Cymbals

For cymbals, start by placing your overhead mics anywhere from about a foot and a half to two feet out from the center of the cymbal and angle in the 45-60 degree range. You primary goal with symbols is get separation from the soundfield to some extent, while reducing any bleed from the toms and snare.

Hi-hat

In most cases, you won't need a dedicated hi-hat microphone. You should get plenty of bleed-through from the other mics to provide good hi-hat. If you've got an extra mic and input, mic about 2 to 4 inches from the side of the hi-hat away from the snare, at an angle of 45-60 degrees.

Triangular Miking

Using a pair of overhead mics, along with a dedicated mic in the kick drum, works quite well for most situations and spaces. This technique is called *triangular miking*, has plenty of soundfield, is less expensive, and takes far less effort to set up.

Give the kick drum its own channel in the mix, and capture everything else using a pair of overhead mics, placed anywhere from 6 inches out from the kit and from 6 inches to several feet apart.

Start by ensuring that the overheads are placed an equal distance from the drums and that the drums are positioned so that they do not block each other from the overheads. You can capture a highly realistic, balanced full-kit sound this way. This method isn't a walk in the park—it takes experimentation to account for the acoustics in the studio and the natural fluctuations in the resonance of the drums and cymbals. But it's the quickest way to get an authentic sound without getting stressed to imperfection!

SM81's are excellent for an overhead-only approach, as are AKG C-408's.

NOTE

Chapter 2, "Setting Up Your Space," discusses an important topic regardless of the mic method you use for your acoustic drums: soundproofing.

Phase Cancellation

With either method—close miking or triangular miking—there is a strong likelihood you'll run into some problems with phase cancellation. Phase cancellation happens when frequencies from one microphone cancel out frequencies in another, and vice-versa; you'll know you've got a phase problem when frequencies drop out or seem to "shift."

When trying to correct a phase problem, the first thing you need to do is isolate the source(s) of the phase. If only part of the mic signal is out of phase (this is typically the case), moving one mic while carefully monitoring the other mics will probably fix the problem. With an overhead setup, sometimes simply changing the height of the mics is very effective.

TIP

When monitoring to check for instruments that may have dropped out due to phase cancellation, check each drum in mono—not stereo. Monitoring in stereo makes it difficult for you trace the exact source of the phase.

Perhaps the most important aspect of detecting and dealing with phase is to do it before you start experimenting with different mic positions, levels, and distances. If you start out with a bunch of phase problems, things will only get worse.

All Skins Are Not Created *Equal*

Different percussion instruments can produce a wide range of frequencies, and the effects those different frequencies will have on the mix will also vary widely.

For a kick drum, the thump is usually in the 60-100 Hz range, while the punchiness of the kick is up a little higher, in the 100-200 Hz area. Snares are not quite as predictable, especially if you are working in the pop/rock or country music genres. Many snares tend to dominate the 1-2 kHz region, but this is by no means the rule; generally, if you need a little more bottom-end in a snare sound, you can boost around the 150 kHz range, while crispiness typically resides in the 2-5 kHz region. Snare sounds are sensitive to equalization, though, as well as reverb, so don't over-EQ your snare. Work with the source sound as much as possible.

Depending on the size and tuning of toms, their effective ranges run anywhere from 100 Hz to 2 kHz; to achieve clearer tom sounds, you'll usually focus on the 1-3 kHz range when it's time to EQ the mix. With cymbals, the effective ranges are about 8 kHz and above, and their overall harmonic frequency range can go well past the range of the human ear. Thankfully, during mixdown you tend to be a little less concerned with boosting or cutting frequencies in cymbals, and more concerned with the attack and delay of the sound.

Drums and EQ

EQ can do wonders for drums; it is also terribly easy to overdo EQ, particularly if you've used triangular miking.

TIP

Before you EQ drums, always check and play with mic placement first. Don't spend an hour playing with EQ when all you had to do in the first place was move the mic an inch to the right. Always check the placement of your mic(s) and evaluate the signal based on location first—then EQ.

If you've got everything on separate tracks (using the first method discussed earlier), it's a bit easier in one sense, since you've got only each individual sound to contend with, and an isolated sound is always easier to EQ than the complexity of an entire soundfield of instruments.

Using equalization with anything is always, to some extent, a trial-and-error, roll-your-sleeves-up kind of proposition, so it's a bit difficult to predict exactly what works in every situation. However, there are some general guidelines:

▶ Adding more thump to the kick drum is usually achieved by boosting frequencies between 100-150 Hz. Clarity and definition like the 3 kHz region.

▶ The snare is always tough, but you will definitely hear a sharper, more banging snare at around 1 kHz, and the sounds get clearer and clearer as you approach 5 kHz or a little higher. Snare also responds to changes in the 100-150 kHz region—just like the kick. However, depending on how the snare is tuned, you will undoubtedly have to mess around with frequencies lower and higher than this range. In addition, at around 1-2 kHz, you'll get a more explosive, snappier sound out of the snare.

NOTE

Be careful when boosting or cutting the same frequencies across several different instruments. For example, boosting both the kick drum and the snare in the same region will tend to diminish the effect you would have gotten from the boost or cut to begin with.

▶ For toms, you'll play around with frequencies almost exclusively in the 100-250 kHz region; much higher than that, you will rapidly begin to muddy up the sound of the toms, especially the floor tom.

TIP

Cutting tom frequencies around 750-850 Hz can help if you need to get rid of "boxiness." Also, if you are losing toms in the mix to guitars or synth, then add some narrow-band EQ up around 3 kHz.

> Cymbals, as well as the hi-hat, travel in roughly the same frequency range. If you cut around 180-200 Hz, you'll tend to get a subtler sound, while you can add tons of presence and crash if you can effectively boost around 500 Hz. For sizzle, boost in the 5-7 kHz range, and for more air, experiment with 7-10 kHz.

Reverb and Compression Are Your Friends

You can use effects with drums—acoustic, MIDI, sampled, or otherwise—just like you can with any other instrument, though you'll discover that compression and reverb are the two most valuable tools in your drum-effects-toolkit.

NOTE

Compression and reverb are covered in more detail in Chapter 11.

If you use close miking, adding effects will probably do more for your mixes than if you use triangular miking, since, presumably, you already have a good deal of natural reverberation from your recording space, and you're most likely already dealing with a relatively thick soundfield. Compression can still be helpful for a triangular-miked mix; it's rather hit-and-miss depending on qualities of your room, but a little compression can thicken up any limp ambient qualities of a room.

With close miking, compression is highly effective for everything but the cymbals; using it judiciously evens the level of the overall kit, by squaring up the decay with the attack. In particular, compression can even the spots where some hits are louder than others.

For example, to create a gunshot snare sound, use a compression ratio of around 1:3 to 1:4 and a threshold of at least –20. Then add reverb to taste. You can also thicken the kick and the toms with a lower compression ratio, around 1:2.

For close-miking, you can introduce a lot of variation by using reverb. If you use large amounts of reverb on the snare, ensure that the length of the reverb syncs up with the song's tempo, so that the reverb finishes decaying before the next snare hit. Otherwise, you'll be swimming in a sea of wishy-washy snare before you know it.

TIP

When adding reverb to drums, lay off the pre-delay. Otherwise, you lose the very essence of any percussion instrument—its attack.

8

All Kinds of Other Instruments

Though most of this book focuses on electronic instruments, this chapter goes into both recording popular acoustic instruments as well as emulating different instruments using sampling technology. The following topics are discussed:

▶ Effective miking for strings, woodwinds, and brass

▶ Acoustic piano techniques

▶ Using high-quality samples with GigaStudio

Live Recording or Recording Live?

The first, most important aspects of any "live" acoustic instrument sounds are the player and the instrument. Bad player + bad instrument (or good instrument + bad player) = bad recording! Of course, you may not exactly be spending your weekends filling in for the first violin chair at the local symphony; in fact, your primary goal just might have a little more to do with that "cool horn section" in the bridge or the string sounds you need to ramp up the chorus. You may have some rudimentary skill with the instruments, but you're not an expert. That leaves you with two choices: acquire the instrument and learn how to play it or use professional-quality samples.

If you use real instruments, you'll need to first consider from whence the sound comes—where the sweet spots are, and vice-versa. The same qualities of an acoustic instrument of any kind that give it character and expressiveness can also sometimes be the most difficult sounds to capture on disk. Which mic to use? How closely do you mic it? From behind, to the side, square in front of it? How important is the sound of the room?

Hopefully, you're aware of the role the instrument will play in your recording. Is it sixteen bars of a pan flute intro or a four-piece string section to carry the verse? Does the composition feature the instrument or does it serve a backup role? Ask these questions and leave the experimentation for the guitar solo on your Les Paul.

For honest-to-goodness acoustic instruments, you should experiment with some recording sessions first. You'll most likely find that it takes a good deal more tinkering to get a good sound, so "roll tape" (or track, or sample—choose your own terminology) more often during practice sessions while you are working on learning the material.

Acoustic Piano Techniques

There are almost more ways to record acoustic piano than there are pianos, which means you'll wind up experimenting a lot more with your particular room and instrument.

The first thing to consider is the piano part itself. For example, if you want to record a piano sound to back a rock tune and your instrument isn't set up for it, it probably isn't going to sound good, since rock pianos have much harder hammers than "normal" pianos and generally sound brighter than most. Similarly, you're not going to get that killer concert grand sound on the $400 Kimball in the living room.

If you're an experienced piano player who has dabbled in any studio, you probably already know these things, and you may even be prepared to shell out the dough to get the right kind of setup for the style of music you're working in. If you're serious about your keys, you've probably already done it.

Once you have a setup you're comfortable with, you'll need a good mic. For rock, pop, and R & B, it's hard to beat a good condenser if you have a little bit of money to burn. The Neumann U 87 and U 89 and Shure SM81 are all good choices but still not cheap. The Rode NT1 and NT2 mics, which are covered in a couple of other places in this book, are better values in the $200-$400 price range.

NOTE
Tube condenser mics like the Neumann U 67 or AKG C 12 are fairly common in professional studios and are excellent for piano miking of all kinds. They are very expensive, though—$2,000 dollars or better. If you've got that kind of bread, you're probably not reading this book.

Dynamic microphones work very well for piano miking, too, and the Shure SM57 is practically the standard for stage miking. The SM58 also gives good results, though they are generally better suited to singers than instruments. Both are cheap, around $100 at the time of this writing. Their size and pickup pattern also cut down on bleed for a recording situation where you are using multiple acoustic instruments at once.

NOTE
Technically speaking, "bleed" occurs when microphones pick up the signals from the output of other microphones. The result can often be muddy, cause feedback, and sometimes introduce phase or phase cancellation into the mix.

Placement of a piano mic is critical. For rock or pop music, you should position the mic as close to where the hammers hit the strings as possible, and cardioid (like the NT1 or SM57) mics are the best pickup pattern to use.

TIP

Positioning a microphone close to where the hammer hits tends to pick up more of the dynamics of the attack of each hammer—and attack is what gives the "punchier" sound needed for most rock/pop music. To decrease the pickup of the attack and mellow the sound, experiment with moving the mic further and further down the strings until you find a spot you like.

For classical piano or jazz piano, omnidirectional pickup patterns work a little better if you've got a room sound you really want to capture with the piano, which is typically the case. Position the mic outside the piano on the open side to allow the room and the instrument to "breathe."

Ideally, two mics (a pair of SM57s, for example) work best. A tried-and-true technique is to pan one hard left and one hard right (while checking in mono and listening carefully for any phase cancellation). With a jazz piano setup, especially if you have other musicians playing along, you'll probably want to space the mics out a bit farther from the piano to capture the live mix in the air.

Woodwinds

To record most woodwind instruments (flute, clarinet, and so on), use a microphone with a cardioid pickup pattern, usually no more than 12 inches in front of the mouthpiece. Most of the overtones of a wind instrument come out at the ends, while the wind tones and resonance come from the mouthpiece, so experimenting with where you position the mic relative to the mouthpiece is highly important. It's not hard to end up capturing too much air.

In addition, try to position the instrument itself equidistant from the floor and the ceiling to avoid phase cancellation.

The following steps are a good way to start experimenting:

▶ Start off with the mic pointing more directly at the mouthpiece and a bit closer, maybe around 8 inches, then work back from there, depending on how much unwanted breath is present in the recording.

▶ Try a condenser mic first, if you have one. Dynamic mics are much harder— especially for the flute—to capture a rich sound.

▶ Try a number of different angles to keep too much air from hitting the mic.

▶ Experiment with a pop filter—but not a wind screen. A wind screen will unacceptably dull most woodwind instruments.

Strings

Strings are bright. Almost always. In fact, this is where an SM57 or SM58 can work rather well, though you may find the sound too dull, depending upon the characteristics of your recording space. A tube condenser microphone, running through a tube-type preamp, will also bring a warmer sound to strings, particularly smaller ensembles such as a quartet.

For placement, the bow sound is a big variable. Positioning the mic more toward the body of the instrument, a little away from the neck, with a slight down-angle, is the best place to start to preserve more of the bow. Bringing the angle up will tend to lose more of the bow and pointing more directly on the neck will give a fuller sound. Work with a range of anywhere from 10 to 15 inches back from the instrument.

Compressing live acoustic strings during recording almost always sounds bad, though you may find a little pre-fade EQ very helpful, especially with a small or less-than-stellar sounding recording space. In general, though, start with the input levels at about two-thirds of the fader and record as dry as possible.

Brass

Ribbon microphones are popular for brass instruments and horn sections (dynamic cardioid pattern mics run a nice, close, cheap second place here, as always). A vintage ribbon model like the RCA 44 will just blow you away, but if you have to ask about the price, you can't afford it!

More reasonable choices are mics like the Coles 4038, which has a high-end roll-off, while the Sony C-37 is a solid choice for a condenser mic.

NOTE

Ribbon microphones are highly sensitive to moisture, so much so that a pop screen is practically required.

You should work anywhere from 2 to 4 feet when placing the microphone, from chest to head level, depending on the instrument.

GigaStudio

This section jumps head first into an alternative to recording live acoustic instruments, via one of the more lauded and well-thought-out pieces of software to be created in the last few years, called GigaSampler, or GigaStudio.

NOTE

GigaStudio was created by a company called NemeSys. It's on the Web at **www.nemesysmusic.com**.

GigaStudio uses the same kind of tack as that of most types of digital sampling software: It streams sounds in real time from your hard drive instead of shuffling them back and forth strictly from memory (like a hardware sampler).

The result is that, with today's fast ATA-66 or higher IDE hard drives, you can play back seriously high quality libraries of sampled acoustic sounds with very long loops or with no looping at all, as well as record your own sounds. For all practical purposes, this means unlimited sampling capability, and the software also allows you to create multiple layers of samples by using MIDI controllers. It's affordable, too, ranging from around $79 for GigaSampler LE (Light Edition) to $699 for the GigaStudio 160, which supports 160 voices! GigaStudio 96 is perhaps the best value at around $400.

Most important, between NemeSys, third-party vendors, and individual musicians online and elsewhere, there are a huge number of samples you can use in GigaSampler format, from Miroslav Vitous' Symphonic Orchestra to NemeSys' own libraries. GigaStudio is also sixty-four-part multitimbral for huge arrangements.

This section is already beginning to sound like marketing copy for GigaStudio, but the fact is, the product is well worth obtaining if you want the sound of live real live acoustic instruments but don't have the money, space, or training on the instrument.

The difference is in the sounds. The sampling capabilities of GigaStudio are so much greater than even the best hardware synths or modules that you can achieve a level of realism that just wasn't possible a few years back. In fact, there are very few film composers these days who don't have this product in their studios.

Setup Notes

GigaStudio 96 or 160 ships with the application itself and various demo sounds in GigaSampler format, as well as the well-known, very kick butt sounding GigaPiano. Its setup is fairly straightforward, like most Windows software applications these days, though there are a few snags.

First, have the space available on your hard drive and install everything. The GigaPiano is 647 MB alone.

GigaStudio defaults to a maximum polyphony of sixty-four voices, which is a good choice for almost all but the most demanding songs. The available range is actually between twelve and 160 voices, but try to stay at sixty-four or lower if possible. The lower the number, the less the program will tax your processor.

If you go beyond sixty-four voices, work with the "Master Attenuation" setting at levels of up to 15 dB to prevent clipping. This is needed because, as more and more voices are sounded, the overall audio level will increase rapidly.

Getting Started with GigaStudio

The majority of GigaStudio's functions are accessed through its main window containing several resizable panes, as shown in Figure 8.1. From the tool and command bar, you can toggle the panes to customize to the way you work.

The navigation bar is a vertical "Outlook" style pane down the left-hand side of the screen, with icons for quick selection of the different main window displays, while the bottom portion of the screen defaults to the Instrument Loader window.

CHAPTER 8

Figure 8.1
The Outlook-like style
of GigaStudio is an
intuitive interface for
recording and playing
sampled instruments.

The Instrument Loader pane looks a bit like Windows Explorer, with treeview folders displayed in the left-hand column and the contents of the folders on the right. You can search for sounds on your hard drive manually or use the "QuickSound" database to quickly type in a search term for the sound. This is a great feature for quickly finding the sound you need.

In the case of GigaStudio 160, the navigation bar contains icons for four MIDI ports, DSP Station, Settings, Diagnostics, and Help (GigaStudio 96 gives you two ports). Each of the ports has a sixteen-channel MIDI mixer that is assigned to one of GigaStudio's MIDI inputs; you can also link any combination of ports to Port 1 to layer up to four sounds on a single MIDI channel.

Each mixer channel strip has mute and solo buttons at the top, along with tune, pan, and volume sliders, as well as a level meter. A compelling benefit to this software is that all three sliders can be reassigned to any other MIDI controller you choose.

Hard Drive

Like other digital audio applications, GigaStudio is almost equally dependent on hard drive speed and processor.

An IDE ATA-66 or better, Ultra DMA, or Ultra Wide SCSI hard drive with a minimum access time of 10 ms is pretty much a requirement. A drive this fast is easy to get and cheap to buy, which is fine if you need or want to buy a new hard drive; if you have an older hard drive that doesn't run to these specifications, though, you'll find it unacceptable. Memorywise, NemeSys recommends a minimum of 64 MB, but use at least 128 MB.

Sound Cards

A sound card with GSIF (GigaSampler Interface)-compatible drivers is ideal, since these provide the lowest latency (3 to 9 ms). When GigaSampler first hit the scene a few years ago, only three or four sound cards worked well with it, and only one supported multiple outputs (the Aark 20/20). Today, GSIF-compatible drivers are available from a number of different sound card manufacturers, with latency in the 3 to 9 ms range. Of course, there are many cards with multiple outputs to choose from, too—a veritable requirement for a digital home studio setup in any case. Aardvark, Echo, Ego Sys, Frontier Design, Midiman, Soundscape, and Terratec all support GSIF. Sound cards like the SB Live! don't, though you can use DirectSound drivers instead, with much slower and somewhat unpredictable results.

NOTE
NemeSys keeps a list of sound cards it has tested on its Web site.

Use It or Lose It

For your home studio, GigaStudio really is the best bang for your buck if you want to record acoustic instruments so real no one can tell the difference (yes, literally). As of this writing, there is little else on the market right now that comes close.

GigaStudio runs on Windows 95 or better, but NemeSys hasn't yet finished a WDM (Windows Driver Model) driver needed for running the application on Windows 2000.

NemeSys recommends the following specifications:

▶ GigaStudio 160 recommended: 800 MHz Pentium III or Athlon processor, 128 MB RAM.

▶ GigaStudio 96 recommended: 600 MHz Pentium III or Athlon processor, 128 MB RAM.

▶ Absolute minimum: 266 MHz Pentium II or 400 MHz AMD K6-2 processor, 64 MB RAM.

These specs are for GigaStudio running by itself. If you plan on running other applications (like a Web browser or another MIDI sequencer) alongside GigaStudio, you should go with a minimum of 600 MHz and 256 MB of RAM.

9

Wading in MIDI

MIDI is unquestionably an important part of most home studios. While it's possible to be a home recording artist without it, MIDI is a powerful tool that can save you time and money, and it can make it easier for you to write and record your compositions. This chapter is an introduction to MIDI and presumes that you have little or no knowledge about it. We'll cover a number of areas, including:

- ▶ What MIDI is and how it works
- ▶ FM and wavetable synthesis
- ▶ Hooking up MIDI devices
- ▶ The three most common configurations
- ▶ Channels and notes
- ▶ Sequencing
- ▶ Connecting to the PC
- ▶ MIDI-to-wave software

What Is MIDI?

The Musical Instrument Digital Interface (MIDI) is a protocol—a standard that is agreed upon and published by a body of experts—for how electronic musical instruments interact with each other or interact with a computer. MIDI has been widely accepted and used by musicians and composers since it was adopted in 1983 and has proven to be a highly creative and useful tool for writing and recording music. MIDI makes it easy for you to quickly record instruments and change tempos, keys, time signatures, instrument sounds—virtually any music editing activity.

With MIDI you can write music that no human could ever perform, because the standard allows you to manipulate musical notes in any way you see fit. Before MIDI, the physical limitations of a keyboard and two hands made it difficult to achieve many sounds on stage that artists were coming up with in the studio. And even in the studio there were limitations to how much layering one could comfortably achieve and experiment with using analog tape recording techniques.

Enter a group of musicians, synth designers, and equipment manufacturers who got together to devise a way to share the sounds of electronic keyboards with each other. What they produced was the MIDI specification, which was presented at the North American Music Manufacturers show in Los Angeles in 1983. Suffice to say, it took off like a rocket.

NOTE

MIDI may have taken off like a rocket, but it was not without a few disagreements between the U.S. and Japan (and between Yamaha and Roland). The result was that, in the U.S., the MMA (MIDI Manufacturers Association) was formed and, in Japan, the JMA (Japan MIDI Association).

For this reason, MIDI implementation of early instruments (1983-85) was a bit dicey; for example, the Yamaha DX-7 keyboard handles only a velocity range of 0-100, while its internal sound generator accepts up to 127—meaning the DX-7 sounds a bit different when it's being controlled by another MIDI device or sequencing software.

How MIDI Works

Any device that is MIDI-enabled can communicate with any other device that speaks MIDI's language. The device is typically a synthesizer or MIDI controller keyboard, but it could also be a drum machine, a rack-mounted effects unit, an external sequencer, a computer, a guitar outfitted with a MIDI interface—the list goes on and on.

So what's the language of MIDI? On one level, it's digital—a transfer of bytes that tells each participating instrument what it can and cannot do. On another level, the information is all musical: MIDI bytes tell an instrument, a sound card, or other MIDI device when to start and stop playing musical notes. MIDI also handles other important musical elements, such as volume and modulation, pitch, pan, when to change instrument sounds, the starting and stopping points of a song, and tempo.

NOTE

It is important to understand that MIDI does not ever produce or transport sound itself: It is a means by which you create and edit *data* to control the sound produced by the hardware or MIDI device.

The best examples of this are the names for MIDI sounds. On a practical level, names are just a guideline. For example, depending on your hardware, selecting the "Piano" sound from one keyboard may produce the "String" sound from another. As Freud said when asked about his family, "They're all relatives." (*botta-bing, botta-bing!*)

TIP

Terminology in the world of MIDI can often be confusing. For example, the terms "sound," "patch," "preset," "instrument," "program," and "voice" don't always mean the same thing to every manufacturer of MIDI hardware—but often they are exactly the same thing. The terms "track" and "channel" are another example. It can be a synonym frenzy at times, so don't let it get to you, just go with it, let it happen, let it be, chill out, take a load off.

NOTE

A byte consists of 8 bits. A bit is the smallest "unit" of data on a computer. Since a single bit is capable of representing only two different values (typically 0 or 1) you might think that there are a very small number of things you can represent with a bit. Actually, there are an infinite number of things you can represent with a single bit, for example, true or false, on or off, male or female, right or wrong, or two different notes, like C# and A. You could even represent two unrelated things with a bit, like Bb and the color white.

Because a byte is 8 bits, that means that a byte can actually represent 256 different values, or 2^8. This means MIDI can transmit a lot of data back and forth, and it does so quickly, too. In fact, MIDI operates internally at a speed of around 7 milliseconds, or 7/1000 of a second!

The bottom line is, MIDI devices communicate with each other by exchanging data. That data could instruct a MIDI device to, for instance, play a note or change pitch or change volume. The data may even cause the device to use a different voice, so that it sounds like a completely different instrument. In the next several sections, you will discover exactly how those data do their thing. Understanding the data process of MIDI allows you to better understand the power and flexibility of MIDI.

MIDI Channels

When MIDI devices speak to each other, they always follow a certain sequence of events. For example, the first thing two MIDI devices do after shaking hands, or exchanging data, is to agree to use the same MIDI *channel*. MIDI can operate on sixteen such channels, which are actually numbered from 0 through 15. Whenever two MIDI devices communicate, they have to agree upon the channel that's going to be used for any useful musical information to be exchanged.

On a technical level, a MIDI channel is part of what's called a status byte, which is a byte that includes the other elements that define the musical note. For example, when the note is being played, when it's not being played, special system exclusive (SysEx) commands, instrument changes (also called "patch changes" or "program changes"), pitch, volume, and so on.

Each of these elements also defines some of its own bytes—for example, the "Note On" byte tells the MIDI device to begin sounding a note, then "Note On" uses two other bytes itself to state the pitch (telling a MIDI device which note to play), and velocity (how loudly to play the note).

All these bytes must be handled successfully by two MIDI devices for MIDI to work. In other words, even if a particular MIDI instrument doesn't recognize the velocity byte, it still has to communicate back to the sending MIDI device or the MIDI message isn't complete.

CHAPTER 9

TIP

You would think that MIDI uses the Note On and Note Off commands as part of the same byte, but they are completely separate. This is because, just as Note On requires two additional bytes to indicate pitch and volume, the Note Off command needs its own two bytes to indicate pitch and volume. To put it another way: If you say, "Note On/Pitch" and "Note On/Volume" to play a note, you have to say, "Note Off/Pitch" and "Note Off/Volume" to stop playing that note.

The MIDI Interface

There are three *ports* that make up a MIDI interface: In, Out, and Thru. The In port processes incoming MIDI bytes—data coming "in" from another MIDI device—and plays the MIDI device according to the incoming data. The Out port transmits MIDI bytes "out" to another MIDI device. For example, if you play a chord on a synthesizer, all the things that define that chord on your keyboard—the notes that make up that chord, the velocity, the type of instrument sound, the value of your keyboard's pitch-bend wheel—go out of the MIDI Out port into the other MIDI device to which the synthesizer is connected.

The Thru port operates a bit differently. Data from the Thru port is just a copy of the data that's coming in through the In port. Hence the name "Thru"—MIDI data is just passing through, and there are no changes to any of the data before leaving the Thru port.

Hooking It All Up

Almost all MIDI-enabled devices will have both an In and an Out port (although, in some cases, you'll see only an Out port, since an In port is not necessary for devices that only *send* data). To hook up two MIDI devices, you connect the In port of one to the Out port of the other, and/or vice versa. You can use both ports or either one of them when you hook up MIDI devices with one another.

NOTE

Most MIDI interfaces use a standard MIDI cable, a special five-pin cable to connect the ports. The length of the cable is important: More than 50 feet between any two MIDI devices can cause problems with data transmission. Most musicians keep MIDI cable to less than 20 feet; 6- and 12-foot lengths are common.

TIP

Technically speaking, only three of the five pins of a MIDI interface are actually used. Originally, the MIDI standards proposal was to use a cannon connector—a connector very similar in design and appearance to an XLR connector, but wired a bit differently—but the five-pin din was less expensive and a computer standard at the time.

If you connect the MIDI Out port of one device to the MIDI In port of a second, when you press a key on the first device, both devices will play. However, pressing a key on the second one causes only the second device to sound. This is because the first one is only sending MIDI data, and the second device is only receiving data—so it has no way to send its data back to the first device.

It follows that if you connect both the In and Out ports of two MIDI devices, you can send and receive MIDI data on both devices, as shown in Figure 9.1.

Figure 9.1
Two keyboards are connected via their MIDI port, and can both send and receive their MIDI bytes.

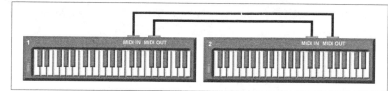

If you're used to using amplifiers or mixing boards, the labeling scheme that MIDI ports use can be a little confusing. It helps to think of a MIDI device the way you think of a mixing board: The MIDI In port is an input into the device and the Out port sends data to another MIDI device. Hence, the In port gets connected to the Out port and vice versa. It will not work the other way around: You cannot hook up the In port to another In port or the Out to another Out.

Masters and Slaves

Figure 9.1 shows a simple MIDI configuration: Both of the keyboards shown in the figure can be either the m*aster* or s*lave*. A master is any MIDI device that sends data through an Out port, while a slave is any MIDI device that will generate sound from the data being passed from, or through, the master.

Masters and slaves are where the Thru port becomes important. Many, though not all, MIDI devices possess a Thru port. Figure 9.2 shows a slightly more complex configuration using the Thru port. Notes played on the master keyboard are sent to the two slave keyboards, which will sound when the master is played.

Figure 9.2
Two slaves can easily serve one master using the Thru port.

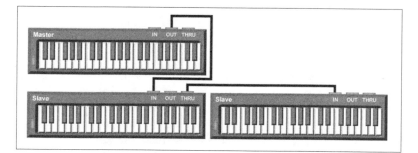

As discussed earlier, the channels of all the devices must be the same. For example, say you set one keyboard (the first slave keyboard) to a lush string sound. Then you set a second keyboard (the second slave) to play a horn section. In order to play the string and horn sounds simultaneously from your master keyboard, you must make sure that the channel you set on both of the slaves is the same as the master channel. It doesn't matter which number you use as long as it's between 0 and 15—and it's the same.

CHAPTER 9

This brings up a question: What if you want to play more than sixteen instrument sounds at once? MIDI allows you only sixteen different channels with which to transmit MIDI data, which means you can never play more than sixteen different instrument sounds at the same time. This doesn't mean you cannot play more than sixteen different slave devices—you can, by simply setting them all to the same channel.

The reason for the sixteen-channel limitation isn't too difficult to figure when you think about it: At the time MIDI was conceived, the most common type of mixing board consisted of sixteen channels. The creators of the MIDI specification presumed that, in most instances, musicians wouldn't need more than sixteen channels.

For most musicians, this limitation isn't a problem. However, there is a workaround in the MIDI specification to enable you to cheat a bit. Though you still cannot play more than sixteen sounds at once, you can switch—on any give note—instrument sounds by sending a program change that will change the instrument sound in midstream. The section "General MIDI: The Standard," later in this chapter, discusses this in more detail.

NOTE

"Polyphony" refers to how many simultaneous notes your electronic instrument can play. A keyboard that has 32-note polyphony simply means that it can generate up to 32 notes at once. Early synthesizers were all monophonic, as are some modern models, meaning that they could play only one note at a time.

Polyphony is important for MIDI. At some point, you are going to be limited as to how much layering or how many different MIDI parts are playing at once by the amount of polyphony in your MIDI keyboard or other device.

Hooking Up 1,000 MIDI Devices

Could you hook up a thousand MIDI devices? Theoretically, yes—but multiple MIDI connections using all three ports can quickly become very complex. For example, consider just four MIDI devices—a synth, a guitar synth, a drum machine, and a direct box for controlling guitar effects. Hooking them together using just one of their possible configurations might go something like this:

> The synth's Out port is connected to the In ports of the drum machine and guitar synth via the drum machine's Thru port. The drum machine's Out port then connects to the In port of the direct box, whose Thru connects to the In port of the synth. A key pressed on the synth sounds the synth itself, the guitar synth, and the drum machine. A pad pressed on the drum machine plays the drum machine and nothing else. A chord played on the guitar synth sounds the guitar synth, the direct box, and the synth, while an effect dialed up on the direct box sounds the effect only. The drum machine does not sound when the guitar synth is pressed, because there is no direct connection between the guitar synth and drum machine. But the drum machine's note, which routes through the direct box, does make it through the synth into the drum machine, because the synth's Thru port is not connected to the drum machine. A note played on the synth does not sound on the direct box for the same reason.

Did you follow all of that? If you did, go to the head of the class, pass Go, collect $200, and the check's in the mail! If you didn't, don't worry—it's genuinely hairy stuff and not at all necessary to be a happy, MIDI-actualized composer. In fact, you can further rid yourself of this kind of complexity by making your real master your computer, as discussed in the section, "MIDI Computing," a bit later in this chapter.

MIDI Is Not Audio, Really

MIDI does not actually sample data or play back "normal" audio data—it does not work the same way as a tape recorder or digital audio hard disk recorder in this regard. For instance, you could not record live instruments or your singing using MIDI. MIDI contains only its MIDI messages, which instruct a *synthesizer* to play sounds by telling it which sounds to use, which notes to play, how loud to play each note, and so on. The actual sounds are then generated by the synthesizer itself and are limited by the quality and capabilities of the synthesizer.

A synthesizer in this context is not just a keyboard—it's any electronic device which contains a built-in set of pre-determined sounds that have already been sampled and hard-coded into hardware or, more recently, into software on a computer. A number of different technologies and algorithms have been created over the years to generate sounds using a circuit board. The two most widely used are FM (frequency modulation) synthesis and wavetable synthesis.

FM Synthesis

FM synthesis uses one timed electronic signal, called a *modulator*, to control the frequency of another signal, referred to as a *carrier signal*. Modulating a carrier signal changes the timbre of the signal, which results in a theoretically unique FM *voice*. Every FM voice needs at least two signal generators, which are commonly referred to as *operators*.

The best FM synthesis techniques will use more than two operators per voice, and the operators will have flexible envelopes which allow you to change, for example, the signal's rate of attack and decay—the coolest knobs on a vintage Moog Sonic Six. The Sonic Six is an analog synthesizer—meaning that the way in which it passes sound around doesn't ever get converted to 0s and 1s—but most modern FM synthesis is done digitally.

To get into any more of the technical detail may cause nasty flashbacks to that physics course you dropped in school—suffice it to say, FM synthesis techniques have created some very expressive, unusual sounds and have been in popular use since the early '70's (the Yamaha DX-7 being, hands-down, the most popular early synth). FM has more recently undergone a big resurgence, which has resulted in synthesizer manufacturers producing new models and more new sounds.

FM synthesis was also the technique used for many years to reproduce instrumental sound on a computer sound card, using MIDI to play the sound card's FM-synthesized bank of sounds. The result was not exactly ear candy, and it was obvious to even the most casual listener that FM synthesis was not at all useful for accurately recreating the sound of an acoustic instrument. In other words, it sucked for realism. In order to achieve a realistic sound, digital sample-based techniques were developed, and wavetable synthesis was born. It has become one of the best games in town.

CHAPTER 9

Wavetable Synthesis

Wavetable synthesis stores sound samples in digital format, allowing you to play those sounds on demand or via MIDI. They use a number of digital signal processing tricks, such as looping, pitch shifting, filtering, and interpolation, to whittle down the memory needed to store the individual sound samples and produce faithful reproductions of acoustic or even other electronic instruments. The word "wavetable" was coined because the samples are organized into a bank, or table, of sound waveforms that can be accessed individually.

NOTE

Digital signal processing—DSP—is everywhere and can mean everything from enhancing sound in the studio by adding digital reverb to using a noise reduction filter in a cell phone. One of the most important aspects of DSP for the home studio artist is A/D and D/A conversion. This is the process of converting analog waveforms to digital format and vice versa. The algorithms and design of A/D and D/A converters can vary widely and can have a great effect on the quality and accuracy of the sound in your final recordings. DSP is covered in more detail in the next chapter, "Diving Deeper Into MIDI."

Nowadays, almost all professional synthesizers, as well as computer sound cards, use some form of wavetable synthesis. Using wavetable synthesis in conjunction with MIDI, you can "play" chords and notes that would be impossible to achieve on the original instrument by yourself. Depending on the polyphony capabilities of your keyboard, for example, you could very easily layer a 24-note chord using an acoustic guitar sound that even three sets of five fingers couldn't handle. You can then use MIDI to sustain, attack, control any number of tempos and volume, and so forth, without ever having to actually play the chord.

The quality of wavetable sounds can really vary. It's often dependent upon the original quality of the sampled instruments themselves, as well as the skill of the musician who played the sample. One thing's for certain: No matter how good a wavetable instrument sounds, you have to have a way to specify the sound, play it, and remember how to access it using MIDI.

Sequencing

Being able to play back beautifully realistic wavetable sounds across your MIDI devices is one thing, but being able to record them together in one place, create a MIDI "song," and play that song back at will, is far more compelling. This is where the real power of MIDI lies.

Recording in MIDI, generally referred to as "sequencing," is more or less the process of recording all of the note events corresponding to what you play. Using an external sequencing device, an on-board sequencer, or, more commonly, sequencing software with your computer, you can record, store, play back, and edit note events.

NOTE

Since software sequencing is the most common—and most powerful—way to sequence MIDI data, it's covered in more detail later in this chapter, in the section entitled "MIDI Computing," which discusses the MIDI file format as well.

In order to sequence MIDI data in a meaningful and organized fashion, you also need some way—other than your ear—to distinguish instrument sounds from one another. For this purpose, there is a standard called General MIDI, often referred to as simply "GM." Though MIDI device manufacturers have come up with their own schemes over the years for categorizing which sounds are which, it wasn't until General MIDI emerged that musicians could share a common structure for which sounds go where and in what order. This is a very necessary thing if you want someone with a different instrument or sound card to hear the same MIDI piano sequence—or any other sequence—that you've recorded.

The General MIDI Standard

When a MIDI sequence begins, a program change message—a kind of MIDI channel traffic cop—is sent on each channel, thereby setting up an instrument's sound. The program change tells the MIDI device which program number, or patch number, should be used on a particular MIDI channel. If the MIDI device receiving the MIDI sequence has already pre-assigned its patch numbers to sounds in exactly the same way the sending MIDI devices has, then the sounds of the notes will all play as expected.

However, if the patch numbers on one device don't match up with the patch numbers of another device, pandemonium ensues, because there is no way you can predict which instruments will sound. Enter the General MIDI (GM) standard, which sets up the relationship between patch numbers and instrument sounds. Any MIDI device that supports GM will usually be able to sound an instrument that corresponds to any other GM device's patch numbers.

The GM standard defines both a GM sound set (a set of patch numbers—also called a patch map) and a GM percussion set (percussion sounds only) and a set of other music-related capabilities, such as the number of voices and the kinds of MIDI messages that should be supported on any GM device.

GM uses MIDI channels 1-9 and 11-16 for instrument sounds, while channel 10 is reserved for percussion. Instrument sounds are grouped into families of similar sounds, as shown in Table 9.1.

CHAPTER 9

Table 9.1
General MIDI Instruments are parts of different families.

Program Number	Family
1-8	Piano
9-16	Chromatic percussion
17-24	Organ
25-32	Guitar
33-40	Bass
41-48	Strings
49-56	Ensemble
57-64	Brass
65-72	Reed instrument sounds
72-80	Pipe
81-88	Synth lead
89-96	Synth pad
97-104	Synth effects
105-112	Ethnic
113-120	Percussive
121-128	Sound effects

For instrument sounds, a note number is sent via a MIDI Note On message to select the pitch of the sound that will be played. For example, if Program Number 1 (acoustic grand piano) is using Channel 1, then playing note number 60 on Channel 1 plays Middle C using the acoustic grand piano sound.

For percussion sounds, a Note On message is used a bit differently: Note numbers select which drum sound will be played rather than sending pitch information. For example, a MIDI Note On message on Channel 10 transmitting note number 38 will play a snare sound and could care less about the snare sound's pitch.

NOTE

Remember how MIDI channels start at 0 and are numbered from 0-15? General MIDI is similar but is a bit more complex. GM specifies sounds using program numbers 1 through 128, but the MIDI program change message used to select these sounds corresponds to decimals numbering from 0 through 127. Hence if you select GM sound number 19, rock organ, a MIDI program change message will have a data byte with the decimal value 18. While most sequencing software uses the numbers 1-128, you will occasionally see 0-127 used.

The General MIDI standard specifies which instrument corresponds with which patch number, but GM does not specify how these sounds are produced. The result, of course, is that the overdriven guitar sound, for example, may not sound the same on two different GM synthesizers. In fact, although the organization that sets MIDI standards (the MIDI Manufacturers Association, or MMA, as noted earlier), set guidelines for developing GM-compatible sound sets that are relatively accurate, they did not set guidelines for the quality of individual sounds. So instrument sounds can vary significantly.

The Cost of Doing General MIDI

This section lists all the program numbers and their corresponding sounds for the GM sound set, but with a twist. The third column in Table 9.2 is a general indication of how much an accurate sound is going to cost you.

In the same way that food critics rate restaurants—with dollar signs ($) to indicate how expensive your meal is going to be—the scheme used here demonstrates that the quality of some instrument sounds can vary considerably, while others change very little. Though much has changed in the worlds of MIDI and wavetable synthesis since their inception, generally speaking, the most accurate, realistic sounds are available only on more expensive MIDI hardware (or sound cards or software synthesizers). Cheaper, less accurate sounds are stereotypical of inexpensive products, though this is not always the case. The ratings are as follows:

▶ **$**—A rating of 1 dollar sign indicates that a realistic instrument sound for this patch is inexpensive and widely available, with, for instance, an inexpensive portable "home" keyboard or a SoundBlaster Live! sound card. At current prices, this could mean anywhere from $50 to $250.

▶ **$$**—2 dollar signs means that you'll have to spend a little more, usually but not always on entry-level professional gear. This means you're probably somewhere over $500.

▶ **$$$**—3 dollar signs means that, while you probably won't have to get a loan to afford it, an accurate instrument sound is going to be reasonably expensive and available only on professional-level equipment. Plan on spending at least $1,000 (and you could easily creep up another thousand or two).

▶ **$$$$**—4 dollar signs means the cream of crop is necessary to get a realistic, accurate instrument sound. Plan on spending some major bucks, whether it's for a rack-mounted synthesizer, a sound card, or a software synth bank.

CHAPTER 9

These ratings are, of course, subjective, as is music in any case. What might be a proper electric grand piano sound to one person may sound like elevator Muzak to another. Indeed, many musicians would agree that some of the sounds in the GM sound set are *impossible* to reproduce accurately.

Use the table as a guideline—not the last word on the subject—to give you a feeling for which end of the cost spectrum you're headed toward in order to obtain an accurate sound for a given instrument.

Table 9.2
The Cost of Doing GM Instruments.

Program#	Instrument Sound	Cost
1	Acoustic Grand Piano	$$$$
2	Bright Acoustic Piano	$$$$
3	Electric Grand Piano	$$$
4	Honky-tonk Piano	$$
5	Electric Piano 1	$$$
6	Electric Piano 2	$$$
7	Harpsichord	$$
8	Clavi	$$$
9	Celesta	$
10	Glockenspiel	$$
11	Music Box	$
12	Vibraphone	$$$
13	Marimba	$$$
14	Xylophone	$$$$
15	Tubular Bells	$
16	Dulcimer	$$$$
17	Drawbar Organ	$$
18	Percussive Organ	$$
19	Rock Organ	$
20	Church Organ	$$$
21	Reed Organ	$$$$
22	Accordion	$$$$
23	Harmonica	$$$
24	Tango Accordion	$$$$

Program#	Instrument Sound	Cost
25	Acoustic Guitar (nylon)	$$$$
26	Acoustic Guitar (steel)	$$$$
27	Electric Guitar (jazz)	$$$$
28	Electric Guitar (clean)	$$$$
29	Electric Guitar (muted)	$$$
30	Overdriven Guitar	$$$$
31	Distortion Guitar	$$$
32	Guitar harmonics	$$$$
33	Acoustic Bass	$$
34	Electric Bass (finger)	$$
35	Electric Bass (pick)	$$
36	Fretless Bass	$$$
37	Slap Bass 1	$$$
38	Slap Bass 2	$$$
39	Synth Bass 1	$
40	Synth Bass 2	$$
41	Violin	$$$
42	Viola	$$$
43	Cello	$$$$
44	Contrabass	$$$
45	Tremolo Strings	$$$
46	Pizzicato Strings	$$$$
47	Orchestral Harp	$$
48	Timpani	$$
49	String Ensemble 1	$$$
50	String Ensemble 2	$$$
51	SynthStrings 1	$$
52	SynthStrings 2	$$
53	Choir Aahs	$$$$
54	Voice Oohs	$$$$
55	Synth Voice	$

CHAPTER 9

Program#	Instrument Sound	Cost
56	Orchestra Hit	$$
57	Trumpet	$$$
58	Trombone	$$$
59	Tuba	$$
60	Muted Trumpet	$$$
61	French Horn	$$$
62	Brass Section	$$
63	SynthBrass 1	$$
64	SynthBrass 2	$$
65	Soprano Sax	$$$$
66	Alto Sax	$$$
67	Tenor Sax	$$$$
68	Baritone Sax	$$$
69	Oboe	$$
70	English Horn	$$
71	Bassoon	$$$
72	Clarinet	$$
73	Piccolo	$$$$
74	Flute	$$$
75	Recorder	$
76	Pan Flute	$$
77	Blown Bottle	$
78	Shakuhachi	$$
79	Whistle	$
80	Ocarina	$
81	Lead 1 (square)	$$
82	Lead 2 (sawtooth)	$$
83	Lead 3 (calliope)	$$$
84	Lead 4 (chiff)	$$$
85	Lead 5 (charang)	$$$
86	Lead 6 (voice)	$$$$

Program#	Instrument Sound	Cost
87	Lead 7 (fifths)	$$$$
88	Lead 8 (bass + lead)	$$
89	Pad 1 (new age)	$$
90	Pad 2 (warm)	$$$
91	Pad 3 (polysynth)	$$$$
92	Pad 4 (choir)	$$$$
93	Pad 5 (bowed)	$$$
94	Pad 6 (metallic)	$$
95	Pad 7 (halo)	$$$$
96	Pad 8 (sweep)	$$
97	FX 1 (rain)	$$
98	FX 2 (soundtrack)	$$$$
99	FX 3 (crystal)	$$$
100	FX 4 (atmosphere)	$$$
101	FX 5 (brightness)	$
102	FX 6 (goblins)	$$$
103	FX 7 (echoes)	$$$
104	FX 8 (sci-fi)	$
105	Sitar	$$$$
106	Banjo	$$$
107	Shamisen	$$
108	Koto	$$$
109	Kalimba	$$
110	Bag pipe	$$$$
111	Fiddle	$$$
112	Shanai	$$$$
113	Tinkle Bell	$
114	Agogo	$$$
115	Steel Drums	$$
116	Woodblock	$
117	Taiko Drum	$$

CHAPTER 9

Program#	Instrument Sound	Cost
118	Melodic Tom	$
119	Synth Drum	$$$
120	Reverse Cymbal	$$$$
121	Guitar Fret Noise	$
122	Breath Noise	$$$$
123	Seashore	$$$$
124	Bird Tweet	$$
125	Telephone Ring	$
126	Helicopter	$$
127	Applause	$$$$
128	Gunshot	$$

The Cost of Doing GM Percussion

Following a somewhat similar format as in the previous section, Table 9.3 lists the MIDI note numbers, using Channel 10, which correspond to different drum sounds. GM-compatible percussion instruments will sound the instruments according to the note number shown in the table. It should be noted that many MIDI devices add additional percussion sounds corresponding to note numbers below or above the GM-specified range, and it's not uncommon for manufacturers to offer full-fledged drum kits based on a "chord" of note combinations as well.

Percussion instruments that make up popular trap set configurations (kick drum, snare, hi-hat, cymbals, toms) are particularly difficult to estimate in terms of realism. One of the unique aspects of a drum kit in popular music is the way the different percussion pieces combine together to create ambience—the way the sounds play off one another. This makes achieving a highly realistic kit sound with MIDI percussion patches very difficult.

Table 9.3
The Cost of Doing Drums.

MIDI Note Number	Drum Sound	Cost
35	Acoustic Bass Drum	$$
36	Bass Drum 1	$$$
37	Side Stick	$$
38	Acoustic Snare	$$$$
39	Hand Clap	$$$$
40	Electric Snare	$$
41	Low Floor Tom	$$$
42	Closed Hi Hat	$$$

MIDI Note Number	Drum Sound	Cost
43	High Floor Tom	$$$$
44	Pedal Hi-Hat	$$
45	Low Tom	$$$
46	Open Hi-Hat	$$$
47	Low-Mid Tom	$$$
48	Hi Mid Tom	$$$
49	Crash Cymbal 1	$$$$
50	High Tom	$$$$
51	Ride Cymbal 1	$$$$
52	Chinese Cymbal	$$$
53	Ride Bell	$$
54	Tambourine	$$
55	Splash Cymbal	$$$$
56	Cowbell	$
57	Crash Cymbal 2	$$$$
58	Vibraslap	$$$
59	Ride Cymbal 2	$$$$
60	Hi Bongo	$$$
61	Low Bongo	$$$
62	Mute Hi Conga	$$
63	Open Hi Conga	$$
64	Low Conga	$$$
65	High Timbale	$$$$
66	Low Timbale	$$
67	High Agogo	$$$
68	Low Agogo	$$
69	Cabasa	$$$
70	Maracas	$$
71	Short Whistle	$
72	Long Whistle	$$
73	Short Guiro	$$$
74	Long Guiro	$$$

MIDI Note Number	Drum Sound	Cost
75	Claves	$$$
76	Hi Wood Block	$
77	Low Wood Block	$
78	Mute Cuica	$$$
79	Open Cuica	$$$$
80	Mute Triangle	$
81	Open Triangle	$$

MIDI Computing

Since MIDI devices and computers speak the same language, a computer is an ideal tool for using MIDI. To control MIDI devices from your computer, you need a MIDI interface for your computer, a cable, and MIDI software. There are many different interfaces available for almost all types of computer systems. Apple supports MIDI in most of its current models, through a USB port. For a PC, most standard sound cards have a MIDI interface built into the joystick port, and a number of interface cards exist with both custom interface designs as well as the standard five-pin MIDI ports for both PCs and Macs.

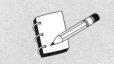

NOTE

USB (universal serial bus) is rapidly becoming the standard for hooking up devices to a PC as well. There are numerous PC peripherals that use a USB port, including joysticks, scanners, digital speakers, digital cameras, and PC telephones. Most PCs on the market today—including notebooks—are USB-ready.

USB is very simple to use, doesn't typically require you to pry open your PC to install an add-in card or set DIP switches, and doesn't need to use IRQs (interrupt requests—the subject of many a Windows user's long nights). USB is also fast—the current 1.1 standard runs at 1.5 MB per second, and you can easily chain together a large number of USB devices, typically using a USB "hub," which is a central box for routing and re-routing all the data. The ability to chain together USB devices is a lot like MIDI, except standard MIDI interfaces run at a speed of 31.5 Mbaud, which is much slower than USB.

More and more MIDI-based devices can use USB, and there are real benefits to USB for MIDI due to the speed increase: better timing accuracy, increased bandwidth, hot swapping (changing connections during data transmission), and easy expansion.

NOTE

See Chapter 11, "Fun-Da-Mental Audio," for excruciating detail on sound cards.

A computer functions in much the same way as any other MIDI device, but it is used a bit differently. A computer works best as the main MIDI data driver, meaning it supplies MIDI data to the rest of your MIDI-enabled instruments. To use a recording analogy, it's your (MIDI) playback console.

This works perfectly with the whole idea of MIDI channels. A computer can send MIDI bytes out on all sixteen MIDI channels simultaneously with ease. For example, if you've connected sixteen different MIDI devices to your computer and assign a different MIDI channel to each one, you can play a different part on each MIDI device and control it all from your computer. This capability has great implications for the home recording studio.

In addition to driving the MIDI data that "plays" your MIDI devices, your computer can function beautifully as the recording device that will capture your MIDI performances, too. Using MIDI software, you can receive incoming MIDI data, record it, play it back while recording new tracks, save it to your hard drive as a file, re-open it later, or share it with anyone who has the ability to play MIDI files on a computer.

You'll need to be able to connect your computer to your MIDI instruments and install software that enables you to use the computer as your own MIDI studio. The following sections will show you how.

Connecting Your Computer

As shown in Figure 9.3, the easiest setup for connecting your computer to another MIDI device is a simple matter of connecting the In port to the Out port and vice versa. With both the In and Out ports in use, you can use a MIDI-enabled synthesizer, for example, to input MIDI data into the computer as well as play MIDI data using the computer to control playback.

Figure 9.3
A typical MIDI connection between a keyboard and a computer is easy.

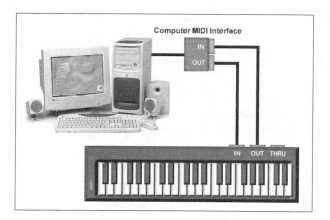

Connecting slaves is also similar to the way the master/slave setup worked earlier in this chapter. Figure 9.4 shows a setup with the computer, one master keyboard, and two slaves.

Figure 9.4
A master/slave MIDI using a computer is slightly more complex.

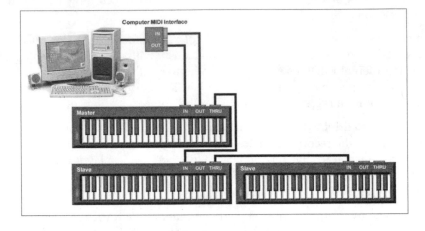

A master/slave setup is most useful if you have one primary MIDI device you'll use to play your songs and several other MIDI devices that you want to trigger from the master, such as external sound modules, rack-mount units with additional instruments and/effects, your computer's sound card, or software synth sounds on your computer's hard drive.

The master/slave setup is *not* the most useful way to set up your connections if you have a number of other devices you want to actually play—like a separate drum machine or electronic drum kit or a guitar synth. In this case, you'll need to be able to both send and receive MIDI data between your computer and each instrument, which is impossible to do with a standard 3-port MIDI interface for a computer. There are two ways around this.

The first way is the most cumbersome—simply disconnect the cables from one MIDI device and connect them to the next device you want to play. If you use more than one MIDI device frequently, you'll quickly tire of having to switch cables.

A much easier way is to buy a separate, external MIDI patch bay, which is a device that allows you to connect all your MIDI devices up to one place, then route it all out of one set of cables into your computer's MIDI interface (see Figure 9.5).

Figure 9.5
A MIDI patch bay enables each MIDI device in your setup to send and receive MIDI data.

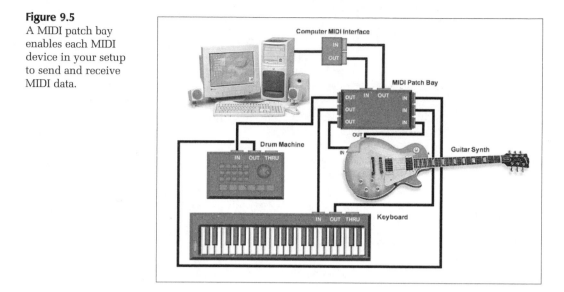

There are dozens of models on the market ranging from $50 to $500. The least expensive units usually offer fewer MIDI ports, typically two In ports and two Out ports (also known as 2 × 2) or 4 × 4) and lack additional features like a SMPTE synchronizer, a pedal switch, or muting. The better units offer at least 8 × 8 and usually provide some kind of software console for easily managing the routing and merging of the MIDI ports. Mark of the Unicorn (**www.motu.com**) makes a line of MIDI expansion boxes that are USB-equipped and allow you to expand your MIDI setup just by adding a standard USB hub. These come in a range of sizes and prices.

NOTE

SMPTE (Society of Motion Picture and Television Engineers) time code, pronounced "Simptee," is a time code synchronization protocol originally developed by NASA to time-stamp satellite data, then adapted for synchronizing audio with videotape.

For example, a multi-track audio tape recorder can use SMPTE to provide time code on one track to keep all the other tracks in sync, or a videotape might use a cue track or one of its audio sound tracks to record and play back the synchronizing SMPTE time code.

MIDI also has its own kind of time code—MTC, or MIDI Time Code. It's a sub-protocol within MIDI used to keep in sync two devices that control any kind of timed performance. MTC is essentially SMPTE mutated for transmission over MIDI, and it's covered in more detail in Chapter 10, "Diving Deeper into MIDI."

CHAPTER 9

The MIDI File Format

MIDI has its own file format, which uses the .MID file extension, to store MIDI data. The format is a binary one, rather than text, so you cannot open it up and view it or edit it directly. The MIDI file format is very efficient compared to storing digital audio. You could create a 30-minute MIDI composition with dozens of instruments and need only a couple of dozen kilobytes on your drive to store all the MIDI information needed to play that file on a computer. Compared to a "real" audio file format like WAV (about 10 MB per minute) or even MP3 (about 1 MB per minute), this is very small.

The MIDI file format specification actually sets up three types of MIDI files: MIDI Format 0, MIDI Format 1, and MIDI Format 2. Format 0 stores all MIDI sequence data in a single track, while Format 1 files store MIDI data as a collection of tracks. For home studio recording with MIDI, Format 1 is the most useful, because you can edit and view individual tracks. Format 2 can store several independent patterns and has some other non-musical capabilities; it is generally not used or supported by most MIDI software.

NOTE

MIDI data files are extremely small when compared to digital audio files. For instance, a typical three-minute pop song in .WAV or .AIFF format recorded in high-quality stereo would need more than 30 MB of space on your hard drive and require about 10 MB of data per minute of sound, while an average MIDI file would take up around 15 KB of space and consume less than 10 KB of data per minute of sound.

The small size of MIDI files also makes the format very well suited to download over the Internet; Web browsers support it, and there are hundreds of thousands of MIDI files available for download across the Net. The MIDI Farm, at **www.midifarm.com**, has a large number of MIDI files online and also links to other MIDI file collections.

The downside is that a MIDI file does not always sound the same on a given computer (particularly so if the MIDI file is not General MIDI!). This is because not all sound cards use the same synthesis techniques for reproducing instrument sounds, as discussed earlier.

In fact, there are as many differences between sound card instruments as there are between different external MIDI devices. Not too many years ago, it was much more consistent: All sound cards used FM-synthesis and they all sounded consistently horrible. Today, almost all sound cards are wavetable-based, so that even the cheapest sound cards sound much better than FM. However, there are differences—sometimes major differences—between the wavetable engine and the sampled sounds (commonly called wavesets) of one sound card versus another. And it's the same rule-of-thumb when it comes to cost: For many sounds, the more you pay, the more realistic the sound, while some instruments sound about the same whether you paid for them in cash or mortgaged your house.

Using MIDI Software

There are dozens, if not hundreds, of software programs that manage virtually anything that can be done with MIDI. Many keyboards have sequencers built on board the keyboard itself, so that if you want to create songs using MIDI instruments, you can store them and play them back at any time. Unfortunately, most on-board sequencers cannot store anywhere near the amount of data that a typical hard drive can, and there's no easy way for you to share your work with other musicians or distribute your work to anyone else without a computer.

In addition, MIDI software has expanded in the last several years to include digital audio recording capabilities. The converse has happened as well—most software that started out focusing on digital audio has added MIDI support.

MIDI software runs the gamut in price, from freeware programs to professional packages that run into the thousands of dollars. Rather than go into an extensive review of every imaginable MIDI program, this section will briefly focus on SONAR—the most popular and best valued, reasonably priced software package available. We'll also survey a few of the other MIDI applications in use today.

SONAR

SONAR (**www.cakewalk.com**) is one of the oldest, best-supported MIDI software packages and is used by many professional musicians and engineers, from Jon Anderson of Yes to George Clinton and The P-Funk All-Stars. SONAR began as Cakewalk, a MIDI sequencer alone, and nine versions later a full-fledged MIDI and digital audio software application; the name "Cakewalk" was retired as the official name of the product with the release of SONAR 1.0, which is a serious, full-featured application that is a master of MIDI, can record and play digital audio, use DirectX 8 audio plug-ins, and even do advanced audio looping.

SONAR will allow you to record an unlimited number of MIDI and digital audio tracks. SONAR also supports 24-bit/96 kHz audio, SMPTE synchronization for film and video, automated volume, and panning. The package also uses control panels (see Figure 9.6), called StudioWare, which simulate the feeling of a mixing board while providing MIDI-based studio automation.

CHAPTER 9

Figure 9.6
SONAR uses a number of intuitive interfaces, including this one, to help make MIDI sequencing easy.

SONAR will also encode to MP3, RealSystem G2, and Windows Media, let you bundle your MIDI recordings into one file with digital audio, and easily create and print music notation, including lyrics. But this just scratches the surface; there are a huge number of other features, so many that an entire book could easily be written to cover them all.

NOTE

Scott Garrigus' book, *SONAR Power!* (Muska & Lipman, 2001, ISBN 1-929685-02-5), is a highly recommended book for discovering all of the ins and outs of getting the most out of SONAR's features. The book has received rave reviews and is well worth your time if you are interested in SONAR.

SONAR employs a number of different interfaces, and its main interface, as shown in Figure 9.7, is highly intuitive.

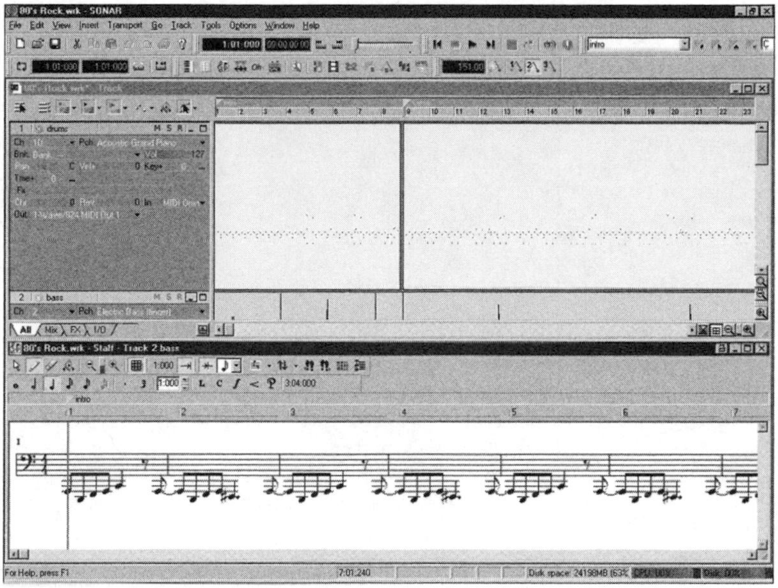

Figure 9.7
SONAR's main interface
is shown on top. Part of
the "Staff" view is
displayed at the bottom.

SONAR uses a simple scheme which displays blocks of MIDI data that you can cut, copy, paste and edit, much like you would edit text in a word processing program. You can also view the MIDI data in other ways: A note list of all MIDI events, a "Piano Roll" view which shows you individual blocks of each MIDI note, a "Staff" view to edit notation, and several others.

These different views of MIDI data allow you to "see" your music in ways you may never have thought of before. For example, the Event List view (Figure 9.8) allows you to manage at a micro-level exactly what every note does, including where patch changes occur. This is highly useful, as mentioned earlier in the chapter, for overcoming MIDI's limit of sixteen simultaneous channels.

CHAPTER 9

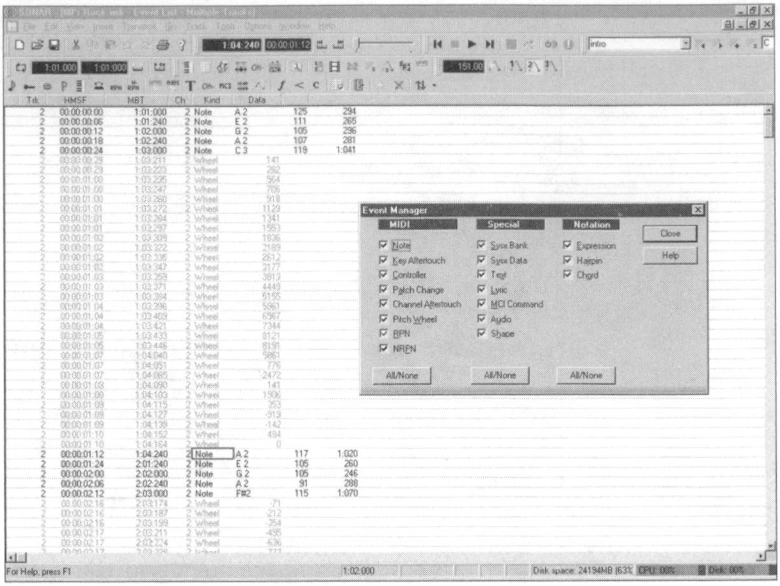

Figure 9.8
SONAR's Event List view is an easy way to make patch changes anywhere in a song. SONAR uses "tracks" in much the same way as a mixing board uses them, too.

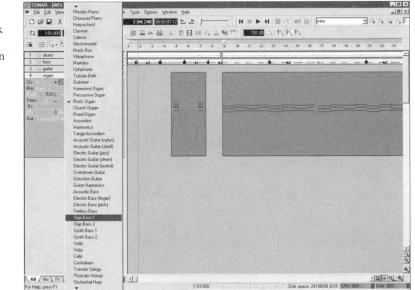

Figure 9.9 shows just how easy it is to assign instruments to a track. It's mostly a matter of scrolling and picking.

Figure 9.9
Use the Patch drop-down box in the Track pane in Track view to select an instrument in SONAR.

In order to use SONAR, you'll need a MIDI interface card in your computer or a sound card that supports MIDI (just about all of them do). During installation, SONAR will automatically detect your audio hardware and set itself up to work with that hardware.

Although SONAR uses a couple of its own proprietary file formats for storing both MIDI and digital audio data, it also fully supports the MIDI file format. In addition to SONAR's Pro Audio package, the company also sells stripped-down version, called SONAR Home Studio, which still offers full MIDI support but more limited digital audio capabilities.

Other MIDI Software

In addition to SONAR, a number of other audio software applications fully support MIDI and offer well-designed interfaces. Arguably, none of these is as easy to get started with as SONAR, and several of them are more expensive. However, they are excellent applications and well worth noting.

▶ Logic Audio (**www.emagic.de**) is a complete digital audio application that offers almost identical interfaces for both Windows and Macintosh. The application is high performance, DSP-rich, and completely redesigned for version 4.0 in 1999. Logic Audio fully supports MIDI, offers 24-bit/96 kHz digital audio recording, and ships with dozens of high-end digital audio plug-ins.

▶ Digital Performer (**www.motu.com**) is a Mac-only integrated digital audio and MIDI sequencing production tool that handles recording, playback, and editing for both MIDI and audio data. The software includes an automated 32-bit digital mixer, reverb, effects, EQ, and compression in addition to its MIDI sequencing capabilities.

▶ Studio Vision Pro (**www.opcode.com**) is a Mac-only MIDI and digital audio recording and sequencing application. Features include full support for advanced DSP, enhanced integration with Apple's QuickTime, and support for all major audio file types. The program is inexpensive and ships with excellent samples in audio and MIDI format.

▶ Cubase VST (**www.steinberg.net**), available in separate versions for both Windows and Mac, is a professional-level application which combines MIDI with digital audio recording. The software performs high-resolution MIDI recording, with audio recording for both 16- or 24-bit formats and an extensive list of custom plug-ins for MIDI and digital audio effects. Cubase VST supports a special type of sound card called ASIO, which is known for its unique design and low latency (fast data transmission).

▶ RocketPower Audio Software (**www.rocketnetwork.com**) makes MIDI software for online collaborative use. The application allows you to connect with other musicians via the Internet and create, record, and "post" audio and MIDI tracks to everyone in an online Internet "recording studio." RocketPower requires the RocketControl application—a specialized chat program—and a Web browser. Only audio software that supports RocketPower works with RocketPower, and that currently includes Cubase VST and Logic Audio.

▶ MIDI Orchestrator Plus (**www.voyetra-turtle-beach.com**) is a cool, inexpensive, dedicated MIDI recording studio. The program supports up to 1,000 tracks of MIDI data, lets you print music from any MIDI file, has a treble clef, bass clef and grand staff view, and includes a wide variety of MIDI music files, drum tracks, and video demos for getting up to speed quickly.

CHAPTER 9

10
Diving Deeper into MIDI

If Chapter 9 was learning how to drive, this chapter is understanding how the engine works. Though the basics of MIDI will take you well down the road to a more powerful home studio setup, understanding the way MIDI works under the hood will put you across the finish line. This chapter will teach you:

▶ How MIDI works behind the scenes using MIDI messages

▶ The types of MIDI messages and what they do

▶ How to record and edit tracks in a MIDI software sequencer

▶ The inner workings behind the MIDI format and where MIDI is headed in the future

Messages, Messages, and More Messages

Dissect for a minute exactly what happens when you play a line on a MIDI device: Each time you create a note, an almost instantaneous stream of digital data travels down your MIDI cable. Any MIDI device, including your computer, that is tuned to the correct MIDI channel immediately responds to each note in the stream and "renders" that note as an audible instrument sound—a bona fide analog sound wave. The analog sound is then piped through an amplifier, routed through a set of speakers and into the air.

Hence, there are two sides: a digital side, and an analog side. You can't hear something that is digital, any more than a computer or an electronic keyboard can "hear" an analog signal. In both cases, a conversion process must take place, from digital to analog and analog to digital, commonly referred to as D/A and A/D.

NOTE

A MIDI device can be anything that sends and/or receives MIDI messages. This is everything from an electronic keyboard to a device that operates based on motion detection to a drum machine.

For convenience's sake, this chapter will generally refer to a MIDI device as an electronic keyboard, which is the simplest and most common method of doing MIDI.

In order for a stream of MIDI information to eventually reach D/A, it needs to contain meaningful bits of data that a D/A converter can use to manipulate audio data and then construct a sound wave. These bits of data are organized into 8-bit chunks, or *bytes*—meaning they are delivered 8 bits at a time—and make up what are called MIDI messages.

Bytes in the Message

Two types of bytes make up a MIDI message: status bytes and data bytes. A status byte comes first. It identifies what kind of MIDI data is being transmitted or received—for example, Note On or Note Off, Velocity, Modulation, Pitch, and so on. A data byte comes next, and it is simply the value of its associated status byte.

As an analogy, think of how a mixing board works: Imagine a board with 128 faders, each with a range of 128 different values. When you move fader 1 to the halfway position, it is like saying, "Fader 1, Value of 64." The instrument on fader 1 will then change its volume to a value of 64.

Now imagine that instead of moving a fader, you tap a note on a MIDI keyboard. When you press the key, a Note On status byte is sent, immediately followed by the data byte for that note, for example, a value of Middle C. It's like saying, "Play a note. The note is Middle C." All MIDI devices receiving your MIDI messages will respond by telling their D/A converters to get ready to render a note and then render it as Middle C. When you release the key, a Note Off status byte and a data byte of Middle C are sent, causing connected MIDI devices stop playing Middle C.

Types of MIDI Messages

There are two basic types of MIDI messages: Channel Messages and System Messages. A Channel Message is channel-specific, meaning there is always a channel number included in its status byte; while a System Message is not channel-specific. System Messages come in three different flavors: System Common, System Real-Time, and System Exclusive Messages.

Channel Messages can be further broken down into three groups: Voice Messages, Controller Messages, and Mode Messages. Voice Messages carry musical data, and make up most of the traffic in a MIDI data stream, while Controller Messages allow you to affect musical data in other ways, such as panning the sound or adding vibrato. Mode Messages work a bit differently: They deal only with the way a receiving MIDI devices respond to Voice Messages.

Voice Messages

There are several important kinds of Voice Messages. They are:

► Note On
► Note Off
► Aftertouch
► Pitch Bend
► Bank Select and Program Change

Each type of Voice Message is discussed in the following sections.

Note On

Note On is the most basic of all MIDI messages. Every time a key is pressed on a MIDI device, a Note On status byte is delivered, followed by Pitch and Velocity data bytes, which are values for the note's pitch and volume, respectively. MIDI devices don't exchange pitch information in terms of traditional letter names, such as Middle C or F#, but use numeric values between 0 and 127. This range is a full three octaves, more than the number of octaves on a piano.

Middle C is always a value of 60, hence a MIDI device that receives a Note On message and a value of 60 will produce a sound with its pitch at Middle C, regardless of the instrument setting.

Velocity refers to how fast the key is struck, which more or less equates to volume. Velocity carries a value range of between 0 and 127 and is obviously a critical data byte for shaping any performance.

Note Off

A Note Off message is just the opposite of Note On and must be sent to a MIDI device for it to release the note. Note Off also must be followed by messages for pitch and velocity. A Note Off/Velocity message combination specifies the rate at which a key is lifted; velocity has a range from 0 to 127.

NOTE

Technically speaking, a Note Off/Velocity combination is called "Release Velocity," and a few instruments (Kurzweil, for example) can change voice parameters based on the rate at which you release keys. It's difficult to use, but extremely cool!

Running Status

A Note On or Note Off message takes about one millisecond (ms) to be sent, which is quick enough that the human ear perceives multiple notes as being played simultaneously. Even if you played a 10-note chord, for example, the time between playback of the chord and when you pressed all the notes (10 ms) wouldn't be noticeable.

However, playing a large number of different parts, such as several tracks from a sequencer, could produce delays that might be noticeable. To prevent this, a technique called "running status" is often used.

Running status takes into account the fact that it's common for a string of MIDI messages to be of the same message type. For instance, when you play that 10-note chord, 10 successive Note On and Note Off messages are pretty much guaranteed to occur. So running status doesn't change status bytes until a different status byte comes through. Running status doesn't work with all types of MIDI messages, but it does work for many important ones, such as Pitch Bend, which can produce a huge number of MIDI messages.

Aftertouch

An Aftertouch message is sent when any key is held and pressed harder or softer after striking the key. Not all MIDI devices support Aftertouch, and ones that do vary, responding differently depending on the type of instrument and the sensitivity of the electronic sensors built in to the MIDI device.

Channel Pressure

The most common, and least expensive, type of Aftertouch is called Channel Pressure. Channel Pressure calculates pressure sensitivity based on an average of all of the keys that you're holding down. In other words, you don't have individual control over each individual key. This type of Aftertouch is better than no Aftertouch but is not nearly as useful as Key Pressure.

Key Pressure

Key Pressure Aftertouch usually means that the MIDI device has a separate pressure sensor for each key or pad on the device. This means you can be much more expressive during a performance. For example, say you've written a horn section and you're playing several parts of the arrangement at the same time. At some point, you're going to want one or more of the instruments to stand out a bit more than the others while you're playing. Using Key Pressure, you can focus on any one note without also making the other instruments' notes brighter. This is a much more realistic horn section, since real brass instruments are capable of a wide range of subtle differences in volume and tone.

TIP

Key Pressure is more expensive to implement, and therefore many MIDI devices don't offer it. The same is true for many sound cards and MIDI sound modules. A MIDI device that supports Key Pressure won't do you much good if you're using a sound card that doesn't support it.

Aftertouch is not just for controlling volume. In fact, one of the most common uses of Aftertouch is for Modulation or Vibrato. The harder you hold down a key, the wider the resulting vibrato. This is very useful for wind and string instruments.

TIP

It's not uncommon for some instruments or sound patches to be overly sensitive to Aftertouch, making it difficult to play notes at high velocity with a vibrato effect, for example. You may have some luck adjusting the sensitivity of the MIDI device itself (if it offers that capability), but the easiest route is to edit the Aftertouch values using your sequencing software after recording the performance.

Pitch Bend

Most MIDI devices have the ability to perform a Pitch Bend on any given note, usually using a toggle or wheel control. Pitch Bend messages are great for accentuating the natural expressiveness of instruments like guitar, flute, and even some percussion.

Pitch bend is measured by combining two data messages. Since a range of 0 to 127 isn't sufficient to create a convincing effect, MIDI combines two data messages to provide 16,384 possible values (128 × 128). This creates a high enough resolution to make pitch changes smooth and continuous.

Bank Select and Program Change

MIDI instruments are organized into a MIDI device's memory by numbered banks, and each bank contains individual sound patches tagged with unique ID numbers. MIDI Bank Select allows a MIDI device to trigger a bank change on any other device with a matching MIDI channel.

A Program Change message will then bring up a sound within the bank that corresponds to the ID being sent. This seems basic enough at first glance, but it's actually quite powerful: Because a Program Change affects only an ID and not any other sound parameters, it can be applied to any MIDI-compatible device, such as an effects unit, a mixer, or even a sampler.

NOTE

General MIDI aside (see Chapter 9, "Wading in MIDI"), there is no standard for numbering patches and banks, nor is there any agreed-upon system for organizing instrument types with ID numbers. Hence, most MIDI devices are packed with sounds that are numbered well beyond the scope of the GM specification, which makes it difficult to share anything beyond GM across multiple MIDI devices.

Controller Messages

Controller Messages are similar to Voice Messages, but they behave a bit differently. These messages provide extended "control" over the sounds or instruments that you associate with them and are typically transmitted using a modulation wheel or other controller on a MIDI device, such as a pedal, slider, touch ribbon, knob, fader, and so on. Controller Messages use a status byte just like a Voice Message, but they use two additional data bytes, rather than just one. The first data byte is the Controller Number, of which there are 128 possible values (numbered 0 to 127). The second byte is similar to the data byte in a Voice Message—it's the actual value of a particular controller.

The idea behind MIDI controllers is that they work while the MIDI device is generating sound, in "real time," so that the effect is immediately noticeable. However, Controller Messages can also be sent from within a MIDI software program, usually through virtual knobs and faders as part of the software interface or by editing a particular value directly.

Many of today's songs use controllers in creative and innovative ways to give a customized, unique expressiveness to a sequence. The next sections cover the most common types of controllers.

Modulation

Most sounds in a MIDI device will respond to Modulation with a vibrato effect. Vibrato is a common and useful type of modulation and can add realism to wind, string, and brass instruments if used carefully. Vibrato can also create some very non-intuitive and unrealistic sounds when applied to other types of instruments, such as piano or percussion, for example. In addition, many electronic instruments respond too abruptly to Modulation, which can create unnatural and sometimes indecipherable mutations.

Devices which control Modulation—such as a Modulation wheel or pedal—typically control the depth of the effect, not the speed; Speed is almost always a preset parameter.

NOTE

Modulation isn't just for wavering the pitch of an instrument, as is the case with Vibrato. It can also be use to produce a trill (with a square wave) or introduce distortion, with noise as the modulation source.

Volume

This message controls a sound's volume. Just like the knob on your home stereo, a Volume Message controls the overall output level. If you manipulate a Volume Message using a software sequencer via a virtual knob or fader, it can create dynamic volume changes.

Volume doesn't affect a given MIDI instrument's Velocity; rather, it adjusts the internal volume of any sounds using it. A good general rule of thumb is to set an instrument's volume to maximum and then use Volume Messages to change the volume. This can be more expressive and accurate than using Velocity strictly for volume control.

Pan

The Pan Controller has a value range of 0 to 127, where 0 is a full left pan and 127 is a full right pan. Most keyboards are equipped with stereo output connections. By connecting both left and right outputs to two channels of a mixer and setting the pan-pots to a corresponding hard left and hard right, automated pan moves can be performed using the Pan Controller and sequencing software.

Sustain Pedal

A critical part of a getting a good piano sound is the use of a sustain pedal. The Sustain Pedal Controller manages the depressing, sustaining, and releasing of a MIDI sustain pedal that you might use during a performance. Connecting a compatible sustain pedal to a master MIDI controller and applying it during the recording of a part is usually enough to initiate Sustain Pedal messages.

Other Controllers

Each Controller Message carries with it a specific number, and though there are 128 possible controller types, not all of them are pre-defined. Table 10.1 shows the defined controller types. Notice the gaps in the left-hand column of numbers: These gaps represent non-defined controller types, which could be just about anything a particular manufacturer wants them to be.

Not all of the defined types are implemented in every MIDI device, either, and often MIDI devices will implement the defined types differently. For example, a device may recognize and respond only to controller number 1, Modulation Wheel (coarse), and not implement controller number 33, Modulation Wheel (fine), to save processing overhead.

NOTE

The difference between "coarse" and "fine," in technical terms, is a difference in the bit-resolution of the controller itself. A fine adjustment is twice the bit-resolution, which translates to a more realistic or intuitive effect but takes more processing power.

Table 10.1
MIDI-Defined Controllers.

Controller Number	Name	Controller Number	Name
0	Bank Select	69	Hold 2 Pedal (on/off)
1	Modulation Wheel (coarse)	70	Sound Variation
2	Breath controller (coarse)	71	Sound Timbre
4	Foot Pedal (coarse)	72	Sound Release Time
5	Portamento Time (coarse)	73	Sound Attack Time
6	Data Entry (coarse)	74	Sound Brightness
7	Volume (coarse)	75	Sound Control 6
8	Balance (coarse)	76	Sound Control 7
10	Pan position (coarse)	77	Sound Control 8
11	Expression (coarse)	78	Sound Control 9
12	Effect Control 1 (coarse)	79	Sound Control 10
13	Effect Control 2 (coarse)	80	General Purpose Button 1 (on/off)
16	General Purpose Slider 1	81	General Purpose Button 2 (on/off)
17	General Purpose Slider 2	82	General Purpose Button 3 (on/off)
18	General Purpose Slider 3	83	General Purpose Button 4 (on/off)
19	General Purpose Slider 4	91	Effects Level
32	Bank Select (fine)	92	Tremulo Level
33	Modulation Wheel (fine)	93	Chorus Level
34	Breath controller (fine)	94	Celeste Level
36	Foot Pedal (fine)	95	Phaser Level
37	Portamento Time (fine)	96	Data Button increment
38	Data Entry (fine)	97	Data Button decrement
39	Volume (fine)	98	Non-registered Parameter (fine)
40	Balance (fine)	99	Non-registered Parameter (coarse)
42	Pan position (fine)	100	Registered Parameter (fine)
43	Expression (fine)	101	Registered Parameter (coarse)
44	Effect Control 1 (fine)	120	All Sound Off
45	Effect Control 2 (fine)	121	All Controllers Off
64	Hold Pedal (on/off)	122	Local Keyboard (on/off)
65	Portamento (on/off)	123	All Notes Off
66	Sustenuto Pedal (on/off)	124	Omni Mode Off
67	Soft Pedal (on/off)	125	Omni Mode On
68	Legato Pedal (on/off)	126	Mono Operation
		127	Poly Operation

Mode Messages

Most MIDI devices have a Mode Setting, which tells the device exactly how to respond to incoming notes on each of its 16 channels. The following Mode Settings are common:

▶ *Omni Mode* means that the MIDI device will respond to note messages on all sixteen channels.

▶ *Poly Mode* indicates that a MIDI device will respond to note messages on the current channel only.

▶ *Mono Mode* specifies that the MIDI device will respond to note messages one note at a time (monophony) on any combination of channels.

▶ *Multi Mode* means that the MIDI device will respond to note messages on any combination of channels but maintain the messages relative to each channel.

Though a particular device's mode setting is usually set locally on the device itself, Mode Messages can control the way a device will respond to other MIDI events from an external master or sequencing software. The types of Mode Messages are:

▶ Omni On/Poly

▶ Omni Off/Poly

▶ Omni On/Mono

▶ Omni Off/Mono

When Omni/Poly is on, a MIDI device will respond to incoming MIDI data on all channels and incoming Note On messages will be played polyphonically—meaning that each note is assigned its own voice, up to the maximum number of voices the MIDI device has available. The result, of course, is that multiple notes are played at the same time.

When Omni/Poly is off, a MIDI device will respond only to MIDI messages on one Channel. This can be useful when several MIDI devices are daisy-chained together using the MIDI Thru port, since each device in the chain can be set to play one part and ignore the information related to the other parts.

When Mono Mode is selected, a single voice is assigned to each MIDI channel, so that only one note can be played on a given Channel at a time.

Most MIDI devices these days default to Omni On/Poly, and, generally speaking, Omni On/Poly will give you the most flexibility and is the easiest with which to work.

All Notes Off

As the name suggests, this Mode Message globally stops all notes that are currently on. This is useful to stop an entire sequence from playing back—when using sequencing software, for example.

Reset All Controllers

This Mode Message resets all MIDI controllers. Most sequencing software will send a Reset All Controllers message immediately following an All Notes Off message when the stop button is pressed.

Local Control Off

In a MIDI configuration with two or more MIDI devices, a Local Control Off message may be very useful. Local Control Off, with a data byte of 0, disables a device's ability to be operated from the device itself, which is helpful when using a software sequencer to change instrument sounds.

System Messages

MIDI System Messages come in three flavors: System Common, System Real-Time, and System Exclusive. System Common Messages are useful for sending information to all the MIDI devices in your setup, and System Real-Time Messages are used to synchronize two or more MIDI devices. System Exclusive Messages, or SysEx, are device-specific and are used to relay information that might be useful only to a specific MIDI device.

System Common Messages

System Common Messages are not something you'll deal with on a regular basis—they typically work behind the scenes, usually as a means of additional communication between your MIDI devices and software. The following are the most common System Common Messages:

►   *MTC Quarter Frame Messages* are part of MIDI Time Code, or MTC, that is used for synchronizing MIDI devices with other equipment, typically audio and video tape machines.

►   *Song Select Messages* are used with sequencers or drum machines to store and recall "songs," or sequenced MIDI tracks, that have been stored in memory.

►   The *Song Position Pointer* allows for playing back a song from any point in a MIDI sequence; though it is a System Common Message, it can be used only with MIDI devices or software which recognizes MIDI System Real-Time Messages, because it derives its ability to keep track of note positions through the use of the MIDI clock.

MIDI Time Code Synchronization

MIDI Time Code synchronization is useful for synchronizing external audio or video data and for letting your software sequencer act as a slave to another MIDI device. It's essentially a way for MIDI to recognize and react to other types of time code, chiefly SMPTE time code. Time code messages are received from an external MIDI device or from a MIDI interface that generates MTC from other time code signal, such as SMPTE. SONAR, for example, uses MTC for this purpose.

Time code is nothing more than an indication of position and timing that specifies the position of data in an audio or video track and the speed of the track. Both MTC and SMTPE label position in terms of hours, minutes, and seconds, while speed is indicated via a frame rate calculation.

Time code is recorded onto tape using a time code generator—a process called "striping." Normally, the start of a tape stripe has a particular time, for example, 00:00:00:00, or 01:00:00:00. The actual audio or video data on the tape may start anywhere, though, after the start of the time code itself.

Most sequencing software—including SONAR—supports the most common time code frame rates, as shown in Table 10.2.

Table 10.2
Typical Time Code Frame Rates.

Time Code Frame Rate	Uses
24 fps	The standard for movies and film
25 fps (also called EBU time code)	PAL/SECAM video, video, and some film in countries that use 50 Hz wall electricity
29.97 fps non drop-frame	NTSC non-broadcast and short video in North America and Japan and some audio applications
29.97 drop-frame	NTSC broadcast and long-format video in North America and Japan
30 fps non drop-frame	Many music projects, some film in North America
30 fps drop-frame	Used only rarely for speed correction and transfer problems

CHAPTER 10

▶ The *Tune Request Message* is useful for analog synths for retuning internal oscillators and is not typically used with digital MIDI devices.

▶ The *End of Exclusive (EOX) Message* is for indicating the end of a System Exclusive message.

System Real-Time Messages

System Real-Time Messages are used to synchronize MIDI clock-based devices such as sequencing software, synthesizers with built-in sequencers, and drum machines. To keep accurate time, System Real-Time messages are given priority over other messages, and these single-byte messages may occur anywhere in a MIDI data stream. System Real-Time Messages include the MIDI Clock, Start, Continue, Stop, Active Sensing, and System Reset. Together, these messages work to keep MIDI notes and other messages in sync and in time.

System Exclusive (SysEx) Messages

System Exclusive Messages allow a MIDI device to send and receive special information that pertains only to a particular MIDI device. A MIDI device that can use SysEx messages will carry with it an assigned manufacturer's ID number that allows it to be distinguished from the other MIDI devices when data is sent or received. SysEx messages are used mostly to transmit custom sound patch settings to a software sequencer or proprietary patch librarian/editor. By doing so, special instrument parameters can be played, stored, or edited along with the rest of the MIDI information for a specific sequence.

Certain SysEx ID numbers are reserved for special activities, such as doing a MIDI Sample Dump, which is a way for MIDI devices to share sampled audio data between them, as well as MIDI Show Control and MIDI Machine Control.

A MIDI Sequencing Tutorial

This section takes you, step by step, through a MIDI sequencing session, including setting up a typical MIDI configuration, the sequencing process itself, and the editing of MIDI tracks. This tutorial uses SONAR (**www.cakewalk.com**), a combination audio/MIDI software package that has been used elsewhere throughout this book. SONAR is full of professional features, is powerful and fast, and represents the best value on the market today for the home recording artist. There are lots of other software packages, but SONAR is the best bang for your buck.

Still, if you are using another brand of software, that's cool: Almost all software sequencers share the same basic functionality, and you generally can't break software simply by pressing a wrong button!

The Setup

The MIDI setup for this tutorial looks like this:

- ▶ SONAR 1.0 or higher
- ▶ Gadget Labs Wave 8/24 sound card
- ▶ Korg TR-Rack synth module
- ▶ MIDI controller keyboard
- ▶ Boss Dr. Rhythm DR-660 drum machine

Hooking It Together

Figure 10.1 is a general diagram of how the devices in this tutorial are connected. The MIDI controller keyboard functions as the Master Controller for a rack synth module, in this case, the Korg TR-Rack; hence, there is a MIDI loop between the TR-Rack and the controller keyboard. From there, the TR-Rack itself is connected to the computer's serial port via a special "PC to host" MIDI cable.

Next, a MIDI loop is created between the drum machine and the computer's sound card—in this instance, the break-out box which comes with the Wave 8/24 sound card, enabling the drum machine to be used as both an input device and a sound generator.

This setup allows both devices—the master controller keyboard, which is controlling sounds from the TR-Rack, and the drum machine—to both send and receive MIDI data from SONAR on the computer. This means that, for drum parts, the pads on the drum machine can be recorded and played back separately from the master controller, and the Korg sounds are independent of the drum machine. These devices are easy to manage separately using SONAR.

The connections are made simple by using the "PC to host" interface provided by the TR-Rack, effectively adding a second MIDI interface, in addition to the Wave 8/24's MIDI ports. Alternatively, you could simply use an external MIDI multiport interface, such as those made by Mark of the Unicorn (**www.motu.com**) or MidiMan (**www.midiman.com**), to keep daisy chaining to a minimum.

Figure 10.1
This MIDI setup is simple and allows for separate control of both sound-generating MIDI devices.

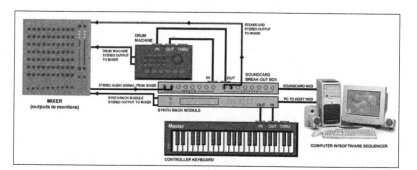

Figure 10.1 also shows how the stereo outputs, which carry the analog audio signals from the different MIDI devices, are routed to a mixing board so that the music can be monitored while recording and playing back MIDI tracks and live performances at the same time. The mixing board, in this case, has channel inserts as well as direct outputs to handle routing output signal mixed with input signal on separate buses. (This tutorial is concerned only with MIDI; for more detail on how to set up the digital audio portion of your home studio, see Chapter 11.)

The SONAR Interface

When SONAR is launched, the first thing you'll see is a blank interface and project space, waiting for you. Toward the top of the screen (see Figure 10.2) you'll find several toolbar icons which control recording, editing, and playing back MIDI sequences.

Figure 10.2
SONAR's default tool bars are just what you'd expect and borrow their look from traditional recording controls.

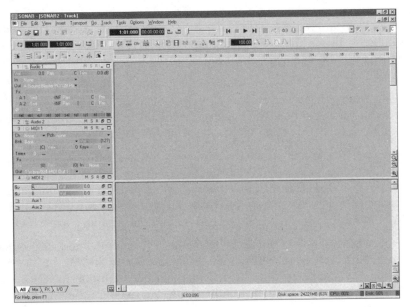

The tool bar contains some familiar buttons, including "play," "stop," and "record." It also contains basic information about the sequence being recorded or played back, such as the tempo setting, position, and time signature.

SONAR, like most MIDI software applications, derives its sequencing power from utilizing one of the System Common Messages discussed earlier, the Song Position Pointer. The Song Position Pointer allows MIDI software to find the location of a sequence down to at least the nearest sixteenth note.

Enabling MIDI Tracks

Below the toolbar, you'll find the main window, which displays track information as well as the recorded sequences once you've recorded them. The right side of the re-sizing bar contains a visual of the MIDI data coming into the computer, which makes locating notes and editing sequences of notes easy.

In order to record a track in SONAR, you must first map it to a MIDI device. As shown in Figure 10.3, Track 5's MIDI Out port is set to "Korg TR-Rack Prog Banks," and in this case, it has been mapped to an instrument sound from the TR-Rack—the Finger Bass. The MIDI channel is set to 2, and in this case there is no special setting for the MIDI In port—it's designated by the "MIDI Omni" setting, which maps the In port from Windows since the TR-Rack uses a proprietary MIDI connection.

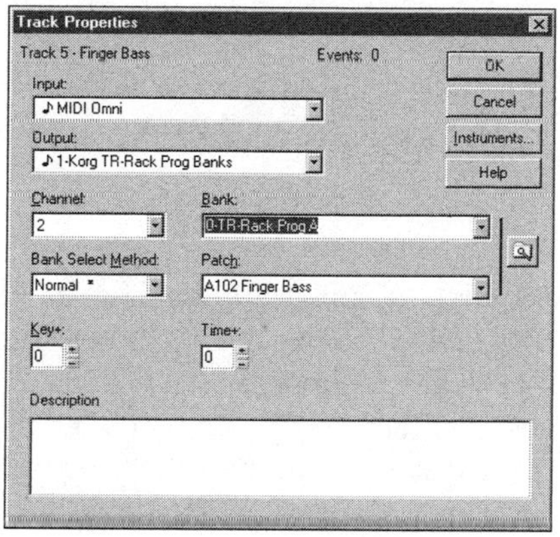

Figure 10.3
Track 5 is set to receive and send MIDI using the TR-Rack's MIDI interface.

The same thing can be done for the drum machine, which is using the MIDI port on the Wave 8/24 sound card. Right-clicking on the track will open up the same dialog box (see Figure 10.4), where you can specify the Input, or In port (MIDI Channel 10) and the Output (Wave 8/24 MIDI Out 1).

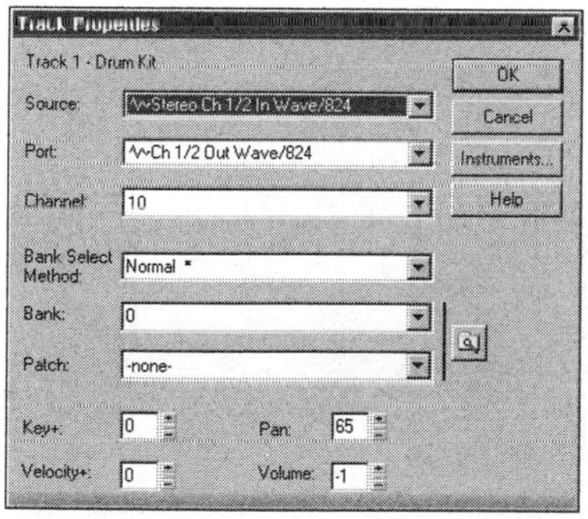

Figure 10.4
Track 1 uses the MIDI interface on the computer's sound card to send and receive MIDI.

NOTE

This tutorial doesn't address installation and basic configuration of SONAR. SONAR has come a long way since its early days, and it now automatically detects your sound cards and MIDI devices and sets them up for you. To see if SONAR has successfully detected your hardware, go to MIDI Devices in the Options menu; you can also select or deselect which previously detected In ports and Out ports you want available for use by SONAR.

The MIDI Recording Process

Once you're hooked up and your MIDI ports have been set, you're ready to begin a MIDI recording session. You can play anything you want, but for the purposes of the tutorial, we'll set up the song a little beforehand.

In this case, it's a basic groove with some drums, bass, and strings—a pop ditty. We'll add a kick drum, snare, hi-hat, toms, and cymbals for the percussion, lay down a bass line, then add some strings for melody and harmony.

You could start with any of the instruments, but in this case, we'll lay down the beat first, which provides a solid anchor for the other parts. In pop music, rhythm is critical, and it's one of the hardest things to get right using MIDI.

Here's the step-by-step:

1. Set the meter and tempo first. In SONAR, click the "4/4" button on the tool bar, then double-click the first note in the pop-up window for meter. For tempo, click the Tempo text box on the tool bar and type in the bpm (beats per minute) you want. For example, you might set the time to 6/8 and the tempo to 120 bpm—both good choices for a pop tune. These settings are essential to laying down the drums properly, and ideally, you want to know what they are before you start. However, you can easily change them later.

2. Next, you'll want to set up the instruments. In SONAR, you can add tracks easily by right-clicking in the Track pane in Track view; choose "Insert MIDI Track" from the right-click menu. Once you've added tracks, you can view all the details either in the Track pane or by double-clicking any of the tracks in the Track pane in Track view or by selecting a track, right-clicking, and selecting "Track Properties." For the tutorial, use the following instruments from the general MIDI Sound and Percussion sets:

    ▶ Track 1: Bass Drum 1

    ▶ Track 2: Acoustic Snare

    ▶ Track 3: Pedal Hi-Hat

    ▶ Track 4: Crash Cymbal 1

    ▶ Track 5: Low Tom

    ▶ Track 6: Low-Mid Tom

    ▶ Track 7: Electric Bass (pick)

    ▶ Track 8: String Ensemble 2

3. You're ready to record your first track, the kick drum. First, highlight the track corresponding to Bass Drum 1 in the Track pane. If you're using a drum machine as in the tutorial, then you'll tap the kick drum pad on the drum machine. If you're using a keyboard, you'll use note number 36, as defined in the GM Percussion Set.

CHAPTER 10

NOTE
Chapter 9, "Wading in MIDI," lists all of the instrument numbers for the GM sound set as well as the note numbers of the GM percussion map.

4. To begin recording in SONAR, arm the track by clicking the "R" button for the track, then either click the Record button on the toolbar, choose Record from the Transport menu, or press "R" on the keyboard. Once you've started recording, you'll hear a metronome from your computer speaker or from your drum machine to keep you in time. Lay down a kick drum sound on every beat, for as long as you like. When you're done, tap the space bar or click the Stop button on the tool bar.

TIP
By default, recording will begin immediately with the sound of the metronome, but you may want to give yourself some lead-in before you start playing. In SONAR, select Project from the Options menu, then the Metronome tab, then change the Count-in scroll box to the number of count-in beats you want.

5. For the snare, highlight the snare track and repeat Step 4 above, this time laying down the snare sound on beats 2 and 4.

6. Repeat Step 4 for the other four percussion instruments, highlighting the associated track before recording each time, with a cymbal crash every 8 beats, 2 hi-hat sounds for each beat, and a few low- and low-mid toms at will.

7. For the bass line, you'll need to decide what you're going to play. For the tutorial, you can play a time-honored pop "walk-up" bass line, which puts the following notes at 8 beats each per measure: E, G, A, B, E. Repeat this for several bars.

8. For strings, lay down a melody of your choice and some backing chords for depth and harmony. In this case, you can begin by selecting Track 8 for strings. Record the first line, then either record on top of the same track (just keep the track selected) or create a new track for each additional string part. Creating a new track for each successive part is by far the easiest way, because it enables you to edit individual notes for different parts later on a per-track basis, which means there are fewer notes to view when editing.

After you record each track, SONAR will play it back as you record subsequent tracks. The beauty of sequencing is its non-linear design: There's no real "rewind," because you can jump later to any point in the sequence and edit individual notes.

Quantizing

Play back everything you've done so far. How does it sound? Unless you're the exception rather than the rule, your timing isn't going to be dead on. This is where the idea of "quantizing" comes in very handy. Quantization is an incredible feature found on every modern sequencer that corrects timing to the nearest metric value that you specify.

In this example, quantizing to the nearest eighth note should correct any stray rhythm issues, though you can quantize up to a thirty-second of a note, as well as in triplets. Start by quantizing each drum track. In SONAR, highlight each drum track and select Quantize from the Edit menu. Set the quantize resolution to an Eighth note. Hit OK, and bingo: You're as tight as a drum.

Many software sequencers provide additional parameters that allow you to further customize the quantization for any selection of notes. This can help with putting some of the natural feeling back into a performance. For example, in SONAR, selecting Groove Quantize from the Edit menu gives you options such as Shuffle Feel, Straight Feel, Pushing Feel, Late Snare, and so on. In addition, several software companies produce DirectX plug-ins that produce some sophisticated quantizing routines.

Copying Tracks

One of the beautiful things about MIDI is how easily you can take one performance and layer it by copying it onto another track, then changing the instrument sound. This was the main impetus for the creation of the MIDI specification to begin with—to be able to create rich compositions by layering sounds.

With any modern software sequencer, copying and pasting tracks is as simple as using a word processor. You start by selecting the MIDI data comprising the track you've recorded, copy it, then paste it to a new track. Once pasted, you simply change instruments for that track until you get something you like!

You can also edit individual notes to make the track vary from the original in any way that you want, or you can change the entire track by raising or lowering all of the notes a half-step at a time, creating instant harmonies using multiple instruments.

Editing MIDI Notes

Editing individual notes is a highly useful and common feature on all modern sequencers. In most applications, including SONAR, this is achieved through a "piano-roll" editor.

The Piano Roll view in SONAR, as shown in Figure 10.5, lists all of the notes for a track on a grid, where the vertical axis shows a virtual piano indicating each note and its pitch and the horizontal axis shows when and where the notes were played. Editing an individual note is as simple as highlighting the note, dragging and dropping it to another pitch, shortening or lengthening it, or deleting it to make mistakes disappear instantly.

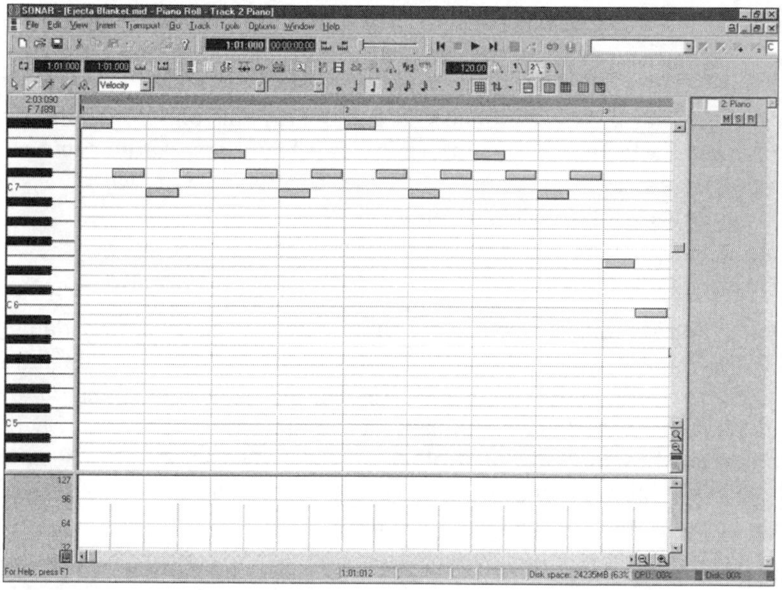

Figure 10.5
The Piano Roll view is a wonderful way to hand-edit your music without having to re-record the performance.

NOTE

It's not hard to see how useful the Piano Roll feature can be. Aside from having the capability to deliberately change pitch and note placement at will, you can easily correct stray notes or that perfect performance that was ruined by one or two flub-ups.

You can also smooth out volume changes using a piano roll editor. Remember that Velocity is a MIDI message that measures how fast each key is pressed?

By making strategic Velocity changes in percussion instruments, for example, you can quickly add a more natural feel to the performance (or unnatural, if that's your gig!) Other instruments can benefit from Velocity editing—for example, adding some punchiness to the bass in the tutorial or creating a smooth string ensemble crescendo.

In fact, most software sequencers that provide a piano roll editor will allow you to graphically edit all of the Controller Messages your devices and/or the software itself supports.

On the Horizon:
New MIDI-Based Audio Technologies

This chapter wouldn't be complete without mention of some of the most exciting MIDI-related technologies that have come about over the last few years. Audio engineers and experts are continuing to leverage the original MIDI specification in new ways that create standards for better and more useful music and audio.

DLS-1

Targeted primarily for CD-ROM and Internet applications, DownLoadable Sounds Level 1 (DLS-1) was created in 1997 to provide a means for game developers and composers to add their own custom sounds to the General MIDI sound set. Any device that conforms to the DLS-1 specification can download a DLS bank of sounds from a hard disk, CD-ROM, or any other digital media, allowing MIDI-controlled music to be easily and freely extended with an infinite number of new instrument sounds, the spoken word, or sound effects—anything and everything that can be captured in a digital audio file.

The result today is the DLS-1 file format, which is essentially a digital audio format that uses MIDI to control the contents of individual digital audio data contained in the file. It's a format that has merged some of the best features of MIDI with wavetable-based synthesis techniques into a single, standardized form for computers and electronic instruments to play.

Though not yet widely adopted, this format holds much promise, since it can effectively allow anyone to store instrument or other sounds in a form that can be used on any supported platform. It's like MIDI with really good (or bad, depending on the composer!) sounds.

DLS-2

At a recent meeting of the Moving Picture Experts Group (MPEG), the attendees decided to further the DLS format to better leverage all the recent advances in wavetable synthesis. That format is DownLoadable Sounds Level 2, or DLS-2. This new format is also known within MPEG as the MPEG-4 Structured Audio Sample Bank Format.

The DLS-2 format is an extension of DLS-1, and it leverages wavetable synthesis to the max. As with DLS-1, samples of digital sound can be accessed and controlled via MIDI messages, providing a greater palette of available instrument sounds and realistic sound effects for composers and sound designers.

DLS-2 represents a significant savings in file size, which makes it particularly beneficial for the Internet, and it is now an open standard that anyone can use. The MIDI Manufacturers Association (**www.midi.org**) has all of the technical details if you want to research DLS-2 further.

DLS-2 is one component of a powerful and flexible suite of tools being developed called MPEG-4 Structured Audio, which is open technology originally developed by the MIT Media Laboratory. In MPEG-4, wavetable synthesis can be used in conjunction with general-purpose software synthesis and mixed with compressed vocals or the sounds of natural musical instruments. For more details on MPEG-4, check out **www.mpeg.org**.

DownLoadable Algorithms

One other cutting edge technology worth mentioning is a novel way of controlling audio data using MIDI, called DownLoadable Algorithms, or simply DLA.

The DLA format was pioneered by the Stanford-based startup Staccato Systems (**www.staccatosystems.com**), is now an integral part of SoundMAX technology (**www.soundmax.com**), and is yet another way of building upon MIDI to produce new, realistic, and highly controllable music and sound.

The idea behind a DLA file is a bit like DLS—in fact, the DLA format supports DLS as a subset—but adds another layer of technology: The ability to control audio data via programming code within the audio file itself, or *algorithmic synthesis*. Algorithmic synthesis is a new concept that gives a composer the ability to structure audio in a particular order—such as a string sound that changes depending on other instruments that are or are not played at the same time—and can model sound effects or instruments based on real-world, physical acoustics or imagined, real, or random events.

A good example of algorithmic synthesis is the engine sound in the game "NASCAR 2000" by Electronic Arts. The game employs the DLA file format to produce highly realistic acceleration and engine sounds that put normal looped, recorded audio data to shame.

11

Fun-Da-Mental Audio

It's time to home in on perhaps the most critical part of successful home studio recording—the sound itself. This chapter focuses on getting to the heart of what makes a great-sounding recording by distilling the science of audio. You'll learn the most important things you need to know in order to get up and running and actually producing something. These include:

▶ The basic principles of audio engineering

▶ The difference between analog and digital recording

▶ Digital audio file formats

▶ What kind of recording gear works best for you

▶ How to choose and install a computer sound card

▶ How to choose headphones for monitoring and mixing

▶ The most common types of DSP

Audio Engineering 101

What makes a "good" sound? Putting the music itself aside for a moment, why is it that some recordings wring emotion out of you like water out of a sponge, while others have little effect at all? It's the sound—the realism, surrealism, or otherwise—that often does it, and, contrary to popular belief, it ain't all that complicated to understand.

A Little Math, Please

In one sense, sound is, pure and simple, a matter of math. The way sound works is a much traversed (and much ballyhooed) piece of science, and there are a number of facts about acoustics and audio that are unavoidable, especially when it comes to music. In fact, the physiology of sound has played a major role in the character and existence of music long before music was, well, music.

Here are some fundamental facts about sound and music—some of them translated for your pleasure into understandable English—from the *Audio Cyclopedia*, by Howard M. Tremaine (Howard Sams and Co., 1978, ASIN 0672206757):

▶ Sound is quantifiable: In humans, hearing takes place whenever vibrations of frequencies between about 15 and 20,000 hertz reach the inner ear.

▶ The hertz, or Hz, is a unit of frequency equaling one vibration, or cycle, per second.

▶ Vibrations reach the inner ear when they are transmitted through the air, and the term "sound" refers to these vibrational "waves." There are sound waves lower and higher than what most humans can hear; for example, sounds of frequencies higher than about 20,000 Hz are called "ultrasonic."

▶ The human ear can easily pick out different frequencies by a factor of two, so most musical systems have naturally evolved around dividing notes where the frequencies of the notes in one group are a factor of two higher or lower than the notes in the another group.

A Brief History of Sound

The ancient Greeks had a great interest in music; Pythagoras, for example, discovered that an octave represents a 2-to-1 frequency ratio, and he stated the law connecting harmonic intervals with numerical ratios. (He also came up with some interesting religious ideas about sound, but that is another book.) Aristotle, too, made a fairly accurate guess concerning the nature of the generation and transmission of sound.

It wasn't until around 1600, however, that serious inroads were made into the scientific study of sound. Galileo formed many of the fundamental laws, including stating the relationship between pitch and frequency and the laws of musical harmony and dissonance. He also theorized that the frequency of sound produced by a stringed instrument depends on the length, weight, and tension of the string.

Since Galileo, there have been a number of advances in the study of sound, including developments by Heinrich Hertz (for which the "hertz" was named) and Alexander Graham Bell (the deci**bel**). Today, there are enough details in existence that some universities even offer Ph.D. programs in acoustics and sound engineering.

▶ In the system with which we're most familiar, the groups are called octaves, and an octave always contains seven major notes (C, D, E, F, G, A, and B) and five minor notes (C#, D#, F#, G#, and A#), for a total of twelve notes equally spaced on the scale.

▶ The American scale starts at C-0 and is located at 16.351 Hz, while the European scale ends at C10 and is located at 16,351 Hz. The C we usually consider to be Middle C is C4 on the American scale and is 261.63 Hz. In the American scale, A4, or A above Middle C, is set at 440 Hz.

There are lots of other facts, but you get the idea: The "standard notation" musical system is a finite system, which operates in a known way and is based on known facts about sound. This means that you can, to some degree, successfully predict and repeat how a performance and/or a recording will sound.

Sound Waves

A sound wave moves in a somewhat linear fashion, meaning that, as the wave motion created by a sound moves outward from the source of the sound, air molecules carry the sound parallel to the direction of wave motion. In this physical sense, a sound wave is a series of air molecules moving back and forth in the air, and after the sound wave has passed, each molecule stays in about the same location.

NOTE
Another way to think of the propagation of sound through air is a Slinky (you know, the toy: "a Slinky, a Slinky, it's fun for a girl and a boy"). While stretching a Slinky out on the ground, quick pulses can be sent down the its length: The coils will compress and expand without the Slinky actually going anywhere. These pulses in the coils are representative of how sound waves travel out from their source.

This is a bit different from other types of physical waves. For example, if you throw a rock into a pond, a cork floating near where the rock hits the water will bob up and down, moving somewhat perpendicular, rather than parallel, to the point of impact. It will show some, but very little, outward motion in the direction of the wave motion.

The way in which sound waves behave has implications for musical notes. In fact, musical notes end up with three basic characteristics which correspond to three physical characteristics:

▶ Pitch refers to how fast the sound wave vibrates, otherwise known as the sound's *frequency*.

▶ Intensity is the loudness of the sound, also known as *amplitude*.

▶ Timbre is the accuracy of the sound frequency, physically described as the sound's *waveform*.

NOTE
A musical note is a simple sound. Noise is a highly complex sound—a mixture of many different frequencies and/or notes that are not harmonically related and cannot be neatly described in terms of pitch, volume and timbre.

Pitch

Pitch, or frequency, of a sound wave is a measure (the hertz) of the number of waves passing a given point in 1 second. Frequency can be controlled independent of amplitude or waveform, as in the case of the notes on a keyboard. Each note is "tuned" to a specific frequency. To illustrate this, consider the sound of a typical fire engine's siren, which consists of a rotating wheel with 44 teeth. The wheel rotates at 10 revolutions per second, with each tooth interrupting an air blast creating 440 vibrations per second, or 440 Hz.

This is equivalent to the A above Middle C on a keyboard. Though the sound of the siren is quite different in quality from that of A above Middle C, they correspond closely in pitch.

Two octaves above Middle C on the piano, A has a frequency of 880 Hz. Similarly, an A one octave below Middle C has a frequency of 220 Hz, and the next octave below has a frequency of 110 Hz, and so on. In fact, an octave, by definition, is the interval between any two notes by a factor of a 2-to-1 ratio.

CHAPTER 11

NOTE

A fundamental law of harmony states that when two notes an octave apart are sounded together, they produce a pleasant sound to the human ear, or a *euphonious* sound.

A fifth and a major third sounded with the "root" note produces a slightly less euphonious sound. In terms of physics, an interval of a fifth consists of two frequencies at a ratio of 3 to 2, while a major third has a ratio of 5 to 4.

The general rule is that two or more notes sound sweet when played together if their frequencies reduce to small, whole numbers; otherwise, the sound is not so sweet and produces dissonance (which, arguably, can be sweet to some ears!). In addition, it's not technically possible to arrange notes on most instruments, including piano and guitar, so that all the ratios hold exactly, so some compromises are made when tuning, resulting in a somewhat altered scale known as the tempered scale.

Volume

The greater the volume, or amplitude, of a wave, the harder the air molecules strike the ear drum, and the sound is perceived as louder. The amplitude of a sound wave can be measured in several ways: the distance of displacement between the air molecules; the pressure difference in the compression and "rarefaction"; and even the actual, physical energy that's produced. Human speech, for example, produces sound energy at the rate of around one hundred-thousandth of a watt. These types of measurements are quite difficult to make, however, so the intensity of a sound is generally expressed by comparing it to a standard reference measurement, the decibel (dB).

The decibel is actually one-tenth of a *bel*, an idea developed by and named after Alexander Graham Bell. The bel is a ratio that compares the intensity of two sounds and is expressed in large, logarithmic values from 10 to 10,000,000,000. Because the bel never really falls into the range of human-perceptible sound, the decibel is used instead. The range is generally about 0 to 120 dB, with a whisper coming in at about 20 dB, a conversation at about 60 dB, and a space shuttle blasting off (or a Pearl Jam concert) around 120 dB.

Graphically, using an oscilloscope or digital editing software, amplitude is represented by how tall the waveform is. Figure 11.1 shows a waveform of a song in SONAR.

Figure 11.1
This waveform of a track in SONAR shows both the frequency and the volume of the sound.

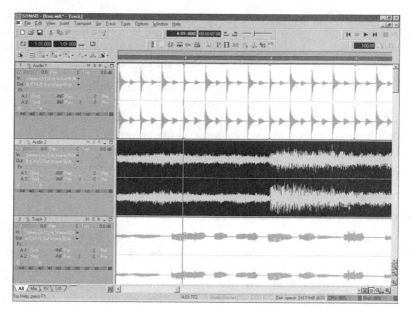

CHAPTER 11

Timbre

If A above Middle C is played on a bass guitar, a piano, and a tuning fork—all at the same volume—the notes have the same frequency and amplitude, but are quite different in quality. Of these three instruments, the simplest tone is produced by the tuning fork, which is almost entirely pure sound waves having a frequency of 440 Hz. The bass guitar and piano are less pure, because they contain other frequencies—in this case, exact multiples of 440, called *harmonics*—which determine the quality, or timbre, of the note. The intensity of these additional frequencies is what makes a piano sound like a piano and a bass guitar sound like a bass guitar.

Of course, the physical ear is not perfect (and not exactly the same for every person), so even the most pure tone of the tuning fork isn't going to reach the brain in pure form in any case.

Tone Reality

The human ear is most sensitive to tones in the range from A above middle C up to A four octaves higher—so sensitive that a sound in this range can be hundreds of times fainter than a sound an octave higher or two octaves lower and still be heard. For tones of slightly different loudness or slightly different frequency, perception is, naturally, much less accurate.

For example, a difference in amplitude of just 1 dB and a difference in frequency of 30 percent (about 1/20 of a note) can be distinguished in sounds of moderate intensity at frequencies in the 1 to 2 kHz range. In this same range, the difference between the softest sound that can be heard and the loudest sound that can be heard is about 120 dB.

This is quite sensitive—but these facts refer to pure tones, such as those produced in a controlled environment by an oscillator. The reality is that, at high volume, the ear is pretty much equally sensitive to most frequencies, but at low volume the ear is much more sensitive to the middle high frequencies than to the lowest and highest notes. In other words, a recording with a lot of mid-level frequencies—not unusual for a typical pop or rock song—will seem to lose its lowest and highest tones when the volume is decreased. In fact, this is exactly why many stereos have a "loudness" switch, which boosts high and low frequencies to compensate for the perceived loss of the lowest and highest tones at low listening volumes.

This imperfection of the human ear is called *masking,* and it will be of concern to you as a home studio recording engineer. As you'll see later in this chapter and in Chapter 13, it can present a problem for getting a mix that will sound consistent across a number of different playback devices; in fact, properly managing the amount of "mid in the mix" can often be a bit tricky. Ample mid-range frequencies usually sound great on a good stereo with the volume pumped up, but it can be almost ruinous on an inexpensive car stereo.

Analog vs. Digital Recording

When Sir George Martin started his relationship with the Fab Four, he had the technological equivalent of a 4-track tape recorder. It was the technology of the time, and it took a great ear and a lot of saavy to translate the abilities and talents of the Beatles to tape. Don't think for a second that issues of equalization, tape hiss, unpredictable equipment, bad microphone response, and inferior instruments weren't very much a part of a day in the life of Sir George.

Whether you're a Beatles fan or not, you can appreciate the fact that Sir George managed to overcome the limits of the technology at the time and produced startlingly good recordings. He did it because he had artistic vision (and awfully good musicians and songwriters to work with) and because he knew all the subtleties and intricacies of every piece of equipment he had to use.

However, Sir George today would probably be the first person to tell you, as a home recording artist, to take advantage of digital recording technology. Why? Because it's easier, it's cheaper, and the result is better than analog for a home studio. While there are still a number of traditional analog or analog-digital hybrid studios all over the world which still churn out hit records, they have a few things you don't, including money, a full-time dedicated engineering staff, and a whole lot of experience. And even with all that professional gear and experience, there are sometimes significant differences in recording quality from studio to studio.

Of course, going digital is not a license to ignore the fundamentals of sound recording, processing, and mixing; for example, whether you compress a bass track with the click of a mouse or you use a rack-mount unit, knowing what compression ratios to use and how to tweak input settings, delay times, and volume levels still applies. However, you will find that the learning curve is not so much a rock-climb as it is a few pushes in the right direction to get you going when it comes to a digital studio.

Digital Is Cheaper, Much Cheaper

Make no mistake about it: The home recording revolution has not happened because professional 24-track mixing boards and 1-inch tape machines suddenly plummeted in price and ease of use. The reason a book like this one even exists is because of the advances made in digital recording technology using a computer or DAW (digital audio workstation), which have, in many cases, reduced a room full of audio equipment down to a handful of software plug-ins. This has enabled hundreds of thousands of home studio artists to produce high-quality recordings because they don't have to mortgage their lives to afford the equipment.

Why compare digital equipment to a professional studio? Isn't it more comparable to an 8-track cassette tape recorder or an inexpensive reel-to-reel quarter-inch tape recorder? Not at all, for two reasons: First, a tape recorder doesn't record as accurately and noiselessly as a good quality sound card or DAW; second, with every generation of tape editing, the original quality of the recording drops significantly. This problem is nonexistent with a digital setup.

NOTE

Analog multi-track cassette tape recorders also suffer from limited surface area on the tape itself, as well as much slower tape speeds than professional equipment. Contrast this with 16-bit, 44.1 kHz digital audio, which is the same whether you're using expensive professional equipment or inexpensive consumer equipment.

With that in mind, Tables 11.1 and 11.2 compare typical core equipment costs of a digital home studio setup with that of a professional studio. You don't have to be math major to immediately see the difference (note that these figures are estimates at the time of this writing).

Table 11.1
The Basic Costs of a Digital Home Studio.

Equipment Type	Cost
Computer*	$750-1,800
Sound Card	$100-1,000
Digital Recording Software	$300-500
Outboard Mixer	$500
Common Effects Plug-ins	$50 each
CD-RW Drive for Mastering	$150
CD-R or CD-RW Media	$1-5 each

*Or good-quality consumer digital audio workstation

Table 11.2
The Basic Costs of a Professional Analog Studio.

Equipment Type	Cost
32-Channel Analog Mixing Board	$5,000
24-Track 2-inch Reel-to-Reel Tape	$5,000
Common Effects Boxes	$1,000 each
DAT for Mastering	$2,500
2-inch Tape Reels	$200 each

CHAPTER 11

It's worth noting that Table 11.1 is a liberal estimate: You could spend as little as $1,000 for a computer setup that will do a fair job and as little as $100 for a sound card. On the other hand, Table 11.2 is a minimal estimate: You could easily double or quadruple these costs depending on the quality of the components.

Digital is Easier

While the raw recording itself is always important, producing a high-quality end-product ultimately comes down to editing and mixing, and this is where digital recording really shines. Unlike recording tape, digital audio files are lossless—meaning the audio quality doesn't decrease with repeated editing, mixing, and re-recording—and the flexibility is enormous. You can perform editing feats in seconds that would require lots of skill, time, and experience using analog tape.

With software like SONAR or Sound Forge, it's easy to record an almost limitless number of tracks using a computer, and with audio plug-in software, you can easily add effects, clean up unwanted frequencies, speed up or slow down the music, even tune the vocals to virtual perfection during mixdown. In addition, you can copy and paste any number of recorded tracks with pinpoint accuracy, making it simple to replace a bad backing track in the second verse with that stellar performance in the first verse.

The bottom line is that the only kind of analog equipment comparable in price to a digital setup is multi-track cassette recording, yet the quality of digital is far better than cassette tape and, arguably, as good or better than reel-to-reel tape. In addition to being expensive, reel-to-reel tape requires a huge amount of maintenance, uses up a lot of tape at speeds of 15 inches per second, and is difficult to edit, requiring you to use a razor blade and editing block with precision. It can take years to get good at it.

Gearing Up

Even with all the advantages of digital technology, there are wide differences in equipment quality and features. To start, there are two routes you can take: computer-based digital recording using software and a sound card or a DAW.

DAW-Gonnit, Maw, I Need to Move

A digital audio workstation has one major advantage over a computer-based digital recording setup: It's much more portable. If portability is critical to you, then a DAW may be a better choice than a computer. In addition, several of today's DAWs include a digital mixer with analog inputs—some even have phantom power for mics that need it.

There are several disadvantages, though. A DAW typically has much smaller storage space available for your recordings, doesn't easily give you the ability to burn your own CDs without adding a computer or an expensive all-in-one CD recording unit, and can't be easily upgraded simply by buying a new sound card and/or software. It also lacks the visuals of a high-color computer screen.

It's not altogether uncommon for a DAW to be used in conjunction with a computer. Though it's virtually twice as expensive, it can provide portability but still afford you all the advantages of your computer. The key to a dual-setup is that both the DAW and your sound card support a digital input and output signal, rather than analog, so that you can transfer digital musical data in its original digital form. Converting to an analog signal, using an analog quarter-inch or eighth-inch jack, opens up the potential for more noise and lower frequency response in your recordings. You'll want to look for a DAW that supports digital transfer protocols like S/PDIF and/or TDIF.

Yamaha, Sony, Tascam, and several other companies offer digital-based DAWs with 8 tracks to 24 tracks or more that are full-featured and sell at consumer-level prices.

> **TIP**
>
> For several years, 4-track DAW and DAW-like standalone units were popular and inexpensive, and there are still a few of them on the market at rock-bottom prices. The biggest disadvantage to these units is not their 4-track limit, since you can ping (record three tracks, then record those three onto the one open track, opening up three more tracks, ad infinitum) tracks back and forth for just about infinity on most of them. It's their general lack of editing, equalization, and effects, their small storage capacities, and the recording quality. If you are on an ultra-slim budget, Sony's 4- or 8-track Mini-Disc is probably still the best choice for price and capacity, though the trade-off is that mini-disc recorders end up using data compression to fit more audio into less storage space, using compression technology called ATRAC, which is a bit better than MP3. This results in lower audio quality for saving audio and/or mastering onto mini-discs.

Professional quality DAWs combine digital mixing, on-board hard disk recording, effects, higher-quality sampling (from 16-bit to 24-bit), and a large number of tracks. Yamaha, Tascam, Korg, and Roland have consistently been some of the most popular brands. You'll want to look for at least a 24-bit, 16-track hard disk recorder, 32-bit digital parametric EQ, compression and reverb effects, and at least 1 gigabyte of storage capacity to even approach the capability of a computer-based setup.

Real Power for the Home Studio: The Computer

With a computer, you will get the most bang for your buck, hands down. Using a computer as the central aspect of your home recording setup affords you the ability to add limitless functionality to your studio, both in software upgrades as newer and better applications become available and storage for keeping all of the data you record accessible and archived for future use.

There are two popular platforms for setting up your digital studio on a computer: Macintosh and PC. This chapter focuses on the PC, though Macintosh has been quite popular in the audio computer sector for many years.

When you get down to the nitty-gritty, the PC is more powerful, cheaper in both hardware and software, and can be used almost simultaneously for other applications like browsing the Internet, reading e-mail, or using a word processing program for your lyrics. If you're a Mac-head, sorry. Now that the Windows platform has begun to solidify and DirectX software plug-ins are a reality, there really is little contest between a Mac and a PC for the home recording artist. Still, if you're currently using a Mac, you should be able to apply some of the basic concepts in this section for tweaking your system. If you're a die-hard Mac fanatic—more power to you—but you may want to just skip the entire section and go directly to "Monitoring and Mixing with Headphones."

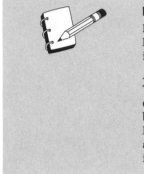

NOTE

If you are considering a Macintosh setup, don't stray any further back than a PowerPC-based machine. Pre-PowerPC Macs came with only 8-bit sound built in, which is not good enough for home recording.

At the time of this writing, the iMac and G4 are the latest MacOS computers. They come standard with an IDE hard drive and CD-ROM drive and fair-quality 16-bit audio hardware. The iMac/G4s are quite fast and easy to use, but they use only USB and FireWire ports for external devices, including MIDI. This means that you'll have to buy a USB MIDI interface or a USB adapter cable, which does not work consistently with all non-USB MIDI interfaces.

Real-World Hardware Choices

There are a number of components you'll need for a PC-based recording, and some are far more important than others. A monitor, for example, is not the most critical thing on your list, while a good hard drive is crucial. Here's the lowdown:

▶ A large and fast hard drive is probably the most important part of doing digital audio on a PC. At the time of this writing, ATA66-based IDE drives in the 30 GB range can be had for around $200, and an ATA66 or better IDE is plenty of speed for all but the most discerning home studios. Look for Maxtor, IBM, and Western Digital brands. On a system with sufficient RAM and a fast processor, simultaneously recording/playback of up to 100 tracks can be expected with little difficulty. Alternatively, SCSI-based drives can be purchased for four to five times the price of an IDE but are, arguably, only marginally better. Five years ago, SCSI was the best value for speed; today, it's ATA66 or better.

▶ Sound cards are as important as a good hard drive. It pays to do your homework—there are a number of cards on the market and there is also a lot of advertising hype and misrepresentation in the market. See the section, "Choosing and Installing a Sound Card" later in this chapter for more details.

NOTE

While it is always ideal to have a dedicated system for audio recording, the speed of most of today's computers, even entry-level hardware, makes a dedicated audio PC unnecessary. There is no reason why you can't use the PC for other applications—just keep in mind that, with every new piece of software or functionality you add to your computer, you increase the likelihood for things to go wrong, crashes to occur, data to be lost, and so on. You can also fill up your hard drive space much faster, which means you may have to add hard drives sooner than you would prefer.

▶ At the time of this writing, 1.3 to 1.5 GHz Pentium 4 processors are becoming the rage, as is the AMD Athlon processor (1GHz+). Where processors were once a problem when it came to solid audio recording on a PC, this is simply not the case anymore. A Pentium 3-level processor clocked to at least 500 MHz or better will do the trick for you for some time to come. Avoid the IBM/Cyrix 6×86, MII, and MIII chips like the plague for audio recording, and know that anything slower than a Pentium II 300 will make it hard to work on digital audio files for CD mastering.

▶ The more RAM you have, the better. The idea is simple, really: RAM is far faster than the fastest hard drive on the planet, and the more you have of it, the fewer trips your audio recording software has to make to the hard drive during actual recording. At the time of this writing, RAM is comparatively very cheap: Go with a minimum of 128 MB of PC-100 RAM or better; 256 MB is ideal, as is the newer, faster RDRAM, which will hold you for several years before you will have to upgrade.

▶ An inexpensive 15-inch or 17-inch monitor will do just fine, since you need only a clean and simple window into the software you'll be using. There is no reason to pay thousands of dollars for a 21-inch Sony flat screen or the newest LCD panel, unless you have money to burn or you plan on playing every new video game or running other graphics-intensive applications on the studio computer.

▶ Chapter 16 covers CD-R and CD-RW drives in detail. Generally, you want the fastest you can get for around $200, which these days means an 8×/8×/24× drive. This is quite fast and will burn a CD before you can finish making a pot of coffee.

CHAPTER 11

NOTE

Dell, Gateway, and Micron computers using Intel processors are usually a safe bet, as each of these manufacturers has a long history of using quality parts and providing something actually resembling customer service when something does go wrong.

If you're building your own PC or upgrading, use known brands and higher-quality parts. Tom's Hardware (**www.tomshardware.com**) and StorageReview.com (**www.storagereview.com**) are excellent resources for reading reviews of the best parts and for seeing what other people use and have had success with.

TIP

If you're building or upgrading your system yourself, watch out for compatibility issues between components, and check the manufacturer's Web site for links to online forums or newsgroups (**www.deja.com** is an excellent resource) where you can read about other users' experiences. A little research goes a long way when it comes to assembling PC components.

One more thing: Understand that the capabilities of computer hardware are going to change over time and get comfortable with the idea. Processors will get faster, hard drives bigger, monitors prettier, and so on. The difference today, compared to just a few years ago, however, is that affordable computer hardware is now fast enough to easily do audio recording on a PC. In other words, if you set up a PIII 500 MHz, 30 GB, 256 MB RAM system today running Windows and SONAR, you have a system that, regardless of the advances that will be made next year or in the next 10 years in hardware, is fast enough to do the job comfortably.

Of course, as hardware gets better, so will software, and the capabilities of your PC-base home studio will grow accordingly if you upgrade every few years. SONAR 18.0 will look as different from SONAR 1.0 as SONAR 1.0 does from the very first version of Cakewalk (SONAR's predecessor) over a decade ago.

Choosing and Installing a Sound Card

The sound card in your home studio system is the heart of it all, and it's important that you choose a full-duplex sound card that is as noiseless as possible.

NOTE

Full-duplex is the ability of a sound card to simultaneously record and play back audio, and this is a requirement for having any kind of real home studio. You can't multi-track without it! Avoid ISA-based, older sound cards even if they are advertised as full-duplex. Older sound cards are full-duplex only in strictest sense of the word, since they can typically only manage playback of previously recorded audio in 8 bits while recording 16-bit audio, and none of them record in 20- or 24-bit audio. The result is that they are noisy and distorted. Stay away.

Almost every sound card is made of the same basic components. The following is the core list:

▶ **Analog-to-Digital Converters**—AD converters convert the incoming analog audio from your microphone and input signals into digital audio data.

▶ **Digital-to-Analog Converters**—DA converters translate digital audio data from your PC into good old-fashioned analog audio that you can hear through speakers or headphones. DA converters are found in electronic keyboards, MIDI modules, Mini-Disc recorders, DAT recorders, and digital mixers.

▶ **Mixer**—This is where crucial functions like volume, input and output signals, and multi-channel recording are handled. For Windows 95 or better, a sound card's mixer is controlled from that little yellow speaker icon in the system tray or sometimes the sound card's own proprietary control panel.

▶ **Codec**—This is usually a dedicated audio chip that controls audio data, including compression, decompression, a mixer, and the AD/DA converters. Codecs can vary widely in quality.

NOTE

Two of the most popular codec manufacturers are Analog Devices (**www.analog.com**) and Sigmatel (**www.sigmatel.com**). In addition to producing codecs for sound cards, these companies have also branched out to provide codecs for inclusion directly onto a computer's motherboard. In other words, built-in sound!

This is an exciting development in the world of PCs, because PC processors are now fast enough to support on-board sound to the extent that the quality is beginning to approach that of professional-grade sound cards. The only drawback is software support, since on-board sound capabilities can only be upgraded through better and more powerful software (or by buying a whole new motherboard!).

The SoundMax product from Analog Devices, in particular, is worth watching, and if current versions of the product are any indication, SoundMax may be an obvious choice for inexpensive, yet high-quality, professional audio within the next couple of years.

▶ **MIDI Ports**—Almost all sound cards have MIDI ports. Cheaper sound cards and consumer-level hardware will typically combine MIDI In and Out ports with the joystick port, which requires a special cable to rig the sound card to your MIDI devices. The cable is widely available. Professional-level sound cards will come with MIDI interfaces sporting either standard 5-pin ports or USB ports.

▶ **MIDI Synthesizer**—In the old days (not all that long ago, actually), sound cards came with FM-synthesis based MIDI synthesizers; these days, almost all PC sound cards build in a wavetable MIDI synthesizer. The quality of the wavetable instrument sounds vary widely—some of them don't sound much better than FM.

▶ **Digital Signal Processor**—DSP is used on most sound cards these days, and it makes it easier for you to perform mixing, resampling, changing the recording quality, and, most importantly, providing effects and EQ to your mixes. While you can still perform these things in software using your computer's main processor, DSP is an extra chip on the sound card that takes some of the load off the main processor for smoother sailing.

So what kind of sound card should you choose? To begin with, there are two consumer-level sound cards that will just about do the trick for under $100 at the time of this writing: Creative Labs' SoundBlaster Live! and Turtle Beach's Santa Cruz. Both cards will run on Pentium or Celeron systems or higher running Windows 95/98/Me/NT/2000.

These sound cards are really designed more for gamers than for musicians, but they'll do as a minimum. SB Live! supports the SoundFont 2 sampling format, and there are a number of SoundFont CD-ROMs available from E-MU and third-party developers; however, for home studio use, the SB Live! is a bit on the noisy side, using a 32-bit DSP which resamples everything to 16-bit 48 kHz and then resamples again to whatever the output format is, typically 16-bit 44.1 kHz. The SB Live! does have S/PDIF, which is a plus, though its quality is questionable and you can purchase a version of the card without it.

Turtle Beach's Santa Cruz offers about the same quality full-duplex digital audio as the SB Live!, has more inputs and outputs, and is a bit less noisy, though it doesn't support the SoundFont standard. Unless you want to use SoundFonts, the Santa Cruz is a better value for the home studio and its drivers are more solid than the SB Live!

Hopefully, you aren't pinched for cash to the point that you have to use these sound cards; there are number of better choices in the $200 to $1,000 price range which are of far superior quality:

▶ Emagic's Audiowerk2 is a good choice at about $200 and includes 18-bit AD and DA converters as well as S/PDIF. This card is not supported on Windows NT.

▶ M-Audio's Delta 44 is a 4-input/4-output sound card and, like many professional-quality sound cards, includes a break-out box that connects to the PCI card you install in the computer. It's 24-bit and can sample up 96 kHz; however, it does not support either S/PDIF or MIDI. It sells for around $300.

▶ Echo's Layla24, at around $800, boasts some impressive new features (besides full 24-bit 96 kHz support) including eight balanced inputs and outputs, eight channels of ADAT I/O, S/PDIF (coax and optical), Word Clock I/O, and on-board MIDI (In, Out, and Thru). This is a very good-sounding sound card that I highly recommended if you can afford it.

▶ Emagic Audiowerk8 is a multichannel audio interface. It has two analog inputs available for simultaneous recording, eight analog outputs, and MIDI I/O, and sells for less than $400, street.

▶ M-Audio's Delta 1010 (around $700) is a combination rack-mount 8-channel analog box plus S/PDIF and PCI card (24-bit, 96 kHz capable) and is competitive with the Layla24 at about the same price and features.

▶ Yamaha's SW1000XG is a feature-rich sound card, using a pair of 20-bit AD converters on a 24-bit internal data path and a very powerful Yamaha XG synthesizer with 20 MB of wavetable ROM, along with seven independent effects processors and more than 1,200 MIDI sounds. There's a lot here for the money at around $600. You can also purchase optional plug-in boards from Yamaha for additional MIDI instrument sounds and effects, such as vocal harmonizing.

▶ E-MU's Paris combines a hardware mixing surface, a PCI interface card with onboard DSP, analog/digital I/O modules, and mixing software to create a powerful audio production system for Windows 95/98 or MacOS 7/8. The 16-channel package comes in at a little over $1,000, a bit on the expensive side (but well worth the extra money).

▶ DigiDesign's ToolBox XP, at under $500, street, couples its excellent Audiomedia III PCI card's high-quality I/O and proven reliability with its award-winning Pro Tools (LE version) software. ToolBox XP has four inputs, four outputs, and two S/PDIFs and is 24-bit.

While almost all sound cards will work with Pentium-based processors, there are occasional problems with AMD-based (K6 or Athlon) systems. In particular, conflicts and complete lockups have been reported using the Echo Layla. There may also be operating system limitations—for example, a sound card might work fine in Windows 98 but have problems in Windows 95 or NT due to lack of driver support or memory requirements. Make sure you read the manufacturer's published system requirements, and it's not a bad idea to check newsgroup posts via Deja (**www.deja.com**) to see if other users have experienced any particularly unusual problems.

Sound Card Installation Notes

All of the sound cards mentioned in the last section are PCI-based cards, meaning they plug into a PCI slot on your computer's motherboard. Physically installing a sound card in one of these slots is rarely a problem—it's about as technical as putting together a mic stand—but there are some general, good practices to prevent problems and make sure the installation goes as smoothly as possible:

▶ In order to put the card in the slot, you'll have to open your computer's case. Before doing anything inside the computer, always unplug the computer completely from its electrical socket—and it's a good rule to touch another piece of metal (such as a piece of metal furniture frame) to ground yourself to prevent damaging any of the components with static electricity.

▶ Proceed carefully and slowly, and read all of the manufacturer's directions for installing the sound card. Pay attention to the other devices in the case (it will usually be crowded and tight), being careful not to accidentally knock a hard drive or floppy drive cable loose.

▶ If you can, keep the sound card as far away from your graphics card as possible to minimize potential interference between the two cards. (In other words, don't plug your graphics card and sound card into adjacent slots.)

CHAPTER 11

▶ In rare cases when you have lots of other PCI device already installed, particularly multiple sound cards, you may get clicks and pops in the audio due to simultaneous heavy activity. If this happens, it may be possible to give your main sound card a higher priority in the internal bus-mastering order by moving it to the slot closest to the AGP graphics slot or CPU. This, of course, contradicts the last bullet, but may be necessary as a last resort. Check your motherboard manual to see how the slot priority is laid out.

▶ Handle the sound card, and any computer hardware for that matter, gently. You can unknowingly crack the circuit board if you flex it too much, which can cause almost untraceable and intermittent problems.

▶ In general, it's best to insert a PCI card by positioning one end of the connector first to get it started, then pushing the connector home with a gentle rocking action.

▶ All PCI cards are held in place by a single screw at the top of the backplate, and this should be tightened firmly to prevent a poor connection.

▶ If you have to use excessive force to get the sound card to fit, stop what you're doing and give the manufacturer a call; the circuit board itself could mistakenly have been cut too wide, and forcing it could damage the PCI slot.

Audio File Formats

For a PC-based digital recording setup, there are a number of audio-based file formats you can deal with. SONAR, for example, can deal with seven different formats. Sonic Foundry handles many more, and programs like Cool Edit or GoldWave can read and write dozens of file formats.

With most of your recording projects, you'll be concerned with only three formats: MIDI files (.MID), wave files (.WAV), and whatever proprietary format the software application uses for storing MIDI and/or wave files with the software's other data.

In SONAR, both the project file (.WRK) and the bundle file (.BUN) are used. Both formats deal with MIDI data just like a MIDI file and digital audio data just like a wave file; the only difference is that a .BUN file actually combines the audio data and MIDI data into one big file, while the .WRK file only references external wave files.

Wave files are usually uncompressed audio files—meaning they are large (a typical three-minute song will take up a bit more than 30 MB of your hard drive) and they sound quite good. The sound quality of a wave file is determined by you when you record it and by the quality of the sound card you're using. Generally, you'll want to work with wave files at the same level of fidelity as the CD music standard, which is a bit depth (or "resolution") of 16 bits and a 44.1 kHz sampling rate.

NOTE

The idea of bit depth is not terribly complicated. Bit depth implies that the string of 0s and 1s representing a slice of audio data can't be more than 16 bits long (a pretty good-size number). Similarly, a sampling rate of 44.1 kHz means that the audio has been sampled 44,100 times per second. The result is that the sound reproduction is quite accurate, but the audio files take up a lot of space. That's why, at 16 bits and 44.1 kHz, you can't pack more than seventy-four minutes or so of audio onto a compact disc.

Bit depth also indicates the highest signal-to-noise ratio and frequency you can record. For example, at 16-bit, the highest signal-to-noise ratio is 96 dB and the highest frequency that can be recorded at 44.1 kHz is 22 kHz.

Figure 11.2 shows a typical SONAR project including both MIDI file and wave files. In this case, MIDI and wave files alike are recorded and played back as separate tracks. In addition to saving wave file data in a SONAR project or bundle file, you can export individual wave file tracks into separate files.

Figure 11.2

This SONAR project shows both digital audio files and MIDI files.

The wave file format is actually a subset of another, more complicated audio format called RIFF. Data is divided up into "chunks," and all wave files require at least two kinds of chunks:

▶ The FMT chunk describes the sample rate, sample width, bit depth, and other digital audio details.

▶ The DATA chunk contains the actual audio sample data.

A wave file can also contain some of the other chunk types supported by its parent RIFF format, including LIST chunks, which are used to store optional kinds of non-musical data such as the copyright date, your name, song title, and so forth.

Wave files are powerful and also support a number of different compression schemes. An entry in the FMT chunk indicates the type of compression; for example, a value of 1 indicates Pulse Code Modulation (PCM), which is a "straight," or uncompressed, encoding of the samples. Values other than 1 indicate some form of compression. Typically, you won't use compression with wave files, because you'll use them as the uncompressed raw audio source when you record.

The MIDI file format is used by musicians extensively, as well as in many popular PC games and entertainment software, and there are loads of MIDI files available on the Internet. A MIDI file does not capture and store audio data; it instead manages a list of events which describe the specific steps that your sound card or computer must take to generate the music. MIDI files are tiny compared to digital audio files, and they are easy to edit, allowing the music to be rearranged, recorded, and played in real-time. Chapter 9 covers the MIDI file format in detail.

Monitoring and Mixing with Headphones

In Chapter 2, you learned some techniques for positioning monitors and a bit about working toward effective, accurate monitor mixes. This section expands on this all-important aspect of your home studio by focusing on the headphone mix—which is critical not only for recording but for monitoring your mixes during both mixdown and mastering.

There are a couple of things to realize about using headphones. First, they are absolutely necessary, and getting a decent pair is crucial. Second, the way you mix using headphones can be deceptive—even with excellent frequency response (in fact, sometimes because of excellent response), a headphone mix can sound quite different than the way your music will sound on a typical home or car stereo.

Choosing Headphones

Whether you're recording or mixing, you want as accurate a sound from your headphones as you can get. This is literally not as simple as it might sound. In one sense, you can evaluate the quality of headphones the same way you do monitors—by how good they sound. At the end of the day, this is more important than what the technical specifications say.

Unlike loudspeaker monitors, though, sound from headphones goes directly into your ears without the spatialization and acoustic shaping—also known as room coloration—that occurs when sound waves interact with your head and the space around you. And, of course, no two heads (or ears, for that matter) are alike, so what sounds good to the drummer may not do it at all for the lead singer!

For these reasons, you should try a number of different brands of headphones before spending your money—don't just go on a friend's (or a book's) rote recommendations. When evaluating headphones, here are some important things to look for:

▶ Smooth, even overall frequency response—not too bright
▶ Deep bass response
▶ A good fit, since any discomfort at all will only get worse the longer you wear them
▶ How durable the headphones are and how easily they can be repaired

▶ The cord length, because you'll need long cords for good mobility between instruments, the mixer, and the computer

▶ An ample power supply which should handle from 100mw up to 1W

▶ The frequency response—20 Hz to 20 kHz is the normal human hearing range, and anything lower or higher than that is unimportant to most music recording

▶ A low distortion factor—the lower, the better, usually less than 1 percent

▶ A sensitivity rating of 100 dB or greater

Comparative Headphone Mixing

Unlike monitors, which exist and create sound in a live acoustic space, headphones tend to sound a bit artificial because each audio channel is isolated to each of your ears. There is no room for sound waves to interact with each other, with your recording space, or with the rest of your head before they reach your eardrums. Therefore, headphone mixes can quickly become a mish-mash of complex phase-shifting which may change, cancel, and/or delay frequencies. The bottom line is that an otherwise smooth headphone mix can sometimes sound downright rough when heard through your monitors.

In terms of panning, or effects like reverb and delay, a headphone mix is generally accurate, unless you're using an excessive amount of phase-shifting effect. On the other hand, achieving any kind of accurate "3-D" type of effect is next to impossible using headphones, because standard headphones trap the entire soundfield in a straight line relative to each side of the stereo field to begin with.

Perhaps the simplest problem to avoid when choosing headphones is to find headphones with excellent bass response and flat frequency response across the entire spectrum. Bad bass response will make your monitor mix sound bad just about every time, and headphones that are too bright will tend to sound muddy coming from your speakers.

It's not easy to match a headphone mix with a monitor mix, but it can be done. Unfortunately, it's not something you can learn from another person or from a book. Good mixdowns with headphones are ultimately a matter of trial and error, which means you should always check the final result with the monitor mix.

TIP

Headwize (**www.headwize.com**) is an excellent resource on the Web for extreme details about everything related to headphones. In particular, there are a number of good technical articles on psychoacoustics (how the brain processes sound) and effective studio headphone use.

CHAPTER 11

Signal Processing Basics

Digital signal processing, or DSP, is simply a way of altering an audio signal. It's achieved electronically, through the use of an external piece of hardware that makes changes to the audio signal or through software plug-ins that do the trick using SONAR or other digital recording software.

Though Chapter 12 covers DSP and audio effects in detail, this section is a brief survey of the most common types of DSP you'll encounter during both recording and mixing, including reverb, compression and delay.

Reverb

Generally speaking, reverb is how sound is reflected in any acoustic space; the rate, distance, and amplitude of that reflection is exactly what is simulated in a reverb box or reverb-capable plug-in. Reverb is all about timing between the original sound of your instrument or voice (or any other sound) and the sound that bounces off surfaces in the range of the original sound.

Because different spaces have different sizes (a football field vs. a shower stall, for example) and surfaces (grandstands vs. ceramic bathroom tile), there is an almost limitless number of the types of reverb. A typical rack-mount device that can process reverb into your recording will offer dozens of different settings, as do the software plug-ins.

Reverb can give music a whole new feel. For example, adding reverb to vocals helps the sound become fuller, more dimensional, and, in many cases, more natural than a straight-up "dry" vocal sound. (This is why most people sound better when they sing in the shower.) Reverb can also be used to make string and percussion instruments sound larger than life or add ambience and spatial qualities that blend harmonies in beautiful ways.

Reverb consists of a number of different components which you typically control while recording or mixing; however, there are two fundamental pieces, which also happen to be the most important:

 The level of the original sound source itself

 Decay, which controls the length of time the reverb takes to stop sounding and the number of reverberations

The first component above is probably too obvious: It's simply the original signal to which the reverb will respond. Reverb will sound different with different instruments and frequencies, as well as the sound's timbre and amplitude.

Decay is the rate at which the sound frequencies in the original sound reflect back, as well as how many times they do so. Depending on the types of frequencies in the original sound, the level of decay can be adjusted to a number of different settings. For example, if high-end frequencies roll off faster than the lower ones, you typically achieve a darker sound, while conversely, where the lowest frequencies take longer to reflect, you'll get a brighter sound.

The advantage of a good digital reverb processor is that it allows you to control the sound of your recording in so many different ways. You can control a variety of parameters, which run the gamut from tripped-out space effects to a concert hall to a warm, intimate-sounding club effect. SONAR comes with a DirectX reverb plug-in (Figure 11.3) which lets you easily apply reverb to individual audio tracks and audition them before making changes to the tracks.

Figure 11.3
SONAR's FXReverb
plug-in can add a new
dimension to your
recordings using reverb.

The downside to reverb is that it's notoriously easy to overuse, which often results in muddy or hard-to-EQ mixes. The best rule for reverb is never to record it to original tracks. Always record as dry and cleanly as you can, then you can add and tweak reverb later till your heart's content.

Compression

Compression restricts the range of sound by attenuating signals that exceed a certain input, or threshold, level. By attenuating the louder signal levels, you limit the dynamic range of the sound, or the difference between the loudest and softest levels in sound. This has the effect of making compressed sounds a bit louder in the mix than the original, non-compressed frequencies; it's also very handy for ensuring that an input signal doesn't get too hot and cause digital distortion. There are four parts to compression:

▶ The level at which you want the compression to begin affecting the sound

▶ The attack time, which is the time it takes for the input gain to decrease to an amount you specify

▶ The release time, which is the time it takes for the gain to return to its original value (usually a 1:1 ratio to the attack time)

▶ The compression ratio itself, which is the increase of signal input in dBs needed to cause a 1 dB increase in the compressor's output signal

Most compressors will have controls for all of these elements. Using different combinations, you can smooth out unevenness in volume, reduce vocal sibilance, increase or decrease sustain quality, and much more. One of the most frequently compressed instruments is the bass guitar; compressing a bass properly can bring up the lowest frequencies without losing the punctuation of the plucked bass strings and add incredible sustain. Compression can also do wonders for overall mixes.

Delay

Delay can be a highly useful tool for fattening tracks, getting cool guitar effects, and augmenting reverb to increase spatialization and the "openness" of your sound. In fact, delay and reverb are often used together. There is really one important piece to controlling delay: its length. Delay lengths are always timed in milliseconds (ms).

Perhaps the most widely utilized range is from 5 ms to 40 ms, which tends to fatten sound, but, unlike higher-length delay, delays in this range are not perceived as discrete, separate sounds. The result is that thinner sounds become fuller and fatter, but without any perceptible echo effect.

TIP

Be wary of using delay lengths below 5 ms or so. This almost always causes phase cancellation.

Delays of 60 ms to 100 ms are commonly referred to as "slap echoes." These can make thin vocals sound a little fuller, while 40 ms to 60 ms delays "double" sound, which causes a vocal track, for example, to sound more like two singers than one. Be careful in both these ranges for vocals—and for any acoustic instrument, for that matter. The downside is that a lot of the natural timbre can become unnatural rather quickly.

Lengths of more than 100 ms are usually heard as echoes. With longer delay, you should also be careful to make sure that the delay effect corresponds to the tempo of the music. If it doesn't fit the tempo, it can quickly throw off the timing of the song.

12

Serious Audio

Chapter 11 covered the fundamentals of audio and is probably all most of you will ever need (maybe even a little more than you'll ever need). For the rest of you, this chapter dives deeper still into some of the more useful details behind digital audio. Warning: There's a little math and a sentence here and there that exists for the sole purpose of making the author sound like he invented the entire theory of digital audio (which, of course, he didn't, but don't tell anyone). The following topics are discussed:

▶ The RIFF file format
▶ Audio buffer data
▶ Oversampling and dithering
▶ Reverb

It's a Pressure Cooker in There

If you've read Chapter 11, you know that sound is, fundamentally, fluctuations in air pressure. Likewise, digital sound is a kind of graph or table of the changes in that air pressure over time.

This idea is easily illustrated. For instance, if you zoom in on an audio track in SONAR, as shown in Figure 12.1, you see a graphical representation of the audio data points, all sampled up and ready. All those wide, ragged edges indicate that there is a lot of air pressure, which your ear knows as loud audio. The wider the audio "graph" of the sounds, the higher the amplitude of the track's audio.

CHAPTER 12

Figure 12.1
This one, Nigel, almost
goes to 11.

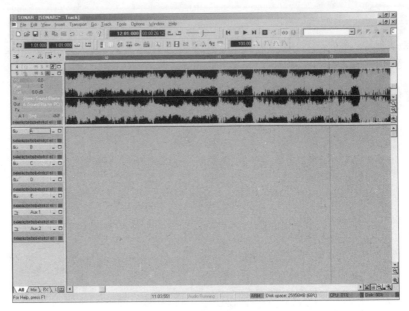

On the other hand, as shown in Figure 12.2, when you zoom in on an area where there is nothing but silence, the image is just a little line in the middle, indicating that there is no change in air pressure. Your ear correspondingly detects that as silence.

Figure 12.2
This one is the sound of
silence.

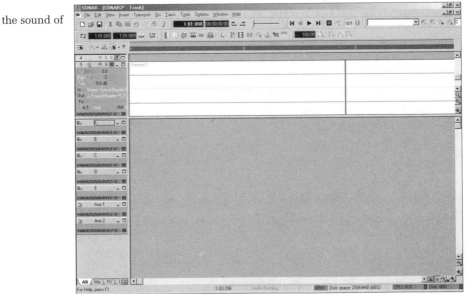

When you record sound, your computer's hardware knows how to process fluctuations in electrical voltage, which your sound card—by way of its A/D converter—measures so-many-times per second. A computer processor changes the signal into numbers, called samples. When you play sound, the whole process is reversed, so that the fluctuations in voltage go to your speakers, happily converted back to a waveform by your sound card's D/A converter.

NOTE

The speed with which your sound card samples audio is called the sampling rate and is expressed in kilohertz (kHz). One kHz is 1,000 samples per second; 44.1 kHz is 44,100 samples per second; 96 kHz is 96,000 samples per second; and so on.

Pulse Code Modulation

As it turns out, there is a standardized way of recording digital audio. Used by both audio CDs and most PC audio files (.WAV files, for example), the most common type of digital audio recording is called PCM, or pulse code modulation.

The process of PCM goes something like this in your computer's hardware:

▶ As discussed in the previous section, an electrical signal is sent down the path from your instrument or microphone.

▶ Your computer's A/D converter then precisely measures the signal at regular intervals—for example, 44,100 samples per second in the case of CD-quality audio.

▶ Each sample is converted into a 16-bit number and contains two channels of data, one for your left ear and one for your right, in order to produce stereo.

▶ The digital stereo image is recorded in alternating fashion, in sequence: left, right, left, right, etc.

It seems almost magical that a sequence of millions of numbers can end up as an accurate audio recording. But it's not magic—it's air pressure (and mathematics!). All these numbers combine to recreate the same waveform that creates the same amount of air pressure over the same period of time, via a set of speakers, that you heard when the audio was first recorded.

Audio Data Storage

When you want to store an audio track or any other digital recording, you write it in some form to your hard drive. Well, you don't actually write it—your digital audio software does. Also, the file actually doesn't directly store anything about a sound's frequency, pitch, or amplitude; instead, it stores certain types of identifying information about the data and the digital samples themselves, in the form of audio buffer data.

A buffer is an area in the computer's memory reserved for data that is not logical code but is, instead, values representative of the audio's waveform. In the case of audio, these values are the samples taken when the audio was recorded—for example, 16-bit numbers for 16-bit audio—which translate into a description of what the audio is supposed to sound like.

A simple analogy is that non-fat latte you had at Starbucks last week: The physical cup itself is like a file, while the name on the cup identifies it as some kind of espresso-based concoction from Starbucks. The coffee itself is kind of like buffer data; opening the lid and taking a sip is analogous to opening an audio file.

The RIFF File Format

RIFF is a file format for storing multimedia data like audio and video; it is based on the concept of "chunks." Each chunk of a RIFF file has a type, represented by a name which is four characters long. A chunk type contains the size of the chunk and then the actual contents—the values representing the audio data—of that chunk.

Wave Files

The wave file format, with the file extension .WAV, is actually a form of the RIFF file format used specifically for storing digital audio. It requires two types of named chunks:

▶ The *fmt* chunk identifies the number of channels (two for stereo, for example), the sample rate, the bit depth, and the type of data compression used to store the buffer data.

▶ The *data* chunk contains the actual samples.

A wave file may also use any other chunk type allowed by the RIFF format, including *list* chunks, which are used to store optional kinds of data such as the copyright date, artist name, song title, and so on. The wave file format is quite powerful because of its RIFF-based structure, which is the principle reason why Microsoft adopted it as the primary audio file format for Windows.

Perfect Digital Audio

In 1928, the only way to record anything was to copy sound waves in wax. Harry Nyquist, an AT&T engineer, thought there might be a better way than wax, so he theorized that sound waves could be "sampled" and then read back to re-plot the original wave—perfectly reproducing the signal.

His idea was simple (the math was complex, though—you don't *want* to see the math): If you sample an analog signal at a rate of at least twice its highest frequency component, you can convert it back to analog, pass it through a low-pass filter, and get back the same thing you put in.

Though his theory was a stroke of genius, it turned out to be a frustrating thing for good old Harry at the time (and he was *good*, a prolific inventor who held more than 100 patents), since it needed at least 22,000 samples per second to really make it worthwhile. In the 1920s, nothing had been invented yet that could measure, record, and store that much information quickly, so Harry had to wait several decades for a binary language and integrated circuits—in other words, computers—to make digital recording and playback a reality.

Of course, there is theory, and there is, as always, reality:

▶ 16-bit samples, even 24-bit samples, are not the pure numbers of Nyquist's theorem, so digital sample values can never be completely accurate. For example, 16 bits is not a very big number when weighed against Nyquist's numbers, and though it ends up as a 96 dB dynamic range, the average level must be much lower than 96 dB in order to make up for peak frequencies. What's worse, at low amplitude, some signals tend to become distorted, causing the somewhat brittle or "cold" sound that some people associate with digital audio.

▶ Nyquist's theory uses samples that are instantaneous values, or "impulses," and reproducing a perfect impulse is impossible. The result is typically a loss of some high frequencies, though adjusting frequency response with filtering does help reduce this problem.

▶ Unfortunately, there is no such thing as the perfect low-pass filter required by Nyquist's theorem. A real filter has a finite, set slope—for instance, a steep filter can produce a lot of phase shift. A technique called "oversampling" was invented to try to overcome this problem.

Today, the audio on a compact disc is a realization of Nyquist's theory, but it is not perfect by any means. For any digital recording that sounds good, there is likely more than a little filtering, dithering, interpolating, slicing, dicing, and julienne fries behind it.

NOTE

The word "good" is a highly subjective term, especially when it comes to digital audio. For the purposes of this book, "good" digital audio is audio that accurately plays back that which it has recorded. The more accurate, the more "good."

Of course, that begs the question, "What exactly is accurate?" The long answer is, "Read the rest of the book." For those of you who want the short answer now: Accurate is "good."

The Big Julienne Fry: Oversampling

Take a look at the way a typical CD audio system plays back audio:

▶ Since the audio was recorded at 44.1 kHz, 16-bit audio samples are sent down the datastream at 44.1 kHz to an anti-aliasing, low-pass filter.

▶ Nyquist's theory says that the highest playback frequency is less than half the recorded rate, so the highest play-backable frequency you can hear is 22.05 kHz.

▶ Frequencies above 22.05 are "aliased" frequencies—essentially reflections of the original sampling frequency; the anti-aliasing filter attempts to block these reflections.

CHAPTER 12

The biggest problem with this process is effectively blocking the reflections; the anti-aliasing filter's cutoff needs to go from around 0 dB attenuation at 20 kHz to somewhere near 90 dB at 22 kHz. This is a steep slope, and a filter this steep has a lot of phase shift as it nears the cutoff. This is not good, since it can produce less-than-stellar audio quality.

NOTE

In the audio world, attenuation is how you affect the strength of an electrical signal; to "attenuate" a signal means to reduce its amplitude, hopefully with little or no distortion. Attenuating a signal usually means you also have to amplify that signal, which typically introduces distortion back into the signal. It's a bit Zen-like, when you think about it.

The solution is to sample at a higher rate to begin with; since reflections of the audio image happen at near the sampling frequency (and multiples of it), sampling at a higher rate moves the reflections farther from the good, happy audio you want to keep.

This is called "oversampling" and is accomplished through interpolation. In mathematics, interpolation is simply estimating the value of something (usually a math function or a series of numbers) between two other, known values, and it's the same kind of thing here: Oversampling calculates the frequency spectrum as if the audio data were sampled with more than 44,100 samples.

For example, eight times as many samples running at eight times the rate is dubbed "8×oversampling," which produces a less-steep cutoff slope. For example, at a 44.1 sampling rate, 8x oversampling would generate 352,800 samples per second! This is almost a bit of magic, really, because oversampling effectively generates more samples from a waveform than what's there, and it works! The tradeoff is that it takes more processing power to interpolate the audio.

NOTE

There is another type of oversampling, at the analog to digital stage, and it's far more complicated and far less interesting. "Oversampling" here refers to the digital to analog conversion stage.

Dithering

The fact is, you can't use 16 bits of data all the time; a digital recording must adjust to allow for peaks that use the full 16 bits, and that means most of the music is recorded at a lower volume using fewer than 16 bits. For instance, at 1 bit in amplitude, waveforms that are sine waves become square waves, a phenomenon which introduces a lot of very bad distortion into the equation. Points smaller than 1 bit won't make it into your recording at all.

This is where dithering can be a big help. Dithering is adding a little low-level noise to the audio signal, on purpose, in exchange for a huge reduction in distortion. The added noise spreads out most of the numeric errors, which would have produced distortion across the frequency spectrum, as broadband noise.

To illustrate this idea, think of sitting in the stands at the starting line of a racetrack. When the cars are all still and lined up before the race, it's impossible for you to look through them. You can't see the road beneath their wheels, or, if you're low enough to the ground, anything to the other side of them.

However, once the race begins, you can always see the road as well as the track's infield on the other side. When the cars come whizzing past you over the starting line, you see a little blur, but that's all. The blur is similar to the noise you get by dithering. You're trading a little bit of noise so that you can clearly and accurately hear what's really there.

Dithering Down

The most fundamental use of dithering is when you reduce the number of bits used to represent the signal—for example, "down-sampling" a recording from 16 bits to 8 bits. Instead of just rounding the 16-bit numbers to 8-bit numbers, which would by itself create unwanted amounts of distortion, dithering spreads the audio spectrum out to fit the samples into the smaller numbers. This decreases harmonic distortion and introduces a little broadband noise into the picture.

Dithering Everywhere

In addition to simply reducing the bit depth of a recording or audio file, there are other types of dither going on all the time, behind the scenes.

For instance, the act of recording itself requires that the infinitely precise numbers of an analog audio signal be reduced to 16 bits, and dithering is going on at this stage, usually by way of the noise already present in your recording chain (the cables and equipment). Yes, that's right—the very presence of all your gear provides the noise necessary to do the dithering for you! Kind of ironic, isn't it?

In addition, almost all types of DSP (digital signal processing) require either some kind of reduction or multiplication of bits; for example, if you add that killer stadium reverb into your vocals, you're actually multiplying 16-bit values together, which results in 32-bit numbers, and you cannot round the extra bits without ruining the vocal, so you must dither.

Volume changes are yet another multiplication-heavy activity, and you do these all the time both during recording and mixdown.

TIP

If you've gotten into the habit of normalizing every track after every edit you make, don't! You're actually increasing noise and distortion, since the noise level is brought up along with the signal and the signal must be re-dithered. Never normalize until you're done recording all of the elements of a composition.

CHAPTER 12

NOTE

The digital audio editing software you use should know when and how to dither—automatically. SONAR, for example, does an effective job of dithering behind the scenes. However, since dithering requires a lot of processing power, dithering routines employed during real-time DSP in SONAR are not quite as effective as DSP applied in non-real-time.

Real-time effects are wonderful, useful, and a major feature of SONAR and other audio software applications, but if you don't have to use them, don't. Do the processing after the track has been recorded.

Reverb Under the Covers

You undoubtedly already know that natural reverberation can have a great effect on music. Natural reverb is the result of sound reflecting off surfaces in a room; sound travels from its source and strikes walls, ceilings, and floors, reflecting off them at different angles. Some of the reflections find your ears immediately and are known as "early reflections." Other reflections may bounce a few more times off other surfaces in the room before finally vibrating your eardrums. A room's size, its contents and materials, and the density of its surfaces give any room its unique sound.

In the digital domain, reverb can be reproduced very effectively; the number of reflections and their frequencies are limited only by processing speed, while the delay of the reflections is limited only by the amount of your computer's memory.

Before digital processing, reverb was difficult to re-create well. "Plate" and "Spring" reverbs were created by emulating a speaker and a microphone at two ends of a metal spring or a suspended metal plate, but they weren't very portable or versatile.

FIR Filters

A finite impulse response (FIR) filter is a method of creating reverb that isn't dependent on time or frequency; it doesn't matter when you play a note, you'll get the same type of reverberation. This type of reverb is characterized by its response to a sound-generating event or its impulse response.

For instance, an F#9 on the guitar, a four-part harmony, even a handclap—any wave-producing action—is a sound-generating event. For FIR-based reverb, it turns out that each sample point of a sound event can be treated as little more than an echo of the event itself. So, any sound event becomes the sum of the other sound events for each individual sample at each of their respective times. This concept is called superposition.

The benefit is that room characteristics can easily be added to any dry digital mix in a fairly straightforward way, but it takes a lot of computing power. Each sample must be multiplied by each sample of the impulse response, then added to the mix. If you have x-number of samples to process, and a sound event itself is y-samples long, you need to perform $(x + y)$ multiplications and additions.

For example, if the impulse response to a sound event is 2 seconds long, and the song is 2 minutes long, your computer's processor will wind up performing many, many trillions of multiplications and about the same number of additions at a 44.1 kHz sampling rate.

Even by today's standards, this method of reverb, while highly accurate, is processor-expensive. Thankfully, there are other ways.

Comb and Allpass Filters

Most digital reverbs today employ a different approach, through the use of multiple delays and feedback which build up a series of dense echoes. Much of this idea is based on the concept of a comb filter.

The impulse response of the comb filter—which gets its name from the comb-like notches in its frequency response pattern—is like a sound event bouncing around between two walls and growing weaker with each bounce—a very simple concept.

The problem is that it takes too many of these reflections to make a smooth reverb, and though a comb filter's phase cancellations can very easily mimic room effects, it can just as easily become harmonically unstable rather quickly and cause ringing.

A slightly better solution is called an allpass filter. In the case of an allpass, the impulse responses are fed both forward and backward to fill in the phase cancellations. Since all frequencies are passed equally, the result is a much smoother frequency response. However, an allpass still affects the phase of the signal, so it, too, can exhibit ringing, particularly with abrupt sound events.

Modern Reverb

Comb filters and allpass filters fall into a category all their own, called infinite impulse response filters, or IIR, and they are often combined to produce digital reverb. M.A. Schroeder, in the '70s, did a lot of the earliest work on digital reverb, and one of his best known reverb designs used four comb filters and two allpass filters, as shown in Figure 12.3.

Figure 12.3
Schroeder's reverberator combined four comb filters and two allpass filters to create a very realistic reverb for its time.

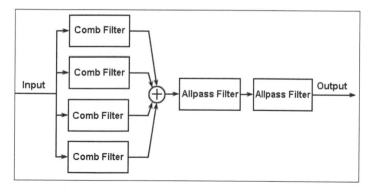

CHAPTER 12

Schroeder's reverberator is a bit primitive when compared to modern reverb algorithms, in which room geometry, surface materials, and location can be taken into account by using both FIR and IIR filters together. For instance, a FIR filter might be used to create early reflections, and then IIR filters create diffuse reverberation of those reflections. Algorithms which attempt to combine the best of both worlds achieve more accurate results and are more versatile, while keeping an eye on processor use.

13
Recording and Mixing

Unlike in much of home recording's sordid past, you are no longer limited to a few noisy analog tracks and cheap equipment. Thanks to the advances made in digital recording software and sound cards, just like the big guys, you have virtually limitless tracks and very little noise to play with.

You've got it better than George Martin had it in the '60s.

But hold on, wait just a second, *caveat emptor*—or something like that: With all this rope, you could easily hang yourself if you don't understand how to turn your performances into high-quality master recordings. That's where the art and science of recording and mixing come in. It can still be a jungle in there if you don't know what you're doing.

We'll swing our machete in the following directions:

- ▶ Recording and mixing fundamentals
- ▶ Monitoring for fun and money
- ▶ Cabling and its role in the chain
- ▶ The mixing process
- ▶ EQ and more EQ
- ▶ Software mixing
- ▶ Understanding the mixing chain
- ▶ Using effects effectively

The Basics

Chapters 2 and 3 helped you get up and running with your studio room and equipment. If you're ready to start recording, where's the best place to begin? Just as with anything else in life, there are a few fundamentals—general skills and knowledge for keeping your nose clean and your frustration meter at low levels.

It Helps to Hear What You're Hearing

As it turns out, we humans don't hear low frequencies (bass frequencies) and high frequencies (treble frequencies) nearly as well at low volumes as we do at high volumes. This was demonstrated by a couple of Bell Labs guys in the '30s, and is called the Fletcher-Munson Effect because of them.

NOTE

Chapter 11 details much more about us humans and our hearing capabilities.

Fletcher and Munson measured human hearing and produced a set of curves (the Fletcher-Munson Curves) showing the human ear's sensitivity to loudness vs. frequency. They showed that human hearing is extremely dependent upon loudness, and that the ear is most sensitive to sounds in the 3-4 kHz region.

Practically speaking, this means that sounds above and below 3-4 kHz must be louder in order to be heard at the same level. It also means that the lower the volume, the harder it is to hear the lows and highs. For example, bass frequencies in the 250 Hz and lower region (bass guitar, low toms, the kick drum) are roughly sixty times harder to hear at low levels than at high levels. In addition, high frequencies above 6 kHz or so (cymbals, vocal breath sounds) are about sixteen times harder to hear.

These facts should tell you something: Your recording and mixing levels will make a huge impact in how the end result sounds.

The best way to smooth out the impact is always to listen to your mix at different volumes and to shoot for a mix that works whether it's soft or loud or in between. This usually means making some trade-offs when calibrating mix levels. For instance, to keep from losing the kick drum in the mix, you may have to pull back on some of its thunderous, snapping ear candy at middle to upper volume levels. Don't be afraid to make lots of adjustments to levels both during recording and mixing; it's virtually impossible to get a satisfying mix if you don't work extensively with levels.

The Mix Behind the Mask

Masking is another human ear limitation you will be dealing with on a regular basis. Masking is when the louder of two sounds around a given frequency keeps the lower of the two from being heard. It's the fundamental reason why individual instrument sounds, when soloed, sound different than they do all mixed together.

This problem isn't as prevalent these days as it was in the days of 4-track cassette recorders; because you've got a multitude of tracks to work with, you can monitor each of the instruments when recording and mixing. You have ample opportunity to adjust each performance's tone so that it works in the mix.

Masking can still rear its ugly head when monitoring while recording, though, if you don't take the time to fine tune the level of the instrument you're on, as well as its tone.

Monitors

Good monitor speakers are an essential part of the home recording process. Like the selection of your home studio's cabling (covered later in this chapter), the value of making a proper choice in monitors is one of those things you can overlook up to a point, but when you reach that point, things can get ugly. In the end, it is your monitors that give an audible voice to the electrical signals that make up your music, and you shouldn't compromise those signals with a poor decision.

In fact, monitor speakers, more often than not, are the weakest link in the home studio chain. This is why it's not unusual for some home recording artists to spend almost as much on speakers as they do on their recording system, in order to achieve a proper balance of quality vs. total investment. Of course, on a practical level, just being able to afford the primary components of the studio (the space, computer, mixer, sound card, and so on) is hard enough, so it's best to regard speakers as one of those items that you should spend as much as you can possibly afford. In the long run, you'll be happier.

Ideally, studio monitors should have an even or flat response across the frequency spectrum. Accuracy is the key objective here, and if your monitors inaccurately color a signal with frequency boosts or gaps, it'll make the mixing process very difficult, particularly EQ. When you start under- or over-compensating for bad monitors, your mixes can easily end up either bass or treble heavy on other loudspeakers, and you'll never know it.

Unfortunately, creating an unbiased monitoring setup at home turns out to a little more brush-to-get to the picnic than what you'd think. Despite long bullet lists of technical claims made by monitor manufacturers, it's a random affair.

You should always compare different monitors with each other in the store, peruse the manufacturer's Web site, and read any reviews online you can find.

NOTE

ProRec, at **www.prorec.com**, is an excellent resource for reviews of studio equipment, and it's is a good place to check for reviews of studio monitors. The site reviews high-quality equipment (and software) with an eye on value.

When comparing monitors, be careful to match levels as closely as possible, since louder music usually sounds better. Listen for clarity and a good tone across frequencies; there should be no distortion or excessive buzz. Of course, once you've made a decision and you get your monitors home, you'll have to contend with the acoustics of your studio space. You can find more on this in Chapter 2.

Monitor Design

Most recipes for a monitor use only two or three ingredients: a speaker, a cabinet, and, in some cases, an amplifier. These aren't terribly complicated pieces of equipment in and of themselves, but their design can vary widely and involve a great deal of engineering.

The design of the cabinet can make a huge difference, and it's one of the most difficult design challenges for engineers who create monitors. For instance, you'll notice that professional-level studio monitors will rarely contain sharp edges. This is because sharp edges on a cabinet can cause something known as *cabinet edge diffraction*. Sound likes smooth, lathed curves, while sharp edges cause sound waves to veer too sharply—which can be ruinous to your stereo mix.

The speakers themselves are designed to provide accurate representations of the sound sent to them. Beyond achieving accuracy, many studio monitors also take into account ear fatigue of a person who listens to them throughout the day. For example, tweeters might be covered in silk or other materials that soften the sound slightly, rather than plastic, which can cause a sharper tweeter sound but ultimately tire the ear.

NOTE

Ear fatigue is what happens when the muscles that normally stabilize the tympanic membrane in your ears begin to tire, as a result of contracting too much in response to repeated frequencies or loud noise. Ear fatigue can cause your ears to ring (after a loud concert, for example) and, more commonly, decrease the ability of your ears to accurately and consistently hear different frequencies.

Crossover

You'll see information about the crossover circuitry of studio monitors in most manufacturers' literature. Because monitors usually have separate speakers for different frequencies (tweeters and woofers), there is also circuitry in the monitor to direct frequencies to the proper speaker.

Most monitors are designed to "cross over" between speakers at or near the low range of the frequency response of the tweeter, around 2 kHz. The quality of the crossover circuitry will affect sounds at or near this "crossover frequency," and monitors with less sophisticated circuitry or lower-quality parts will cause the sound in that region to become vague or distorted.

Nearfield Monitors

Nearfield monitors, also called close-field monitors, are designed so that they sound best at a distance of 3 to 4 feet, and they are an excellent choice for your home studio.

The purpose of nearfield is to cut down on room reflections or other unwanted resonance, meaning that home studio spaces that are tight, rooms that sound bad, or rooms that haven't been acoustically treated can really benefit from a pair of nearfields. If you plan on purchasing nearfield monitors, bear in mind that the technology is not perfect. To get the most out of them, take the following into consideration:

▶ Position the monitors equidistant from the walls to each side of them.

▶ Make sure your ears are about the same distance from the monitors as they are from each other. Think of an equilateral triangle, where the monitors are the two points of the base of the triangle and your head is the third point.

▶ Adjust the horizontal angle of the monitors to your ears. A tip for doing this is to place a mirror on the front of the speaker and have someone else vary the angle of the speaker until you see yourself. In other words, see what the speaker sees (make sure you look all pretty and stuff).

Tannoy makes good professional-quality nearfield monitors. Their System 600, with a frequency response of 52 to 20 kHz and power handling up to 160 watts, can be found (at the time of this writing) for around $500 per speaker, street. The System 600 is a pioneering design that actually puts the tweeter behind the center of the bass cone, causing all the sound to come from a single point, mimicking the way sound is created in nature.

TIP

Remember—your home studio is not a venue for a Pearl Jam concert; a range of 100-150 watts is generally sufficient for accurate monitoring in most home studios.

Yamaha NS10s (MS) are also an industry standard and a good choice, with a frequency response of 60 to 20 kHz and power handling up to 120 watts. They can be found just about anywhere for a little under $400 a pair.

Passive Monitors

Both the Tannoy System 600 and Yamaha NS10 are *passive* monitors, meaning they require an external amplifier to produce sound. Like most home stereo systems, passive monitors are connected to the amplifier via speaker cables.

NOTE

For an amplifier to drive a passive speaker efficiently, proper impedance matching is important. Essentially, impedance is the electrical resistance in a circuit, measured in ohms. Every speaker has a rated impedance, generally 4, 8, or 16 ohms. A power amplifier needs to drive a certain amount of ohms per channel (two channels in a standard stereo setup); otherwise, the amp could overheat, distort audio, or not deliver wattage correctly.

Bottom line: Make sure you match impedances between your amplifier and monitors.

With any passive monitor setup, your amp can alter what you are hearing over your speakers by coloring the output sound. The trick is simply to match up the monitors with your amp so that any coloring is at a minimum. Some manufacturers will have recommendations and even sell amplifiers that are already matched with monitors; a knowledgeable salesperson should also know what matches well and what doesn't. The ultimate decision is yours, of course, so compare combinations before you buy.

Active Monitors

Active monitors—monitors that come with their own built-in amp—are another option, but they are generally a bit more expensive and a bit less rugged. The Mackie HR 824 is an award-winning, killer-sounding choice and sells for a little less than $700 per speaker, street.

NOTE
A budget-minded alternative to the Mackie HR 824 is the Alesis M1 Active, which currently sells for less than $500, street, per pair. Event and Yamaha also produce good-quality active monitors with more palatable price ranges for the budget conscious.

Because active monitors have a built-in amp, a host of potential problems with a passive configuration can be eliminated, giving you improved performance in some key areas:

▶ **Frequency response**—The internal circuitry of an active setup vastly improves its frequency response characteristics. On-board active electronic circuitry allows for precise control over crossover slope, while minimizing phase shifts and distortion.

▶ **Overload protection**—Passive monitors have no control over input power and rely on a somewhat crude fuse to keep the speakers from toasting. An active system has sophisticated electronics that precisely control power going to the speakers.

▶ **Bi-amplification**—Most active systems, like the HR 824, for example, use separate amplifiers to drive each tweeter and woofer, greatly enhancing the monitor's damping and accuracy.

Sub Woofers

Sub woofers deliver the deep driving bass sound into a sound landscape created by smaller or nearfield monitors. They can be used to supplement passive or active monitor configurations and typically handle frequencies in the 25-150 Hz range. If you use a sub woofer, configure your system, if possible, to keep the sub woofer's frequencies to below 100 Hz. This will keep the sub woofer omnidirectional.

Placement of sub woofers is less critical than nearfields. Bass frequencies are by nature omnidirectional and fill the room from just about any position. Just make sure the front of your sub woofer isn't fully obstructed by any of your larger gear or furniture.

Digital Monitors

A digital monitor is not strictly digital—the term "digital" in this case means that the monitor is an active system that takes digital inputs. While 24-bit/96 kHz digital inputs certainly go a ways toward eliminating noise and hum problems associated with analog cabling, really good analog cabling can do just about the same thing. Digital monitors are still a fairly new technology, so you may want to stay away from them until more manufacturers adopt the technology and the jury comes back with a verdict.

The Importance of Sound Cabling

With so many considerations to be made in assembling a functional home studio, it's easy to lose sight of something as seemingly minor as cables. But in reality, the quality of your studio's final output can only be as good as the cables used in it. It's not enough to just plug in whatever happens to be available. If you were looking for good string sounds on a module or keyboard, would you settle for the lowest end model?

An important factor to consider in cable selection is the conducting wire itself. Poor wire can contribute to degradations in harmonic structure, clarity, and frequency response.

A good quality copper wire is the most cost-effective solution, while silver is costly enough that hooking up an entire studio with it could add up to a big investment.

TIP

Some manufacturers offer "oxygen-free" copper in their cables; by limiting the formation of trapped oxygen bubbles when the copper is extruded, internal corrosion is minimized, hence making the copper a better conductor of signal.

Whether a cable is silver or copper, long or short, analog or digital, it must have a quality termination. Examine a cable's termination before you purchase it. Check out the molding on the termination. If it has a metal termination, unscrew it and observe the soldering. If it looks or feels flimsy, you're better off without that cable. A poorly constructed termination can quickly lead to audio headaches down the line.

NOTE

You'll often see gold used in cable connectors, but that's not because gold is a superior conductor—it's because gold is good for protecting connector terminals from corrosion. Non-gold connectors are not necessarily poorer in quality, though they might require a little more maintenance.

TIP

When plugging in cables, use a firm grip around the termination. Never pull out a cable from beyond the termination along the regular insulated section. This can lead to damage of both the hardware and cable terminals. It will also damage your ego.

NOTE

Cabling and connectors are discussed in excruciating detail in Chapter 3.

It's All in the Mix

The heart of any recording studio is its mixer. Also referred to as a mixing board, the desk, the console, and, occasionally, your explicative of choice, depending on how well a session is going, a mixer pumps all of the various audio signals connected to it through its channels and blends them together into one single stereo signal. Mixers also serve as the place for enhancing your music with effects, DSP, equalization (EQ), and the like.

Mixers these days come in a wide range of sophistication and costs. Some mixers are more suited for live sound than studio recording, and recently, the digital mixer has been introduced with rave reviews, packing a powerful punch in a relatively small package. It's important to try and delineate precisely what you expect out of a mixer before you make the investment, whether it be a software-only solution or an external mixer/combination.

This section details the elements common to all mixers and shows you how to use one. Whether you're using your fingertips to turn knobs or your mouse to turn faders—or both—you'll be armed with the principles you'll need to do some great recording.

Preamps

Preamplifiers are used to boost the weak output levels of microphones to levels that are about line level. A preamp, also sometimes called the "trim," is the first link in the mixing chain—the first circuit that processes a microphone signal connected to a mixer.

NOTE
Practically speaking, "line level" is the signal level of the electrical signal running through your cables and gear. For inputs, it determines the sensitivity and loudness of your music, and for outputs, the loudness. The two most common types of line level settings are –10 dBV (consumer level, fine for home recording), and +4 dBV (professional, much hotter, and a little harder to work with).

Every input channel in a mixer has a gain control, which controls gain of the preamp. If you have a mic on a channel, you'll need a lot of the preamp, but if the channel is being used for a line level signal like the bass, synth, monitor mix, or DAT player, the preamp goes practically unused.

NOTE
Preamps are designed to operate within a certain gain range. When you operate the gain or trim on a mixer's input channel, you generally are adjusting the gain of the preamplifier. If operated at unity gain (no amplification), many preamps will become unstable and may start to distort or tend to oscillate. Hence, designers of mixers usually provide attenuator pads before and/or after (usually before) the preamp, enabling the signal to be knocked down so that the preamp can always be operated with some gain.

For example, a microphone that puts out an audio signal level of –60 dBu is producing a weak signal by design: The diaphragm moves a little bit and a small current is produced. Without a preamp, the mixer just cannot work with this weak signal without introducing significant noise into the signal path. A DAT recorder, on the other hand, which produces an output level of +4 dBu, most likely doesn't need the preamp at all. Using a lot of preamp with a strong signal such as +4 dBu will overload the preamp and start clipping like Edward Scissorhands. Clipping happens when the input signal is too strong for the device it is driving; the device will "clip" the audio signal above this threshold and you get distortion.

Input Channels

You can plug a lot of stuff into a mixer: microphones, outputs of musical instruments, synthesizers, samplers, outboard effects, outputs of tape decks, TVs, DVDs, your computer's sound card—anything and everything that has an audio output. The mixer then allows you to control the volume of each input and do all sorts of things to change, enhance, or muck up the sound quality. You can route the signal back out to an effects processor or your software and back again into the mixer, blend all of the different sounds into an output for monitoring or recording to disk or tape, and do both at the same time.

The primary element of a mixer is where you plug in—the input channel. In fact, a mixer is characterized by how many input channels it has: A 32-channel mixer has double the input capacity of a 16-channel mixer, for example.

There are generally two types of physical input connections—balanced and unbalanced—and two types of signals—line level (as noted earlier) and mic-level. In pro-audio, mic-level connections are balanced connections that use an XLR connector. Line-level connections may be either balanced or unbalanced, and typically use quarter-inch input connectors.

NOTE

On some mixers, you may find the designation "Lo-Z" and "Hi-Z." These terms refer to impedance. Most professional-quality microphones are "Lo-Z," or low impedance, which means that you can have long lengths of balanced cable without little signal attenuation. Cheap microphones, and most "computer microphones," are "Hi-Z," or high impedance, which means that if your cable is longer than about 25 (unbalanced line) feet, you're going get hum and some other nasty side effects. Stay away from Hi-Z mics, period. Unbalanced line level gear, on the other hand, is just fine.

Inputs are modular, meaning all the knobs and faders and buttons that control each input are typically organized together. So, although a 32-channel console may seem rather menacing at first, with hundreds of little knobs to turn, in reality, as soon as you've mastered one input module, you've got the other thirty-one down cold. Figure 13.1 shows the structure of a channel module or strip.

Figure 13.1

This basic anatomy of a channel strip includes the gain, EQ, aux, pan, and channel fader.

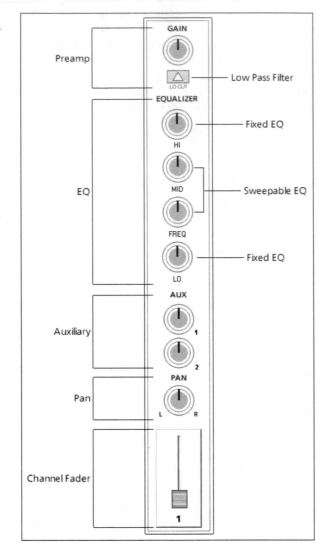

The Mic Preamp

The mic preamp is the site on an input channel where microphones are connected. In general, microphones produce small voltage levels and require a special three-pronged XLR connector.

The mic preamp itself is a female XLR panel mount. XLR connectors (see Figure 13.2) are better quality than cable with quarter-inch standard connectors and are balanced, since the signal passes through a 3 conductor cable and works with balanced input and output transformer on either end of the signal. They also use a screen between their conductors to reduce electronic interference.

Figure 13.2
XLR connectors
make high-quality
connections.

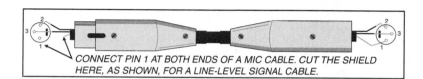

CONNECT PIN 1 AT BOTH ENDS OF A MIC CABLE. CUT THE SHIELD
HERE, AS SHOWN, FOR A LINE-LEVEL SIGNAL CABLE.

XLR connectors can also accommodate microphones that utilize phantom power—a +48 volt DC signal that powers the microphone's internal amplifier. Condenser microphones that need power for charging their internal elements will almost always need phantom power. Most modern mixers can provide phantom power to any one of its input channels and are usually engaged by depressing a button labeled "+48V" or "Phantom Power" elsewhere on the console.

NOTE

Take special care when using phantom power. Serious microphone damage can result from improper use, especially with microphones that do not support phantom power (refer to your microphone and mixer manuals for proper use). In addition, phantom power only can be supplied over a balanced line.

A mic preamp performs an important amplifying function when a microphone is connected to it: Without it, the mic's signal is too weak and will be colored by unwanted ambient or circuit noise. Correspondingly, when the channel's fader is raised, the noise gets even worse.

The relationship between this kind of noise and the input signal is called the "signal-to-noise" ratio. Generally speaking, it's best to record with as strong or "hot" a signal as possible, to minimize unwanted noise by tipping the signal-to-noise ratio in favor of the input signal. If you listen carefully to older, pure analog recordings ("Stairway to Heaven" comes to mind—but you can't play it while reading this book!), you can clearly hear noise during sparse, dynamically soft passages where the signal-to-noise ratio is bad.

The amount of amplification, also called "gain," can be adjusted with the gain knob located on the channel strip.

Headroom

Every mixer has a nominal level at which it operates. But mixers are designed to handle fairly dynamic swings in level. When a signal's level "peaks," it means that it has gone beyond the mixer's audio capabilities. An excessive "peak" can cause clipping, and the results are rarely pretty.

On any given mixer, the difference between the nominal operating level and the level where clipping occurs is called headroom. There is usually an LED on most mixers which indicates when you're clipping, and, of course, you can hear it as well! You'll know it when you hear it.

Line Level Input

A line level input is used to connect equipment that carries the voltage level needed by the mixer to process the signal properly. This is typically –10 dB for most equipment, such as a keyboard or drum machine, for example.

Physically, the line level input is usually a female quarter-inch jack with its own dedicated gain, which lets you calibrate the level for best results. An unbalanced standard quarter-inch inch cable can be used to connect a piece of equipment to the line level input.

Filters

Near the XLR or quarter-inch input jacks, you are likely to find a filter button. A filter removes specific frequencies from an input signal. In particular, a high-pass filter is one that removes undesirable low frequencies sounds and is often found on today's mixers. The filter may be labeled with a number like 70 or 90. This refers to the cutoff frequency; in other words, if it is labeled with a 70, all frequencies below 70 Hz will be filtered out. All of the frequencies above 70 Hz will be allowed to "pass" through, as discussed earlier in this chapter. This filter may also be referred to as a "lo cut" or "low pad."

Get on the Bus

Once an audio signal enters a mixer's domain by way of an input channel, it is assigned to a bus.

In electronics, a bus is defined as a connection that has three or more circuits in common. For all practical purposes, buses are what give a mixer its unique blending capabilities; the most basic type of bus on a mixer is the main output bus.

The main output is actually two buses—one for the left and one for right. The pan control found on any input channel can assign a signal to a point anywhere along the spectrum between these left and right output buses.

Of course, if blending a handful of external inputs to one stereo output were enough, this chapter would be smaller, and mixers a whole lot cheaper. But a good mixer must be capable of handling a variety of other studio needs. These could include the addition of a DAT (digital audio tape), an external effects processor, or a computer-based digital setup. To accomplish these tasks, most mixers are outfitted with supplemental busing systems.

For example, if one of the mixer's input channels were connected to a vocal microphone during a recording session, the ultimate destination wouldn't necessarily be the final mix; rather, the signal would probably need to be sent to one of the inputs of your hard-disk recorder or computer. By connecting the multi-track inputs to another bus' outputs, the same vocal signal could then be assigned to the new bus and be delivered to the multi-track. In fact, the flexible nature of the bus connection permits any signal assigned to it to be transported to the same destination.

Groups

The groups section of a mixer takes its busing capabilities a step further by providing special "group" faders. This means that all of the signals assigned to a particular bus can be manipulated by moving one volume control. This is especially valuable for mixing recordings that involve many tracks. For instance, if you were mixing a tune that featured a gospel choir backup, and you used three microphones to capture the group vocal and decided to double track them for an even bigger effect, you would be left with six faders to keep track of, let alone the rest of your instrumentation and lead vocal!

This is where group faders come in: By assigning the six choir tracks to a bus that feeds a couple of group faders, a stereo choir sub-mix can be easily achieved. The original six faders can be adjusted to get just the right sub-mix, and for the final mix, the group faders can be assigned to the main stereo output, bus, rejoining the other vocals and instrumentation. The two group faders allow you to set the relative level of the choir as a whole to the rest of the tracks during final mix-down. Think of the whole process as ganging input channels together.

Auxiliary Buses

A good mixer offers a lot of flexibility for routing audio signals, almost like a good traffic cop. In addition to buses and groups, auxiliary buses, known simply as the "aux," transport one or more additional signals to the inputs of an external effects unit.

Most of the time, this means effects, from reverb to delay to flanging to compression. Effects are covered in more detail later in this chapter.

The number of auxes on a mixer will vary, though most good mixers will carry more than a handful. The outputs from the auxiliary buses are usually grouped together with corresponding knobs in the auxiliary section of each input channel. Each respective aux input connector introduces the processed signal back to the mixer and then can be re-applied to the main stereo output buses, joining all of the other music tracks before, ahem, "history is made."

EQ

Equalizing—or EQ—is the process of adjusting the signal levels of frequency ranges. Whether the capability is in your software or in the mixer (or both), equalization is the core audio tool you have for shaping your music during both recording and mixing.

Remember that the human ear can detect sounds falling within a range of 20 to 20,000 Hz. This makes for a formidable challenge when lots of different instruments and voices are combined together. Each individual instrument has its own sonic characteristics that require equalizer modifications. Once these tracks are blended together at mixdown, more EQ decisions need to be made to achieve a balanced master recording.

Achieving that balance is the domain of EQ.

Cut-and-Boost

EQ got started way back in the days when a telephone was a piece of luxury equipment; in those days, a significant amount of signal loss was quite common, and though increasing the whole signal's amplitude could more or less make up for that loss, the loss was very frequency-dependent.

EQ was developed in response to that frequency-dependent signal loss, in order to boost only the frequencies that suffered the most attenuation. EQ effectively leveled out all the frequencies in the signal, hence the name "equalizer."

EQ circuitry then was strictly a matter of boosting frequencies, though; today, cutting a frequency is just as important in the process of "EQ'ing" a mix. Cutting—without boosting first—is achieved by using a filter, which is kind of the same thing as archaic EQ, but a bit different. By cutting frequencies, you are effectively boosting the frequencies you're not cutting, so the end-result is a boost, but the process is not identical. For instance, a "low pass" filter is not actually boosting anything—it's allowing all frequencies below a certain point, called the *cutoff frequency*, to pass without attenuation, while it cuts off all frequencies above the cutoff.

NOTE

Every mixer organizes its EQ section a little differently, with varying degrees of sophistication. At the very least, you will encounter low and high pots that will apply a boost or cut at a fixed frequency. The knob may be labeled with a number representing its setting. For example, a "60" refers to a low-end 60 hertz setting, while a "12K" label would refer to a much higher 12,000 hertz setting.

Boosting and cutting combined make up most EQ devices today, whether in software, a mixing board, or a piece of other outboard gear. It's all a matter of boost and cut, cut and boost. The degree to which the boosts and cuts can be combined, layered, and ordered, and the range of frequencies they can operate on, have produced several basic types of EQ.

Fixed EQ

The most basic type of EQ is the tone control on an amplifier or car stereo. This type of EQ works with only two bands: bass and treble. When you turn up the bass, you get around 10 dB of boost near 100 Hz, with less and less effect above that frequency. Below 100 Hz, boosting and cutting doesn't vary too much, so that the slope of the changes in frequency is almost horizontal. In fact, it looks a bit like a shelf, which is why the term "shelving EQ" exists. Typical treble is a mirror image of the way simple bass EQ works, only on the other end of the frequency spectrum.

A typical mixer may have a two-band equalizer for each input channel, but better mixers are more likely to have more sophisticated, separate controls that work with three frequency bands or more, as illustrated in Figure 13.3.

Figure 13.3
Many affordable mixing consoles use four bands of fixed EQ: High, Hi Mid, Low Mid, and Low.

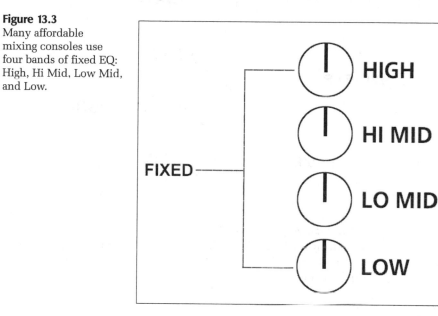

This type of simple equalization has its limits, though. Even a mixer which covers a few dozen discrete frequencies using a half-dozen different bands can have its limitations, which is why a few other types of EQ have been developed.

Sweepable EQ

A lot of consoles in the middle-of-the-road price range will have a high and low fixed EQ and one or two mid, "sweepable" (sometimes called "semi-parametric") frequencies. Instead of having to cut or boost one set frequency as you do on a fixed EQ, sweepable EQ will let you target the frequency you want to adjust with one knob and adjust the volume for that frequency with another knob. Figure 13.4 shows a typical channel strip configuration.

NOTE
The terminology for a channel strip (sometimes called a channel module, too) can be a bit different in the digital domain. A channel strip is analogous to a "control surface." You'll also see "control surface" sometimes used with analog/digital combo mixers.

Figure 13.4
A sweepable EQ, in this case three bands, including one with sweepable midrange, gives you greater power to adjust frequencies across a given range.

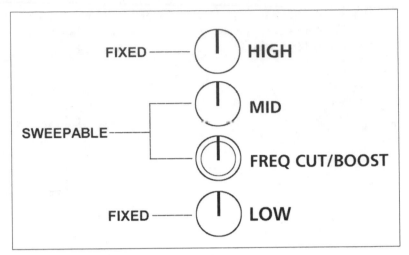

In fact, fixed/sweepable EQ is what you can expect these days for most analog mixers up to around $2,000 or a bit higher. The Behringer MX 2642A or Mackie 1642 VLZ Pro are both good examples in the $500 price range, and when used as a part of your digital recording setup, they provide solid, basic EQ alongside the greater capabilities of your recording software.

Parametric EQ

With both fixed and sweepable EQs, the steepness of the EQ curve is fixed. With any given boost or cut, the amount of the audio frequency which can be affected—whether it's fixed at one frequency or encompasses a specific range—has been set in the hardware and cannot be changed.

A parametric EQ goes beyond fixed and sweepables; all of its parameters can be adjusted to any amount, including:

▶ Center frequency
▶ The amount of boost or cut in gain
▶ The bandwidth

Most often, you'll find one or two sets of controls, labeled "High Mid" or "Low Mid" or possibly just "Mid." Although the natural sound spectrum is vast, having at least one parametric control paired with fixed High and Low knobs is an ideal way to handle even the most demanding audio signals.

The frequency value is the most elemental setting on a parametric control. Usually, High Mid can be set to a frequency center between 1000 and 20,00 Hertz (1-20 kHz), while Low Mid lies predictably between 45 and 3000 Hz.

The bandwidth, or "Q" setting, refers to how broad or narrow the EQ treatment will be. Bandwidth is measured in terms of octaves or fractions of one octave. On a piano, an octave is the distance from one "C" pitch to the next one. In Hertz, if a pitch comes in at 440 (A above Middle C), its octave would be 880. Most equalizers allow the user to select a bandwidth between 0.10 and 4 octave(s), where a standard setting is 1 octave.

Finally, the amplitude of the EQ treatment is set via the cut/boost knob, which adds or subtracts the frequency plus bandwidth by decibels. Typically, the amplitude on a parametric EQ can be adjusted up to +/− 16-20 dB.

Graphic EQ

You are doubtless familiar with graphic EQ. A graphic equalizer can work simultaneously with eight or more frequency bands, usually with one octave or one-third octave band centers. Most graphic EQs employ both attenuation and boost filters.

A graphic EQ is called "graphic" because the sliders which represent each of the frequencies create a visual image that, when set, looks like the overall frequency response curve of the EQ taking place.

Graphic EQ reduces the effect of resonant peaks and dips in monitor response and, to a lesser degree, in the acoustic recording space itself, by reducing the tendency for acoustic feedback to occur.

As the overall gain of any sound system increases, feedback will first occur at peak frequencies, starting as a slight ringing, and then morphing into a loud, sometimes piercing howl. By using a graphic equalizer to attenuate the first peak, the overall system gain can be increased until the next lower peak begins to feedback. That peak can then be attenuated using another graphic EQ band and system gain can be increased a little more, until the peaks have all been leveled to the extent possible with all the bands. Using bands this way, with a graphic EQ, may increase overall gain from 6-10 dB above the initial gain.

Another use of graphic EQ is to model the contour of a mixer's frequency response to get the best overall response pattern for the mixer. In the real world, flat response is seldom what you will want. You'll probably tend to stay reasonably flat over the middle of the spectrum, but effects—especially reverb—will have you boosting the low end, and you'll roll off the high end to varying degrees, depending on the song.

Sometimes the midrange (1-5 kHz) can be effective in increasing or decreasing sibilance, especially when sounds in this region have been masked by other, nearby frequencies.

NOTE
Sibilance is noise associated with vocal sounding of words with, usually, "s," "sch," "ch," "z," and "j" sounds or syllables. The noise created by sibilance is a type of narrow band noise in the high frequency range (5-10 kHz).

A graphic EQ is not something you'll typically find on board an analog mixing console, though most software setups (such as SONAR) will include a graphic EQ along with fixed, sweepable, and parametric EQs.

Auxiliary Section

Depending on how many auxiliary buses your mixer has, you'll find a corresponding knob for each one of them in the auxiliary (often simply called "Aux") section of each channel strip. These knobs are most commonly used to apply outboard effects to the audio signal of any given channel; by turning the aux pot clockwise, more signal is bused to the effects unit, and more effect will be returned and blended into the final stereo mix. The relationship between the original signal and the affected signal is called the wet/dry balance. For example, a wet vocal is one that has a lot of reverb effect applied to it; and, a vocal with no effect whatsoever would be considered very dry. In general, you'll make less use of auxes during recording, since you normally want the source tracks as dry as possible.

Many aux sends also have a pre-fader and post-fader switch that sends the exact amount of signal you dial in or the amount that tracks the fader, respectively.

Mixers are so flexible, auxes don't absolutely have to be used to set up effects subroutines, even though it is their most common use. An auxiliary bus can also be used to create a separate sub-mix, for example.

Channel Inserts

Sometimes an audio signal on a particular channel strip needs special processing apart from everything else. Many mixers are equipped with channel insert plugs that can be used in conjunction with another signal (an outboard processor, for example). Inserts don't function like auxiliary buses. Unlike an aux, the signal using a channel insert will be returned at the same point at which it was tapped.

Inserts are often used with compressors or noise gates to extend more control over certain signals during mix-down. You can also use them as extra single-channel outputs.

Mix B

When you're tracking, the performer (the instrumentalist or singer or you, if you're a one-person band), is monitoring everything with headphones—a very necessary thing to do unless he or she is John Cage.

The Mix B function of a mixer allows you to design a custom mix—also known as a cue or rollover mix—that can be assigned to the headphones output without affecting the main mix. For instance, if you're tracking the singer in the band, using Mix B, you could assemble the perfect mix for his egotistical, self-serving needs in his headphones while independently manipulating the primary mix in your studio monitors. This lets you isolate the vocal and check for errors in performance, as well as make subtle adjustments without distracting the vocalist in mid-delivery.

In addition, if you're a one-stop shop, you may want to adjust Mix B to your own preferences according to each track you're laying down, while keeping the main mix you're working with piped out through main bus. You might want to listen to your voice with 42 milliseconds of delay, for example, but not send it to disk that way.

CHAPTER 13

TIP
Many mixers provide supplemental quarter-inch input jacks that feed Mix B fader knobs. This can be a handy feature when you find yourself running out of channel inputs.

Pan

The Pan control allows you to place the audio signal associated with its channel strip anywhere along the horizontal stereo panorama, from left to right. The Pan control is usually labeled "L" for left and "R" for right, where a straight up 12 o'clock setting results in no pan. This is similar to the left and right stereo control knobs found on just about every home stereo in the universe (except on Mars, because Martians, as it turns out, have only one ear).

The Pan control also plays an important role while tracking. Internal buses are typically organized into stereo pairs. So when an input signal such as a bass guitar is bused to an external tape machine, the Pan control is used to select which one of the two buses will carry the signal. If buses 1 and 2 are connected to the first two inputs of your sound card, for instance, a hard left pan would send the signal to input 1 and a hard right pan to input 2.

In the case of a tape machine, many tape machines can be set up to an input mode where the remaining track inputs can be accessed in complimentary pairs via inputs 1 and 2. On an 8-track tape machine, the Pan control selects whether a signal is bused to an odd numbered track (1, 3, 5, 7) or an even numbered track (2, 4, 6, 8). The same is true for a sound card, but the assignments are handled in software. SONAR, for example, lets you assign left and right signals to a track as well as the overall stereo image coming from any given channel.

Mute and Solo

The Mute and Solo buttons affect a channel and its surrounding modules in different ways. The Mute button, sometimes called Cut, completely silences a channel. This feature is an all-or-nothing "on" or "off" status without any gradation. The same applies to the Solo button; the only difference is that all surrounding channels are muted, effectively "soloing" the original channel's audio signal.

Solo can be a valuable tool for calibrating the gain amount on an input channel when many different signals are being managed. In this way, a signal can be carefully monitored for distortion and set to an ideal recording level. In addition, precise EQ modifications can be made so that the most ideal signal is sent to tape.

You'll also find solo and mute features on any respectable recording software.

The Fader

When people think of mixers, the piece most people envision first is the fader. A channel's fader is a vertical slider that allows you to continuously vary the signal level. This form and functionality has been around for decades and is very efficient at minimizing "cross talk"—the bleeding of audio from one channel to another.

Faders are usually present for individual channels, groups, and the main mix. They will sometimes be labeled with an "infinity" symbol, representing no signal or full fade, and a "0" or "U" for unity gain, representing no fade.

Faders are easy to use and many can be manipulated at the same time (also called "ganging" sliders). In fact, one of the coolest developments to come about in the last several years is the automation of faders (as well as all of the other controllers).

Automation is a really simple concept: Record the movements and settings of your controls and then "play" them back. It allows for an incredible amount of flexibility for a given mix and, most important, lets you take sequences of controller movements and settings from one situation and re-apply them anywhere else.

In SONAR, for example, the process of automation is a breeze. To use automation in Console view, you simply:

1.   Rewind to the beginning of a project.

2.   Move the faders, pans, and any other controls to the initial settings you want.

3.   Enable Automation recording by clicking on the Record Automation button.

4.   Begin playback and move the faders as needed so that the balance and mix you want is where you want it.

5.   If you've grouped faders together, grabbing any of them will change the values of all the controllers in the group.

Once you've stopped recording, you've now automated your mix. To listen to it again, and watch the faders move automatically:

1.   Rewind to the beginning.

2.   To make sure the faders show their current value, select the Update option.

3.   Click Play. You'll see the faders move just the way they moved when you recorded their movements.

Of course, automation can get a bit more complicated than this, especially when you start dealing with real-time effects and complicated layouts. But you get the idea.

Bus Assignments

On mixers that have extended internal busing capabilities, you will encounter separate bus assignments buttons on each channel module. They are clearly marked with numbered pairs (1-2, 3-4, 5-6, 7-8). These are the assignment buttons used to group signals together or bus input signals, as discussed earlier. An "L/R" label found on most mixers represents the main stereo output bus. This assignment is used during final mixdown. The master fader controls the level of this signal.

Other Functions

More elaborate mixers come with additional functions that allow you to monitor signals in a host of other ways. One of these is the PFL, or pre-fade listen function.

PFL is always associated with a corresponding fader. When you enable it, the signal being fed to the fader can be bused to monitors or to headphones. This can allow you to:

▶ Check that the correct signal is being recorded

▶ Check the recording level

▶ Check the quality of a given signal

Another supplemental function is called "talkback." Talkback lets you communicate directly with other musicians in a separate room from your control room space. A lower quality in-line microphone installed directly on the mixer control surface makes the talkback utility possible; by hitting the talkback button, the mic signal can be bused to a pair of headphones.

Common Controller Functions

Every switch, knob, and fader on a mixer performs at least one of three basic functions, as follows:

▶ A controller can select where a signal is coming from. These are known as source controllers and they determine the input source of a signal. A Mic/Line switch is an example of this controller, because it selects the source of the channel input.

▶ A controller can process the signal in some way. These are generally described according to the function they perform. EQ and gain controls are examples of this type of controller, because they alter the frequency response or set the gain of a signal, as opposed to determining its input or output.

▶ A controller can route where the signal is going. These are known as assign or routing switches, and they route signals to different buses or outputs. Channel Routing switches, for instance, route the channel signal to the Main Mix or Group buses.

Software Mixers

Computers have come a long way and are still newborns compared to the history of the mixer. Yet, the computer and the mixer are two partner pieces of equipment that will only grow closer with time.

There are software programs available for some mixers that allow you to control each channel by manipulating images on a computer screen rather than physically moving the various controls yourself.

Most important, there are fully capable mixers within some software, such as SONAR, shown in Figure 13.5, which do an incredibly effective job of manipulating, routing, and bussing your music.

Figure 13.5
SONAR's Console
view emulates mixers
in the physical world
in software.

Most software mixers have been designed to emulate mixers in the physical world, with many
of the same functions. Some of them are simpler in design than SONAR but quite powerful
behind the scenes, while some are limited only to faders that control each channel of input. The
inputs to software mixers can come from your sound card or from any audio present on your
system (such as CD-ROM or DVD-ROM).

Sound Forge is another example of an application that includes a software mixer. Figure 13.6
shows the simple mixer as fade controls. The mixer allows six inputs: two wave file inputs,
two inputs from MIDI devices or MIDI software, and two auxiliary inputs from devices like the
CD-ROM drive.

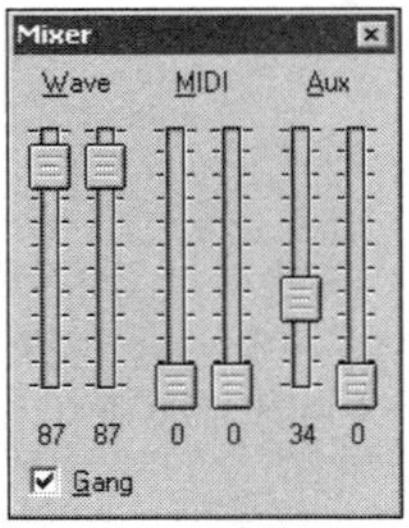

Figure 13.6
Don't be fooled by the
apparent simplicity of
the Sound Forge mixer.

Don't be fooled by the simplicity of the Sound Forge mixer. You can manipulate sound with incredible control by selecting settings from the Sound Forge pull-down menu. For example, the effects menu has the following selections:

▶ Amplitude Modulation

▶ Chorus

▶ Delay/Echo

▶ Distortion

▶ Dynamics

▶ Envelope

▶ Flange/Wah-wah

▶ Gapper/Snipper

▶ Noise Gate

▶ Pitch

▶ Reverb

▶ Vibrato

Rather than forcing you to go out and buy expensive effects processors, Sound Forge, just like SONAR, allows you to create most any effect in software, including using DirectX plug-ins for your effects. Figure 13.7 shows the detail of control you have in the chorus effect, for example.

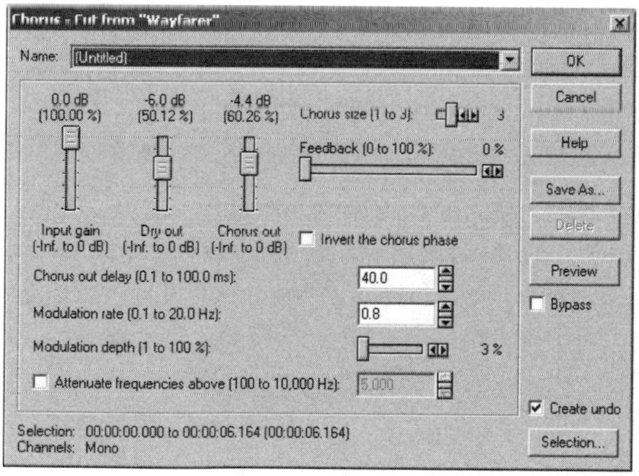

Figure 13.7
You have incredible control over your effects in software.

Stepping through the Mixing Chain

To recap, let's step through the mixing chain and attempt to picture the process of mixing as a series of steps. Of course, your mileage will vary, sometimes widely, because there are almost unlimited configurations and setups with a capable mixer. But there is a basic process behind the scenes at all times. We'll do it in seven steps—Input, EQ, Pan, Fade, Group, Aux, Listen—to keep it easy to remember:

1. **Input**—The mixer takes inputs, from a vocal microphone to your direct bass line to your synth—anything and everything capable of electrical audio signal. It is an input master. This is also where you set the trim.

2. **EQ**—EQs come in several flavors, from an external graphic EQ to a 2-pot tone control to SONAR's software mixing console. Most mixers have 3- or 4-band EQ, including a high band, which boosts or cuts around 1 kHz; a low band, which boosts or cuts around 100 Hz; and 1+ mid bands, which can either be fixed or sweepable. Better mixers and more capable software also employ parametric EQ, which gives you enormous control over most of the human ear's hearing spectrum.

3. **Pan**—The pan control manages how much of the signal goes to the left bus vs. the right bus or any number of available buses, depending on the capability of the mixer. The pan pot (also known in tongue-twisting form as "panoramic potentiometer") directs the signal over left-right, like a traffic cop on a three-way street.

4. **Fade**—The audio signal next goes to individual channel faders, which control the level of the channel before it is routed to corresponding outputs. Sometimes a channel strip will also offer a mute switch and the very important PFL switch, which allows you to preview the channel through a monitor bus pre-fader.

5. **Group**—If present, special "group" faders take a mixer's busing capabilities a step further by giving you the ability to access all of the signals on a particular bus at once. Think of a group as an anal-retentive output.

6. **Aux**—Auxiliary buses are most commonly used to apply effects or other additive signals to an individual channel's signal.

7. **Listen**—Finally, the signal makes its way from the outputs into your monitor or headphones.

The above steps can vary a bit, since most good-quality mixers have the added capability of being able to let you determine whether a signal is being routed pre-fade (before it hits the output bus(es)), or post-fade (after the signal passes through the output bus(es)). But you get the idea! Now go create art!

Using Effects Effectively

Wait a minute. Scratch the last sentence of the last section. You may want to use some effects in your mixes. In fact, if you're like most hot-blooded musicians and audiophiles on the planet, you can't live without a little reverb here, a little delay there, and some compression to top it all off.

Reverb, compression, and delay are all covered in Chapter 11, with a more detailed look at reverb in Chapter 12. In the next section, we'll take a look at a few other, less fundamental—but very powerful—signal processors, or effects.

Noise Gates

A noise gate is a signal processor that turns down or turns off an audio signal when the level falls below where you set it. The idea is that the audio will pass through and kind of leave behind any low-level noise or leakage from other things in the mix you don't want. In this way, you can think of a noise gate as an adjustable noise housecleaner. You tell it how much house to clean and how much time to spend cleaning. How much cleaning a noise gate does is called its threshold.

Noise gates are good for temporarily muting mics. In complex, multichannel setups, the use of a noise gate can also improve the overall system sound without mucking up the mix. It's most effective if your groups use a separate noise gate for each group, and it's remarkably effective if you use a separate noise gate on individual input channels.

Noise gates are particularly suited to the guitar. Careful use of a noise gate in your guitar's signal chain is an ideal scenario: It keeps noise from the guitar at bay until it's time for you to put out and can save you from having to spend a lot of time muting parts of a track during mixdown.

Setting the threshold for a guitar is a by-ear proposition; generally, if you use a lot of gain or distortion and you're playing hard, you should start by setting a high threshold and work down from there until you hear the sweetest spot. With a high threshold, the noise gate is less sensitive to a little more banging and force.

If you're miking an acoustic, on the other hand, you can start with a much lower threshold, since, presumably, you won't be tempted to start having Pete Townshend flashbacks.

Phase Shifters

A phase shifter, or phaser, creates little notches at different frequencies which cut out sounds where the notches are. A phase shifter can control the number of notches, where each notch is located, and the size of the notches.

This is accomplished through the judicious use of deep, high "Q" filters; the source signal is split, with some of it going to the filter and some not. The actual shifting takes place mainly to either side of the notch. The notch is swept up and down the available frequencies in the mix, then mixed with the original signal, causing predictable phase cancellation.

Think of creating a paper airplane and then cutting tiny random notches where the wings are folded (nothing too elaborate, mind you, this is not quite a paper snowflake), then throwing the airplane. The resulting air flow around the notches is a bit like phase. (Note: If you try this example, you really won't hear anything—it's just an analogy. If you want to cut notches in a paper airplane anyway, just ensure that no one's watching. You could be perceived as being mentally phase-cancelled.)

Flanger and Chorus

Flangers turn out to be a special case of phase shifting. They also introduce phase cancellation into the signal path by mixing the output of a signal with a notched copy of itself, then re-timing everything so that the original and copy are out of phase.

The big difference is that flanging notches are always equally spaced. Delay times are also usually in a range from 1-10 milliseconds; this is what produces a flanger's characteristic sweeping sound.

The idea has been around for a while, and the flanger actually takes its name from the flanges of a reel-to-reel tape. By using pressure against the flanges of the tape reel, early explorers of flanging were able to alter the timing of each machine's playback, causing all kinds of interesting, calculated phase cancellations.

It turned out to be a little math, actually: With equally-spaced notches, if one signal is delayed, then immediately mixed back differently (either as a completely different signal or a copy of the original), the result is cancellation at a frequency equal to about twice the delay time. Pretty cool, huh?

Chorus is similar to flanging, with two important differences:

▶ The delay is larger, usually between 20-30 milliseconds, so you don't get the sweeping sound of a flanger.

▶ Chorus makes no use of feedback.

The result is a type of delay that replicates not only the delay between sounds in a natural setting but also pitch differences. By the delay and pitch modulation together, you hear the unmistakable sound of a chorus effect.

Other Effects

There are lots of other effects you can use, and most of them can be had these days in the form of DirectX plug-in packages. Using DirectX plug-ins (or native plug-ins for your particular software) is a way to keep from spending enormous sums on separate, external units, with an added bonus of having to run only a setup program, instead of physically hooking all this gear up.

It's really beyond the scope of this book to try to cover all the different signal processing permutations available these days. There are literally thousands of different effects and dozens of manufacturers. A good place to start online is **www.harmonycentral.com**. The site has links, reviews, and loads of information about most of the plug-ins that have been released over the last several years. Many of the software companies also offer free demos of their plug-ins for download.

In addition, a well-equipped music retailer will typically carry a large selection of DirectX plug-ins, and a knowledgeable salesperson should be more than happy to let you check them out.

Arboretum Software (pronounced "R-BO-REE-TUM), online at **www.arboretum.com**, carries a DirectX plug-in suite called Hyperprism, which is a very strong offering in the let's-try-and-be-everything-to-everyone category; the package includes some killer effects, and lots of them, for about $199 from the company's Web site. Hyperprism includes the following effects plug-ins:

- ▶ Band Pass Filter
- ▶ Band Reject Filter
- ▶ Bass Maximizer
- ▶ Chorus
- ▶ Compressor
- ▶ Echo
- ▶ Flanger
- ▶ Formant Pitch Shifter
- ▶ Frequency Shifter
- ▶ Granulator
- ▶ Hall Reverb
- ▶ Harmonic Exciter
- ▶ High Pass Filter
- ▶ HyperPhaser
- ▶ HyperVerb
- ▶ Limiter
- ▶ Low Pass Filter

- ▶ M-S Matrix
- ▶ More Stereo
- ▶ Multi Delay
- ▶ Noise Gate
- ▶ Pan
- ▶ Phaser
- ▶ Pitch Changer
- ▶ Quasi Stereo
- ▶ Ring Modulator
- ▶ Room Reverb
- ▶ Single Delay
- ▶ Sonic Decimator
- ▶ Stereo Dynamics
- ▶ Tremolo
- ▶ Tube/Tape Saturator
- ▶ Vibrato
- ▶ Vocoder

Ironically, the EQ and compressor plug-ins are worst part of this package, but the rest is well worth taking a look at.

14

Step-By-Step:
Your First 8-Track Song

This chapter will step you through recording, mixing, and mastering a simple 8-track song. Each section is a specific step in the process, from setting up your recording preferences to exporting the finished product as both a wave file master and an MP3 file.

This chapter uses SONAR to handle recording, most of the mixing, and to master the song. If you use a different digital recording application, you should be able to follow along to some extent, but if you use an external mixing console and/or external hard drive exclusively, this won't be as valuable a chapter for you.

Step 1: A Little Preparation

In the world of professional recording studios, good recording engineers maintain fairly detailed records most of the time about setups, settings, mix levels, and so on. A "track sheet" is their primary means of documentation.

It makes sense that you should have your own track sheet of sorts, too, but yours need not be quite as detailed, since most of it is virtually done for you in SONAR. You could also keep hand-written records if you prefer, though having them is not strictly necessary.

1. The first thing to do is really easy: Launch SONAR from the Program Menu in Windows or from the folder in which you installed it.

2. After the default project appears, immediately maximize the window, as shown in Figure 14.1. Note that the project starts with two MIDI tracks, which you won't be using. Right-click on them and choose Delete.

Figure 14.1
Sonar's default layout.

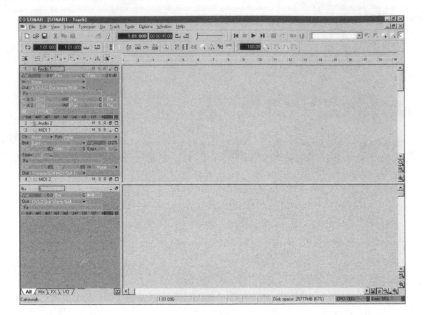

3. Since you're doing an 8-track project, you'll need to add six more audio tracks to the layout. You can do this by minimizing the tracks in the left-hand Track view, right-clicking, and choosing Insert Audio Track from the menu (Figure 14.2) or by choosing Insert > Audio Track from the main menu bar.

Figure 14.2
Set up your
audio tracks.

4. After you've added the tracks, give each one a name. You can do this by double-clicking the default names and typing in new names at the cursor. For this session, we'll use two tracks for drums, one track for bass guitar, two tracks for guitars, one for a keyboard, and two for vocals, as shown in Figure 14.3.

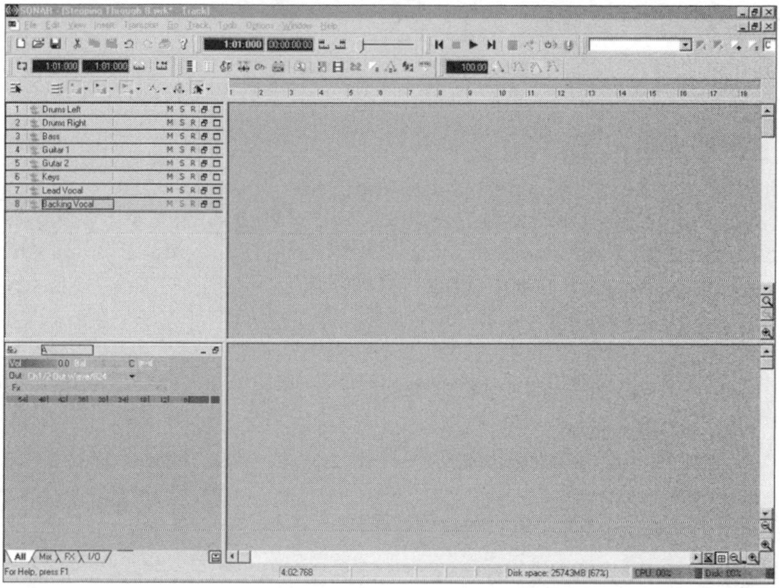

Figure 14.3
Name your tracks.

5. Next, save your layout. Give it the name "Stepping Through 8" and save it as a .WRK file. You can also save it as a SONAR template, but you don't have to for this example.

6. Maximize each individual track (see Figure 14.4) and make sure your Ins and Outs are set up properly. For the two drums tracks, this session uses a mono Left and mono Right track, respectively. For the rest of the tracks, the inputs are all stereo Ins, which can be panned later during the mix. The outputs for this session all go to two main buses—tracks one and two of the sound card.

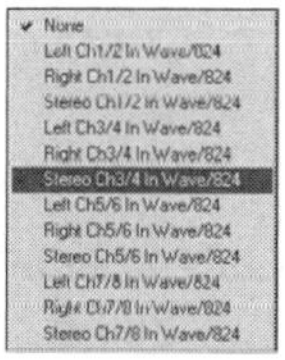

Figure 14.4
Set up your Ins and Outs.

7. Finally, ensure that Vol is at 0.0, Pan is at center, and Trim is at 0.0 dB for each track. Save your work again.

Step 2: Setting Up SONAR

Step 2 involves making sure that the global audio settings for SONAR are set up properly.

Set the Sampling Rate

A fundamental aspect of doing digital audio involves setting the sampling rate. You can't have different sample rates for different tracks; one setting does it all. What should you set it to? Well, you're limited, first off, by your sound card: you can't set it any higher than what the hardware supports. For CD-quality sound, use 44100 Hz.

To set the sampling rate:

1. Choose Options > Audio to open the Audio Options dialog box (see Figure 14.5).
2. Click the General tab.
3. Under Default Settings for New Projects, select 44100 Hz.

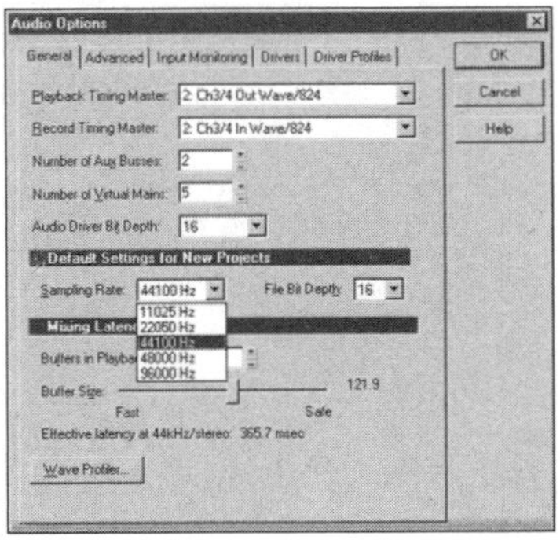

Figure 14.5
Set the sampling rate to 44100.

4. Click OK.

Set the Bit Depths

The drivers for most sound cards use anywhere from 16 to 24 bits to handle audio processing. CD quality uses 16 bits, and though you can arguably get a better sound by recording at 24 bits and converting back 16 bits after mixdown, it does consume a lot more of your processor and memory, which leaves you less overhead for more tracks and real-time effects.

To set your sound card's bit depth:

1. Go to Options > Audio and open the Audio Options dialog box.
2. On the General tab, find the Audio Driver Bit Depth field and select one of the options. Set it to 16.
3. Click OK.

In addition to setting the bit depth for the sound card, you'll need to tell SONAR how to allocate memory as well. You'll use 16 bits for this setting, too. While still in the Audio Options dialog box, find the File Bit Depth field and select 16.

Step 3: Recording a Track

Now it's time to record something. What you record is, of course, completely up to you. For the purposes of this tutorial, we're using a couple of drum tracks, bass, guitars, a simple keyboard line, and vocals, as mentioned earlier.

Before you can start really performing, however, there is one more thing you need to do.

Input Levels

Before you record for real, you'll need to check and/or calibrate your input levels. This is a critical step no matter what kind of setup you're using.

If your audio input is too low, it will be lost in the background noise, while if it's too high, it will overload the input channel and cause distortion. Double-check to make sure the Show Record VU Meter, just above the topmost track in the Track view, is pressed. It should be on by default. To check input levels, follow these steps:

1. Arm the first track by clicking the "R" button.

2. Do a test performance, concentrating just on volumes with no regard for making the performance perfect. Watch the meter: It should be moving with your test performance. If it isn't, raise the volume of your source sound (the instrument or vocal) and try to get the meter as high as possible without it reaching maximum (the red area).

NOTE

If you see absolutely no meter movement of any kind, there is most likely a problem with the physical audio input itself or possibly a Windows sound level problem. Check the Windows sound mixer from the Multimedia icon in Control Panel first.

Rolling Tape—Er, Disk, That Is

It's time to record for real. For this session, a drum machine will be handling the two drums tracks, with the kick, snare, and toms on "Drums Left" and the cymbals and hi-hat on "Drums Right." Bass is recorded on one stereo track, as are the guitars, keys, and vocals.

Which instrument you lay down first has everything to do with your songwriting style and instrument preferences. We'll pretend that this song is a heavy rock song, so we'll lay down the basic drum beat first, on Track 1.

1. Go to Options > Project and click on the Metronome tab; you'll want to set SONAR's metronome—or click track—to keep you in time. Set it up for 1 measure's worth of count, as shown Figure 14.6.

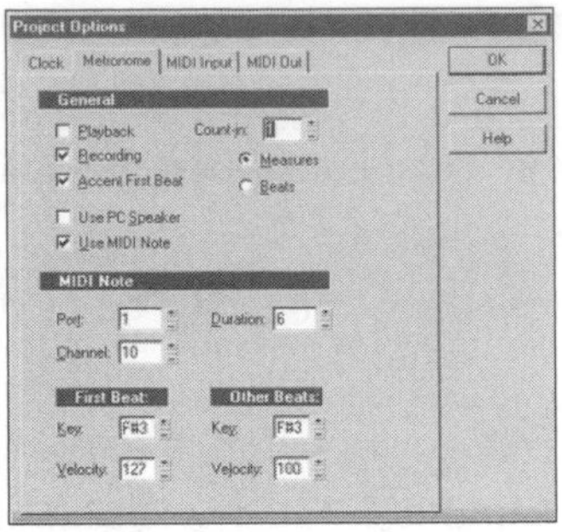

Figure 14.6
A click-track or metronome is critical for getting a consistent beat.

2. Arm the track for recording.

3. Click the Record button on the toolbar—the red button—or simply press "R" on your computer keyboard. The count-in will begin immediately.

4. Play something—anything.

5. When you're finished laying down the track, press the spacebar or click the stop button on the toolbar.

Your recorded track will show up in SONAR's Clips pane (see Figure 14.7).

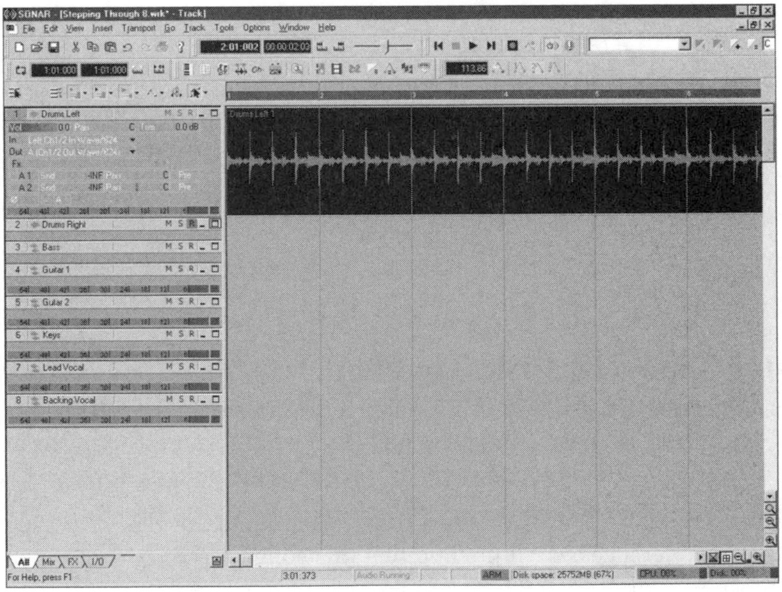

Figure 14.7
It's not exactly Keith Moon, but it's a drum track!

6. Next, arm Track 2 while keeping Track 1 armed, and get ready to record Track 2.

7. Click "R" to record the performance.

8. When you're finished, press the spacebar. You should have something that looks like Figure 14.8.

Figure 14.8
The first two tracks of drums are in.

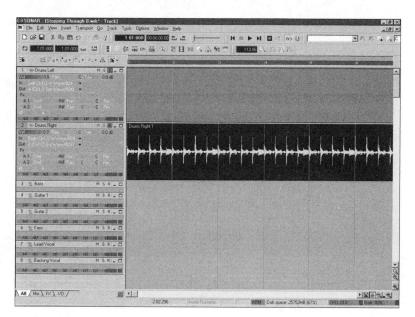

What you actually did was to record the new Track 2, as well as record an additional track on Track 1—effectively creating your second drum track, along with a copy of it available to the first track.

Your first performance is still there—the audio data in the Clips view in SONAR is behind the clip you see in Track 1 in the figure (Drums Left 2).

The idea behind this technique is flexibility; by recording multiple mono tracks for an instrument like drums, you will have a greater degree of flexibility when mixdown arrives.

The final step is to lay down the other instruments, in this case one at a time (since you're working along for this tutorial). Obviously, as you record each new track, the tracks you've already recorded will play back and their individual track meters will indicate that they're playing.

When you're done with tracking the other six instruments, you'll have something like Figure 14.9 on your screen.

CHAPTER 14

Figure 14.9
Eight tracks in software.

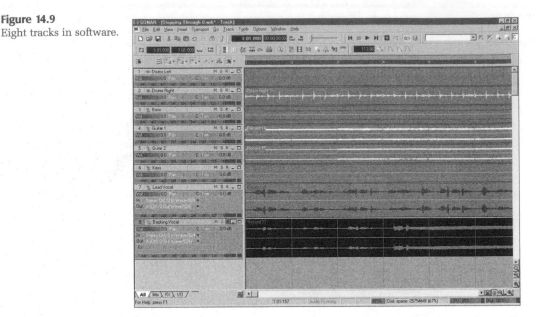

When you're ready to play it back, simply push the spacebar or the Play button on the toolbar. This is a good time to take a close look at the level meters again and make sure you're getting hot signal across all the tracks.

Input Monitoring: What Goes In There

SONAR, and most good-quality recording software for that matter, has an *input monitoring* feature that mimics the live monitoring you can do with an analog board. In other words, you can hear any instrument that is plugged into your sound card whether you're recording it or not.

This includes any plug-in effects as well. You can enable input monitoring in SONAR by going to Options > Audio and highlighting the name of your sound card on the Input Monitoring tab. After you close the dialog box, you can also click the Audio Engine button on the toolbar to turn input monitoring on or off.

Of course, if you're routing your instruments through an external mixing console, mic, or line mixer, you can monitor everything live in any case; this feature is strictly a digital recording situation where you are running directly from the output of the sound card to one external monitoring bus.

A word of caution: Input monitoring can double the effects of feedback if you are routing the outputs of your sound card back into an external mixer, so use the feature carefully.

Step 4: Using Looping

One of the beauties of digital software is the ability to easily loop tracks in real-time. Loop recording, or looping, is a natural for computers, and it lets you start recording and record as many takes as you like, all in a single step.

SONAR loops between "loop start" and "loop end" times, letting you record one take during each loop range. The program creates a new clip for each take, and the clips can be stored either in a single track (kind of like what we saw earlier with two tracks on the first drum track), automatically overwrite everything each go-round, or be recorded to separate tracks every time.

If you use the first method, you'll hear every take every time, making for some very interesting ways to experiment with vocal harmonies quickly and easily. If you store each looped performance to different tracks, they automatically mute, and so you don't hear them each time.

To use looping:

1. Choose the last vocal track and arm the track.
2. Set the loop start and end times in either the Loop/Auto Shuttle dialog box or in the Loop toolbar.
3. Choose Transport > Record Options and choose to stack all takes in a single track.
4. Click OK to close the Record Options dialog and set the Now time to the point in the project where you want to start loop recording.
5. Click "R" and start singing! At each end time in the loop, SONAR will return to the start of the loop and you can record the next take.
6. Click the spacebar when you're ready to stop.

Step 5: Punch-In Edits

Punch-in is a technique that is essential to recording—it gives you the flexibility to replace any section in a track without having to re-record the entire track.

NOTE

The term "punch-in" comes from the days when recording engineers had to physically punch the record button, while the tape was rolling.

In this session, pretend that during the fourth measure of the lead vocal you just completely went flat when you were singing—but the rest of the track is more than acceptable.

By punching in, you can play the entire vocal performance over, so that you're into the song and melody, then sing over the area you need to correct. It's really very simple: SONAR simply automatically deletes the previous performance between the start and end times of the punch and records into the same spot.

CHAPTER 14

To use punch recording, follow these steps:

1. Enable punch recording, from the Transport > Record Options dialog, as shown in Figure 14.10.

2. Set the start and end times of the punch.

3. Start recording, and press the spacebar when you're done.

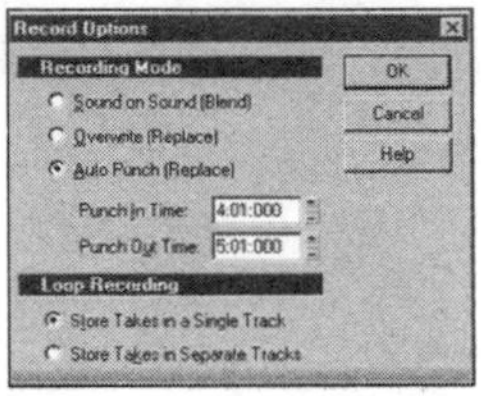

Figure 14.10
Use punch-in to correct mistakes.

When punch recording is enabled, the punch times are indicated by special markers in the Time Ruler, which is at the top of the Clips pane. Figure 14.11 shows both the markers and end result of punching in between measures 4 and 5 in the last vocal track for the session.

Figure 14.11
The punch-in was a success.

You can also combine loop and punch recording to record several takes of a punch. Say you are working on that perfect take of a guitar solo and you need to hear a couple of bars of the project as "pre-roll" before you punch in. By combining looping with punch, you can have each take begin before you start to play and still have the solo cut in at the appropriate instant.

To punch in during looping:

1. Arm the track.

2. Set the loop start and end times.

3. Set the punch start and end times, as shown earlier.

4. Choose Transport > Record Options, or click on the Record toolbar, to display the Record Options dialog box.

5. Choose to stack all takes in a single track or to store them in separate tracks.

6. Set the Now time to the beginning of the loop.

7. Click "R" to record, and play. At the end of the loop, the software will return to the start of the loop and you can record the next take.

8. If you want to erase the most recent take while loop recording is underway, press Ctrl+Spacebar.

9. Press the spacebar to stop.

Editing with a Crossfade

Solo the two guitar tracks and listen to the project. We are going to combine these two tracks and create an automatic crossfade between them. Before you start, hide the beginning of the second guitar part so it doesn't affect the crossfade by using "slip editing."

1. Click the Snap to Grid button to turn off Snap to Grid. The Snap to Grid settings control slip editing as well as drag-and-drop.

2. Move the cursor over the beginning of the second guitar clip.

3. When the cursor turns into a rectangle, click and drag the beginning of the clip until you have reached the beginning of the waveform.

The beginning of the clip is now hidden. The data is not lost.

Let's combine these two tracks and create a crossfade.

1. Enable automatic crossfades by clicking the Automatic Crossfades button located next to the Snap to Grid button.

2. Make sure no clips are selected, then hold down the Shift key and drag the second guitar clip on top of the first guitar track and drop it.

The two clips are now on the same track with a crossfade marker where they overlap. The first guitar track fades out as the second guitar fades in.

CHAPTER 14

Step 6: Mixing Some Effect In

For this session, we'll limit our mixing activities to the basic task of introducing some effects into the mix. First, we'll add some flange to the first guitar track, then add a little reverb to both the vocal tracks.

1. In the Track view, in the guitar track's "Fx" field (accessible by clicking on the Fx tab at the bottom), delete any existing effects by right-clicking the name of each effect and choosing Delete from the popup menu.

2. Add the flange effect to this track by right-clicking the Fx field and choosing Audio Effects > Cakewalk > Flanger from the popup menu (see Figure 14.12).

Figure 14.12
Adding flanger using SONAR's DirectX flanger plug-in almost couldn't be easier.

3. Choose "YoYo Flange" from the drop-down box. You'll see the knobs move to their preset values.

4. Play the song and try soloing to hear the exact effect the flange is having on the guitar. You may want to try out some of the other presets or create a custom preset as well for use in a future project.

5. For the vocal tracks, repeat steps 1-4 above. Note that the SONAR Reverb contains the settings you'd find on any external reverb unit: dry mix, wet mix, decay, and low- and high-pass filter. Experiment with the different settings just as you would with a piece of outboard gear.

When you're done tinkering with all of the effects, listen closely to the overall mix. A tried-and-true method for auditioning individual effects is to first audition the whole song, then solo each track to check noise level and saturation, then try different combinations of the effected tracks with other tracks in the mix by selectively muting.

NOTE

As discussed in Chapter 11 and elsewhere in the book, in general, don't get carried away with effects. For example, using a different reverb on several tracks at once can cause some nasty harmonic modulation. You want *moderation*—not modulation!

Step 7: Mastering to a File

In a very short amount of time, you've recorded eight tracks of audio, crossfaded a couple of tracks together, corrected a mistake or two, and added some basic effects to individual tracks.

Normally, you'd obviously spend more time than this, not only getting the performances the way you want them, but with EQ both during recording and mixing, as well as backup tracks, doubling tracks, quantization for MIDI tracks, and much more.

Now, let's complete this session by mastering the project off to both wave and MP3 formats.

NOTE

SONAR also gives you the ability to save to the Real Audio and Windows Media formats.

To import the song as a wave file:

1. Choose File > Export Audio to display the Export Audio dialog box, as show in Figure 14.13.

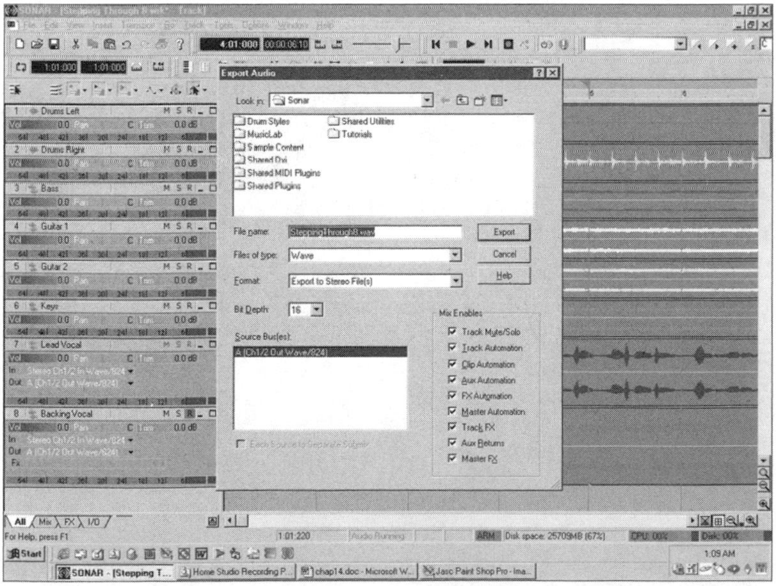

Figure 14.13

Mastering your song to a wave file from software involves a few clicks of mouse button—not much more.

CHAPTER 14

2. Select a folder to save to, and name your file "SteppingThrough8."

3. Choose "Wave" from the drop-down box.

4. In the Format field, select "Export to Stereo File(s)."

5. In the Bit Depth field, select the bit depth that you want your exported file to use.

6. In the Mix Enables field, select the effects you want to include in your new file. In this case, select all the options.

7. Click Export.

NOTE

Selecting the Track Mute/Solo option causes muted tracks to be left out of the exported mix and soloed tracks to be the only tracks exported. This is actually very handy and takes less time than if you were exporting only a few tracks rather than the whole project.

You're done! After a few seconds, SONAR will save the file as a wave file on your computer's hard drive. From here, you can prepare the file to be permanently mastered as an audio track onto disk, convert it to yet another file format, open it in Windows Media Player or any other Wave player to listen to it, or even import it back into SONAR. Note that if you do import it back into SONAR, it will appear as one track.

Finally, here's the good news: To save to MP3 format, you simply follow all the same steps outlined above for the wave file format. The difference is that you select "MP3" in the Files of Type drop-down box.

NOTE

For some annoying reason, SONAR has opted to follow the same path when it comes to MP3 files that a couple of other manufacturers have: You get only a trial version of the software's MP3 encoder and must shell out a little more chump change ($29 at the time of this writing) to get unlimited MP3 encoding.

Hence, you will see an additional dialog box—the Cakewalk MP3 Encoder (Trial Version) dialog—which will inform you that you have 30 days free and then you'll have to pay.

Why the manufacturer of such an excellent product—which already gets $300 of your money—wants another $29 so that you can participate in the biggest music-listening revolution since the concept album is, simply put, beyond the scope of this book!

15

Tracking Tips and Techniques

Sometimes it takes a lot of mistakes and costs a lot of money (that wasn't there to begin with) to learn how to be good at something. Double that for home recording. It's not hard to get tripped up, move a bit too fast, or head the wrong direction with a project.

In that spirit, this chapter offers some of those tidbits of information that come only with lots of late nights and black coffee.

Plan the Session

It's not exactly most musicians' penchant to plan. Nor do most musicians consider much more than a set list a useful way to plan anything.

This is wrong. All wrong. It always pays to put some forethought into a project. Whether your aim is to record a slew of songs and get a roster up on MP3.com or cut demo CDs and selectively try to get them in the hands of the recording industry, going to the trouble of planning the recording session will save you time in the long run, and you'll produce better work. By forcing yourself to sit down and list what you hope to accomplish and envisioning what the result will be, you're making yourself focus on the task of finishing the song.

Say your goal is to record enough material to release your own homegrown CD, but the catch is that you need a little help in the rhythm section. There are several pre-production tasks that make sense:

> ► Record a demo first, rather than going right into the first "real" session, to familiarize the other musicians with the material. Unless your gig is avant garde or free jazz, you don't want to waste sessions teaching everybody else the song.

> ► The flavor of the demo should be about the song, not the sound. Don't try to get a great sound or spend time mixing tracks; the demo should be a general sketch of each arrangement and rhythm.

> ► Think about how you will record the first session. If each instrument needs its own track, you need to configure your mixing console or software beforehand. You may need to double up on some tracks due to limited equipment, for example, so plan for it; don't figure you'll fix it in the mix. In fact, never count on fixing *anything* in the mix. Writing down a pre-track list that spells out each instrument and where it goes in the song will really keep you focused.

▶ Zeroing out all of the knobs and faders on your equipment is also good practice to give you a fresh session each time and avoid mistakenly using settings from the last session. Do the same for your software: For example, you can set up a basic template in SONAR by saving the track and instrument configurations you use most often to a template (.TPL) file.

▶ Keep any first session with other musicians open and relaxed, by having something to drink on hand, and have a schedule. Plan a specific block of time—that's what the pros do—and stick to that timeframe. If someone is going off in a direction you don't like, say simply, "I like what you're doing, but we really need to keep to the original arrangement" and move on. If your fellow musician has a problem with that, he has no business being within a mile of your music.

Quick Basic EQ Settings

While EQ can, in many cases, be a highly subjective aspect of recording, it helps to have a quick and dirty, basic configuration to start with and, most important, to learn from.

NOTE
Chapter 13 has all the gory details for getting the most out of your mixes.

Table 15.1 represents some fundamental EQ settings for a typical instrument setup: drums, guitar, bass, and vocals. This is not by any means the only way to EQ—in fact, your mileage will vary greatly, especially with the guitars and vocals.

These recommendations will give you a place to start, however, by giving you a feel for which instruments typically respond to which frequency ranges the most. The emphasis is on a warmer, more balanced mix.

Table 15.1
Example Basic EQ Settings.

Instrument	Value	Frequency Range
Drums	+6 dB	High
	−8 dB	Mid-range
	+10 dB	Low
Bass Guitar	+2 dB	Low
	+4 dB at 250 Hz	Mid-range
Rhythm Guitar	+6 dB at 2.5 kHz	Mid-range
	+1.5 dB	Low
Lead Guitar	+3 dB	High
	+6 dB	Mid-range
Lead Vocal	+3 dB at 3-4 kHz	High
	+3 dB	Mid-range
Backing Vocals	+2 dB	High
	−6 dB at 2.5 kHz	Mid-range
	+0.5 dB	Low

Cut, Copy, and Paste

One of the most effective and time-honored ways (it's been happening almost since a multi-track studio was in existence) to save time and get the best recording possible is to re-use material whenever, and wherever, you can.

For example, in SONAR (and any other digital recording software worth its salt), you accomplish this by moving or copying clips to new tracks or existing tracks by cutting or copying and then pasting—just like a word processor. There are a couple of different ways to do it.

The first way is the most tedious, but it is great for pin-point accuracy: Launch the Clip Properties dialog in SONAR and change the start time for the currently selected clip, as shown in Figure 15.1.

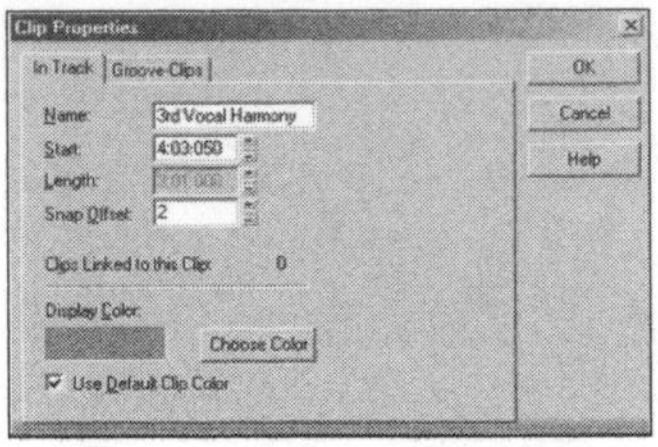

Figure 15.1
The In Track tab in Clip
Properties lets you
quickly move a section
of the track to another
area within the track.

The simplest and easiest way, however, is to do it the Windows way: Click and drag the clip to
its new location in the same track or to a different track with your mouse. Almost all digital
recording software gives you this capability.

SONAR gives you several options for moving or copying audio data, too, by using the Drag and
Drop Options dialog box (see Figure 15.2).

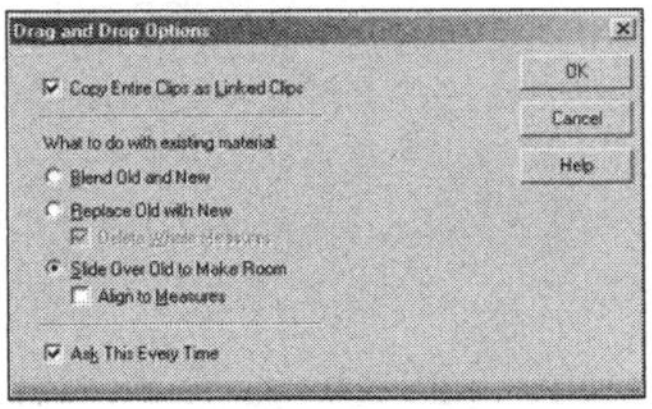

Figure 15.2
The Drag and Drop
dialog box gives you
three options for
dragging and dropping
clips in SONAR.

You can just add the audio you're moving with the destination audio you're moving it to—
automatically—by selecting the Blend Old And New option, and you can replace or change
the positing/timing of the destination clips with the other two options in the Drag and Drop
dialog box.

The real power comes with splitting and copying clips, though. By splitting out a new clip that
contains audio you want to re-use in the song (those eight bars of perfect backing vocals, for
example), you can put the best performances right where you need them, when you need them.

Right-clicking anywhere on a clip in SONAR and selecting Split launches the Split Clips dialog
box, as shown in Figure 15.3.

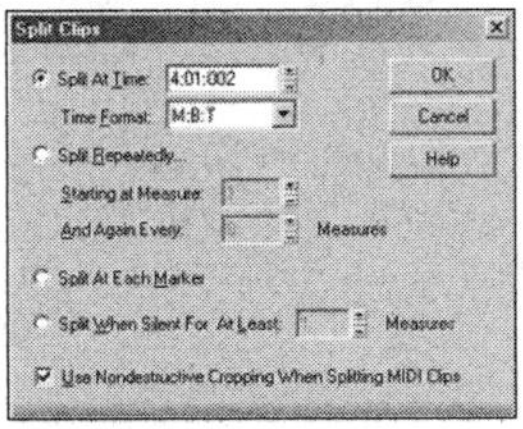

Figure 15.3
Split Clips cuts the area
of the track into smaller
sections but leaves its
sound untouched.

To split a clip, you click on OK to close the Split Clips dialog box and split the clip. Then select the clip you want to copy; to copy the clip, it couldn't be easier:

1. Select the clip you want to copy.

2. Select Edit > Copy. The Copy dialog box will appear.

3. Choose how you'll copy the audio data in the clip.

4. Click OK. ·

5. Click on the track number or click in the clip area of the track where you want to paste the split clip.

6. Set the Now time to the point where you're pasting—or simply right-click the point you want to paste in the Clip View.

7. Select Edit > Paste to open the Paste dialog box. Click OK, and you're done!

As you can see, in SONAR, the process of re-using your music in different locations throughout your song is particularly easy. Not too many years ago, it was a bit more difficult with analog equipment, but the result was still the same. It's a huge time-saver!

Using a Patchbay

A patchbay is a very effective way to cut down on frustration as well as time when connecting all of your studio equipment. A patchbay is a rack-mountable piece of gear with front and back cable jacks, which help you easily direct the signals coming from each piece of gear in your setup. It's the best way to keep your cables organized.

Most patchbays align rows of sixteen to twenty-four jacks in two columns, so that you can permanently plug in all the inputs and outputs of your gear, rather than having to re-patch cables each time a session requires a change of instrument or track on the mixer.

There is no hard and fast rule as to how you set up a patchbay. The traditional way uses the top row for outputs and the bottom for inputs, but you *can* roll your own. There are three types of jacks, though, which a patchbay uses, and you should be aware of their differences before you go hooking things up:

▶ *Denormaled* jacks simply send input from the top and bottom back jacks directly to the front jacks.

▶ *Normaled* jacks route a top jack in the back of the patchbay to a bottom jack in the back when the front jacks aren't being used. These are for cases where you don't need the front jacks—with aux returns from your mixer, for example.

▶ *Half-normaled* jacks essentially allow you to have two copies of the signal from a given output jack, which is very useful for processing two different EQ configurations at the same time.

There are a lot of patchbay models you can buy, and you can even buy plans to build your own or build one from scratch. Switchcraft, Tascam, and Fostex all make affordable and good-quality models, usually in the $200-400 price range. Patchbay cables are also cheap and plentiful.

CHAPTER 15

Master with Care

In the professional recording world, mastering is actually a wholly separate art and science unto itself. Mastering engineers have a different type of process—and even different (usually very expensive) types of equipment, for example, compressors that can control the highs and lows independently and EQ which can affect both right and left channels independently as well as relative to the audio signal.

In the home studio, you can still master, even if your equipment is more limited. You should go through a mastering process: Fix glitches, clean up fades, order your songs correctly and set the timing between tracks on CDs if you're cutting a CD.

This is also the time to pay attention to the dynamics of the song(s) you're mastering. Normalizing, for example, should be done at this stage. By the same token, noise reduction is just as important, and you ideally shouldn't normalize more than once or twice to keep noise at a minimum.

Mastering is your final stab at making the compositions as clear and full of impact as possible. It's the polish. How much time should you spend on it? Depending on what you have to work with (the quality, dynamics, and clarity of the mix), you should plan at least an evening to two evenings just for mastering. You should also get as many people as you can to listen to your mixes closely to see if there is something missing in the mix before you master. Take notes: If you get many of the same comments, it's probably something you should fix or an area of the song that needs attention. If you get a lot of varied input, however, you can pretty safely ignore all of it.

In general, keep these goals in mind when mastering:

> ▶ Don't master right after the "final" take. Give your ears at least a 24-hour break before a mastering session. It's kind of like eating a rich dessert on a full stomach: you have no idea how the dessert really tastes, and there's a good chance you'll get sick!

> ▶ Stay away from limiters, and, in general, don't compress an entire mix.

> ▶ If you do use compression, think "well-balanced" performance. Use only as much compression as you absolutely need to make tweaks to the sound.

> ▶ In general, keep the vocals, bass, and kick near the center of the mix, and pay close attention to the how the high frequencies sit next to each other—guitars and cymbals, for example.

> ▶ Don't use aural exciters: They're wonderful for putting new life into older recordings, but not as a piece of mastering equipment.

> ▶ Get as hot as you can with the mastered signal. For a digital setup, signals tend to clip badly past 0 dB.

TIP

If you aren't the only home studio aficionado on the block and you trust a friend or someone else who is, discuss the serious possibility of exchanging mastering tasks with each other. A fresh pair of ears is probably the single most important advantage the big studios have over you when it comes to mastering.

Track Sheets

After you've got a final mix and a master, then cut it to CD or DAT (hopefully, using the techniques in Chapter 16), you're done—right? The answer is "just about."

If you ever have a problem with a master or need to fix mistakes, you'll need a track sheet. Even with recording software like SONAR, it's really a good idea to keep a separate track sheet in Microsoft Word or another word processor. It's ultimately up to you, but if you don't want to find yourself in a frustrating situation down the road, spend a few minutes documenting the recording.

As a minimum, you should always document the following information:

► Performer(s)
► Song title
► Master title
► Positions
► Fader values
► EQ settings
► Pan, effects, and send/return settings

It's particularly easy to get used to not using track sheets with digital recording software; your mix and the audio are always automatically stored for you. Doesn't matter: Take the extra precaution of double-documenting. Fifteen extra minutes now could mean saving a few days sometime in the future.

CHAPTER 15

16
Pack It and Ship It

It wasn't too long ago that CD recorders were expensive toys for software creators. Not any more: These days, CD-R and CD-RW drives alike are capable of creating CD audio disks and CD-ROMs at consumer prices. This chapter will guide you through selecting and using a CD recording drive and provide you with some tips and tricks for creating and packaging your CDs. This chapter focuses on:

▶ Burning your music to a CD

▶ Mixing your audio tracks with other data

▶ Sleeves, liner notes, and graphics

Putting Your Music on CD

The ability to create audio CDs has become quite popular now that the hardware is affordable. In fact, more and more consumers are using them because they're cheap and easy to install. Instead of having to continually insert CDs just to play particular songs, users are buying economical CD-R drives and a few software tools, and, voila: They've got a higher-tech version of a compilation tape!

Of course, you can do the same thing—but as a recording artist, you can also put a CD recording drive to real use. Even if your primary goal is to distribute your music via the Internet, a CD "burner" can save you money and time by enabling you to archive your performances and recordings instead of buying more expensive and less reliable hard drives.

The Technology is Better and Faster

Not long ago, burning a CD was a frustrating exercise in patience. Buffer-underrun problems, slow recording speeds, and inferior software turned a lot of well-intentioned CD mastering projects into coasters.

NOTE

A buffer underrun used to be an all-too-common problem. A buffer underrun is what occurs when the data stream from the PC to the CD recording drive is interrupted. Though it can still happen, these days it's less likely, thanks to bigger buffers to hold incoming data, faster PCs, and better-designed software to manage high-speed CD recording drives.

There are dozens of CD drive models on the market, produced by companies such as Sony, Phillips, and Toshiba. At the time of this writing, prices for these drives range anywhere from $150 to $300, and most of them include basic software to get you up and going. Two types of drives exist—CD-R and CD-RW.

The Cutting Edge: DVD

Actually, there is a third type of drive just coming into the consumer market: DVD-R. DVD (digital versatile disc) recordable technology does the same thing with DVDs that CD recording technology does with CDs. DVD-R is a write-once medium that can hold any type of information normally stored on DVD discs, such as video, audio, images, data files, and multimedia programs. Depending on the type of information you record, DVD-R discs are usable on virtually any compatible DVD playback device, including most DVD-ROM drives and DVD video players.

The DVD-R drives that are currently becoming available will write only single layer discs which will hold 2.25 GB per side (for a total of 4.5 GB). Professional writers will do dual layer, double-side, which will hold a total of 9 GB, but these are much more expensive than the single-layer disc drives. In addition to the thousands of dollars you'll currently spend on DVD-R, good DVD-R creation software is in the $500-$1,000 range. DVD-R is a little more geared for video enthusiasts, due to the more massive amounts of space needed for delivering digital video.

Another DVD option is DVD-RAM, which was affordable long before DVD-R, and is a bit easier on your wallet, typically at under $500 (at time of this writing). DVD-RAM drives don't need special software, looking and acting more like a fast hard drive, which makes them ideal for storing and transferring lots of simultaneous projects. DVD-RAM discs come in a protective cartridge, like the old CD-ROM caddies (only non-removable) to help minimize dust and fingerprints, can be single- or double-sided, and will hold anywhere from 2.25 to 4.5 GB of data on one disc.

Finally, DVD-audio—which has been up in the air for a number of years—has emerged, with a first crop of consumer players starting at around $500. The format holds a lot of promise, and artists like Neil Young are reportedly getting behind the format because of its larger bitrates and higher sampling rates. DVD-audio also supports full multi-channel (2, 4, 5.1, or 7.1 channels) at a full PCM bitrate rather than the compressed Dolby Digital bit stream. DVD-audio discs support a highly flexible format structure including bitrates that range from 16 to 24 bits and sampling rates of 44.1, 48, 88.2, 96, 176.4, and even 192 kHz! Hello! This means you could choose, for example, 2-channel stereo, 24-bit audio at 192 kHz for the highest fidelity—or go with 6-channel, surround sound, 24-bit audio at 96 kHz for multi-channel surround (like 5.1). You can even mix and match three front channels at 24-bit, 96 kHz and surround channels at 20-bit, 48 kHz, as well as store video clips, graphics, lyrics, bios, games, and other data. Look for great things to come with the DVD-audio format.

CD-R

"CD-R" stands for compact disk-recordable. It is a type of disk drive that can create CD-ROMs and audio CDs once and once only—meaning that you can't reuse the disk once you've written data to it.

CD-R drives have not only dropped dramatically in price, they have increased rapidly in speed since the mid-1990s. Two years ago, CD-Rs could write data at $4\times$ speed and read data at $12\times$ speed (known as $4\times/12\times$). By the end of 1999, performance had doubled to $8\times/24\times$, and today's drives go as fast as $12\times/32\times$.

With prices almost as low as some CD-ROM drives, CD-Rs are still viable as a storage or back-up device, but because they waste resources, i.e., disks, CD-Rs are not the best solution available. You'll get more for your mileage with a CD-rewritable (CD-RW).

CD-RW

CD-RW drives are dual function, offering both CD-R and CD-RW recording, so you can choose which method works best according to what you want to record. CD-RW differs from CD-R in that it uses a different type of disk that can be reused, or re-written.

CD-RW disks are not writable by CD-R drives; although most new CD-ROM drives do support CD-RW, not all of them will read CD-RW disks at full speed. The important thing to know is that, although many new audio CD players can handle CD-RW discs, most older ones cannot. If you want to create audio CDs using CD-RW disks, you're taking chances with it working successfully.

The best bet is to use CD-R disks with a CD-RW drive. That way you're assured of compatibility with most CD players, but you still have the advantage of being able to use CD-RW disks for storage, archiving, and testing.

The best drives are capable of writing CD-R/CD-RW media at $10\times/12\times$ and they read at $32\times$. It's typical to find a CD-RW at about $8\times/8\times/24\times$ these days for less than $200.

CD Recording Software

Nearly all CD-RW drives sold today are bundled with some kind of CD recording software. Some of the bundled software will work fine for burning audio CDs, while some of it may not work consistently or very well. We'll use Easy CD Creator from Roxio (formerly known as Adaptec) in this chapter to walk you through the process of burning an audio CD, since it comes with many of the drives on the market and has proven to be reliable and easy to use.

If you don't have Easy CD Creator, it can be purchased through your local software or on the Web from **http://www.roxio.com/**. At the time of this writing, it can be bought for around $89— a reasonable price considering its quality and many features. Easy CD Creator is a PC-only product, but Roxio also makes its Macintosh twin, Toast, which is almost identical in features and functionality.

NOTE

Many CD recording drives come with a "packet writing" utility, often Roxio's Direct CD, which is a more flexible way to make data-only disks (packet writing cannot be used on audio CDs).

Packet writing software lets you selectively overwrite files, unlike Easy CD Creator, which forces you to erase the whole CD-RW disk before you can rewrite it. Unfortunately, packet writing is also much slower and generally less reliable.

TIP

The files you will create as you go through the process of burning CDs are very big and will take up a lot of space on your hard drive. Before you get started, you will want to make sure you have at least 600 MB free on your hard drive.

Getting Started with Easy CD Creator

Installing Easy CD Creator is mostly a matter of deciding where to put it on your PC's hard drive—it's a typical installation wizard, so we won't cover it here.

Once you've installed Easy CD Creator, you can launch the program from either the Windows Start Menu or by double-clicking the Easy CD Creator icon in the system tray.

Figure 18.1 shows the startup screen you'll see when the program launches. You're presented with five options: Audio, Data CD, CD Copier, Jewel Case Creator, and Photo & Video:

▶ The *Audio* option points to two different programs—the standard CD audio recording application and Spin Doctor, a program which will record audio CDs but also give you options for recording files to your hard drive as well as the ability to remove clicks, pops, and hisses from the audio source.

▶ The *Data CD* option is for creating CD-ROMs. CD-ROMs are useful for backing up your important files or archiving source music tracks. A CD-ROM is used for data storage only and cannot be played on a CD player.

▶ *CD Copier* is the quick and dirty method for making backup copies of any type of CD supported by your CD recording drive.

▶ *Jewel Case Creator* is an application to help you design custom jewel case inserts and CD labels for your CDs. Though Jewel Case Creator comes with several pre-built themes, you can also add your own graphics, change backgrounds, and change the layout and style of text.

▶ *Photo & Video* provides applications for creating and recording a photo album, creating video postcards, and recording MPEG video clips to disk.

Figure 18.1
Easy CD Creator
offers all the options
you'd expect.

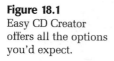

The Audio option is the one you want to select. When you click on it, the menu changes and offers you two more options (see Figure 18.2): Audio CD and Spin Doctor. Select Spin Doctor.

Figure 18.2
Easy CD Creator
offers two ways to
record audio CDs.

Spin Doctor is a very simple-looking program with many features. Its default interface is a simple-looking wizard-like dialog box with three steps, called the "123 Window." The first step is to select a music source; from there, it only gets easier:

1. The Select Music Source dialog box appears.
2. Select the Music Source Type from which you want to record.
3. Click Select.
4. You can add WAV files or MP3 files from your hard drive, a CD-ROM drive, or the CD recording drive itself. In the Select Tracks(s) to Record dialog box, select the tracks you want to record and click OK.
5. The list of tracks that you want to record appears in the Track/Title list. To add more tracks, click Select Track(s) to Record.

The next step, after you've selected the files you want to copy, is to choose a destination for the files. There are three options:

▶ **CD Recorder**—Select this option when you are ready to permanently record your songs to CD.

▶ **File(s) on hard drive**—This option actually allows you to record songs directly to your hard drive as wave files (.WAV), rather than going straight to a CD disk. This is quick and easy for making backup copies of your source audio on your hard drive.

▶ **Audio**—This lets you to listen to your source files before recording them to CD. You can also listen to tracks that have been recorded to a CD that is not yet closed.

TIP

For most sound cards, if you have another audio application open, you may not be able to hear playback when you select the Audio option. If you don't hear the music playing, check to make sure none of your other audio software is currently up and running.

The last step is to record the CD. Spin Doctor keeps a running total of how many tracks you have added and how much space is required on the CD to record the tracks. You can record up to a maximum of 99 tracks or 74 minutes of music (depending on the quality of the CD disk you're using, this may vary slightly).

Mixed CDs

Easy CD Creator will also allow you to combine music and data on the same CD. This is a nice option to have if you want to create a mix of files like promotional images, videos, music tracks, and/or personal info on the same CD.

There are two different approaches to recording a mixed CD in Easy CD: Mixed-Mode and CD Extra. If you want your music to be able to play from a CD player, use CD Extra. A CD Extra CD writes the first "session" as audio files, so a home or car stereo CD player can play them, and then records the data in a second session that can be read from a CD-ROM drive.

Mixed-mode does just the opposite: It writes the data files first, then the audio. This is why you want to avoid using mixed-mode—if the data tracks are written first, you can't play the audio tracks in a CD player, and there is some risk of damaging the CD player and/or the speakers.

When you create a CD Extra CD, the CD Layout naturally contains both an Audio and a Data section. First you add wave files or MP3 files to the Audio CD Layout, then your data files and folders to the CD Layout data area.

TIP

While the Audio CD Layout area is identified as "Audio CD Layout" on the left-hand side of the interface, the place to drop your data files is not identified as such. By default, Easy CD Creator creates a root-level folder labeled with the date (year:month:day) and a default session ID (next to the shiny CD icon). You can rename this default folder to anything you want.

Here is the step-by-step:

1. Open Easy CD Creator from the Start menu. Click Start > Programs > Roxio Easy CD Creator 4 > Features, and then select Easy CD Creator.

2. To open a CD Extra CD Layout, click the small arrow next to the New button on the toolbar and select CD Extra from the drop-down list. A CD Extra CD Layout appears.

3. Insert a blank CD into your CD-Recorder (the destination drive).

4. Add the audio files you want to record to the audio section of the CD Extra Layout, as shown in Figure 18.3.

Figure 18.3
Drag-and-drop your
wave and MP3 files to
the audio section of the
CD Extra Layout.

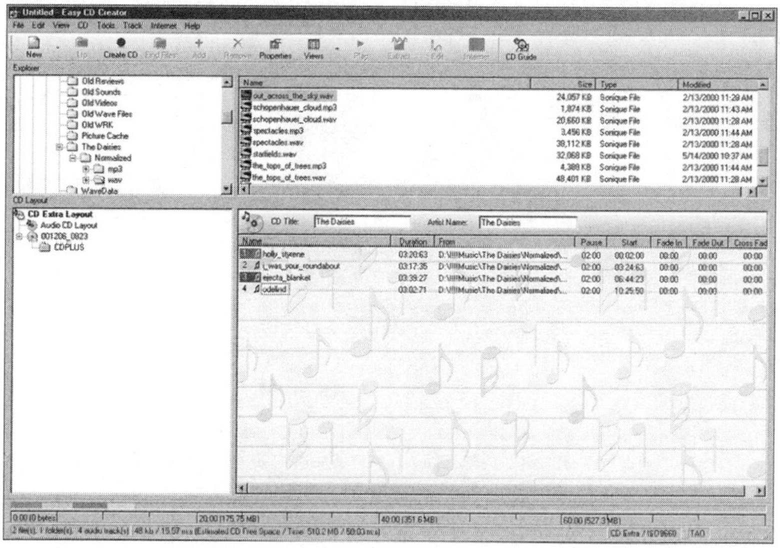

5. Select the Audio CD Layout icon in the left pane of the CD Extra Layout window.

6. If you are recording tracks from an existing music CD, insert the music CD into your CD-ROM drive (the source drive). If you are recording WAV or MP3 files, continue with the next step.

NOTE

You can record any combination of WAV files or MP3 files to an audio CD, in any order. You can also add existing CD tracks in any order.

7. In the left pane of the Explorer section, select the CD-ROM drive containing the music CD; a list of the tracks on the CD appears to the right. If you are recording WAV or MP3 files, select the folder where your files are located.

8. In the right pane of the Explorer section, select the track, WAV, or MP3 file that you want to record, and then click Add, or drag-and-drop the files. Repeat until the Audio CD Layout contains all of the tracks and files that you want to record.

TIP

If you are adding tracks from more than one CD, repeat steps 6-8 for each CD. During the actual recording process, Easy CD will prompt you to reinsert the appropriate music CD for the music track being recorded.

9. After adding all the audio files that you want to record into the Audio CD Layout, click the Data CD Layout icon in the left pane of the CD Extra Layout window.

10. In the Explorer section, select the data files or folders you want to record, and then click Add, or drag-and-drop (Figure 18.4).

Figure 18.4
Add data files and
folders to the CD Extra
Layout.

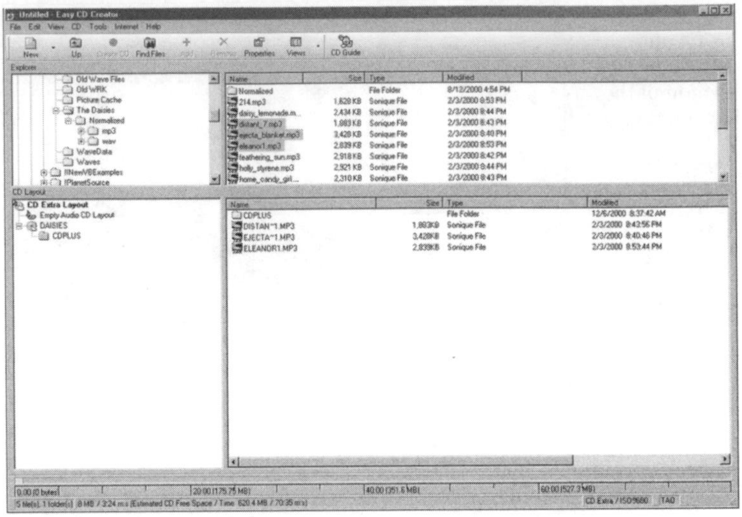

11. After all your files are added, click Create CD. The CD Creation Setup box appears.

12. Click OK to start recording.

Sleeves, Liner Notes, and Graphics

Creating a package design for your audio CD can be straightforward with the right software—or quite difficult if you intend to produce sparkling, professional-looking collateral.

This section will focus on DIY—doing it yourself—because it's the most cost-effective route for a starving artist. Unless you have no visual sense whatsoever, doing your own design and printing will give you acceptable results.

The biggest expense to doing it yourself is a good quality color printer—typically an inkjet-based device—which can range in price from $50 to $500. At the time of this writing, an average price for a color inkjet with a reasonable dpi (dots per inch) rating of at least 600×600 averages about $100.

Aside from that, you'll need to purchase the paper supplies (labels and glossy insert stock), as well as the CD-R media itself. The paper supplies *can* get expensive, but generally speaking, they are a minor expense, available from most office-supply stores.

If you truly don't have any visual sense to speak of, you may want to consider hiring a graphic artist to do the design work for you. If you go this route, you will still need to communicate your own sense of design and expectations about the art that will accompany your music. Here are some tips:

▶ If you have any kind of design concept in mind, try to sketch it out, regardless of how bad you might think it looks. Even a page of doodles will help.

▶ Browse your own music collection, select covers that you like the most, and take note of the things you like about them, such as the type of design and use of color and text.

▶ Browse through recent releases in your music genre at the music store. Write down what you think works and what doesn't.

▶ Talk to other musicians and see if they have used a graphic artist they will recommend. Of course, before you use their recommendation, take a look at their CDs and see if you like the design!

Jewel Case Creator

Easy CD Creator's Jewel Case Creator is a great program for quickly creating your CD's sleeve and label. It's a matter of changing text, dropping in a graphics files, and moving everything around to position it how you want. You can also use twenty pre-built themes—graphics and layouts—and simply fill in the blanks.

But the program does have some drawbacks. For example, though you can define a front cover and an inside cover, any graphics you insert for either one automatically gets used for both, meaning you cannot choose a different image for the front cover and another image for the inside cover. You'll also notice that any images you add are resized and their color depth is set to a limit of 256 colors.

Advanced Media Labeling Tools

For more features and better functionality, MicroVision Development's SureThing CD Labeler is a better choice than Jewel Case Creator. You can download a demo of the program from **www.mvd.com**. SureThing can create the standard CD labels and jewel case inserts, as well as other types of removable computer media, and the full version of the software also includes a good-sized collection of background images and clip art.

In addition to the simple text and graphic additions that Jewel Case Creator provides, SureThing supports a number of special text effects and can import high-color images. Well-written help and a tutorial are available, but you probably won't need them.

You can also create CD labels and jewel case liners using popular desktop publishing software, like Corel Print House (**www.corel.com**) or Broderbund Print Shop Deluxe (**www.broderbund.com**). These programs come with huge collections of good quality images and clip art if you need a large selection of art from which to choose.

NOTE

Graphics programs like PhotoShop, Image Composer, and Paint Shop Pro are the ultimate choices for complete control over your own designs. However, getting the correct sizes for the jewel case insert and CD label will be difficult (for example, a standard-size jewel case is 5 1/2 × 4 7/8 inches) and time-consuming with these professional-level image-authoring applications.

TIP
If you're one of those people who finds jewel cases unwieldy or prefers to use plastic sleeves to store your CDs, Mirage Inkjet Technologies (**www.mirageinkjet.com**) produces glossy photo label paper and silver reflective film. In addition, LabelGear.com (**www.labelgear.com**) carries a large selection of insert and labeling supplies online.

Doing a Big Burn

If you're burning even a dozen CDs a day, a CD recording drive will handle the load with relative ease. But if you find yourself in the enviable position of needing to produce CDs in higher quantities (like hundreds, or thousands), you may want to look into using a professional shop to burn your CDs from one master.

A short- to medium-sized run of CDs—or CD-ROMs—is not as expensive as it used to be. Many vendors advertise rates as low as $1 per disk, which usually includes two-color labeling. Though CD-R disks and label supplies are relatively cheap, you will save a lot of time and wear on your equipment by using a shop to burn large quantities.

17

Wired for Sound: The Internet

Quite simply, the Internet is the biggest thing to happen to music in a long time. For the first time in "recorded" history, artists have a cheap and easy outlet for getting their music heard by millions of potential listeners.

Whether you've already decided you're second in line for a direct Web-jack into your brain or you're just getting good at e-mail, this chapter is for you. You'll learn:

▶ The differences between online audio file formats

▶ How to package your music for the Internet

▶ Tips for the design and setup of your own Web site

▶ How to protect your intellectual property

The Internet Music Craze

It's hard not to have heard about MP3, Real Audio, Napster, streaming audio, and Windows Media. These technologies are rapidly becoming almost ubiquitous parts of the popular music experience.

Not convinced? Take a trip down to your local software chain store and check out the music software section: A couple of years ago, you would have been hard-pressed to find even a handful of titles there—and you would have been lucky if more than one of them was in stock. Today, hundreds of boxes representing dozens of available titles line the shelf. This is because software makers are responding to the huge numbers of online music lovers—and musicians— that have grown because of the Internet.

At the time of this writing, MP3 remains the most used, transferred, shared, encoded, decoded, copied—you name it—music format on the Internet. MP3 became popular so quickly because, around the time it was introduced, online music was either 1) delivered in small files but of very poor playback quality; or 2) of good sound fidelity but unacceptably slow to download because of huge file sizes.

Unless you had the patience of a saint, listening to music then was like listening to a song that had been recorded off an AM radio station—not a very compelling prospect, to say the least. MP3 changed all that by providing much higher quality sound while keeping the average file size manageable.

So how does it work? To understand how MP3 works, you have to first understand a little about audio file formats.

NOTE

While this chapter focuses on the handful of audio file formats that are popular on the Internet, there are dozens of other audio file formats. See Chapter 11 for general coverage of file formats as well as digital audio.

How Audio File Formats Work

An audio file isn't much different than any other file on a computer: It's a piece of data that adheres to a specific set of rules defining how all the data bits (the 0s and 1s) should be stored on your hard drive. A "format" is simply the set of rules.

Of course, there is more than one set of rules. For example, CD music always follows the rule that audio data must be stored using a bit depth (or "resolution") of 16 bits and a 44.1 kHz sampling rate. This means that a string of 0s and 1s representing a slice of audio data can't be more than 16 bits long (a pretty good-size number), and that the music has been sampled 44,100 times per second. The result is that the sound reproduction is quite accurate, but the audio files take up a lot of space. That's why, at 16 bits and 44.1 kHz, you can't pack more than seventy-four minutes or so of audio onto a CD.

TIP

The seventy-four minutes of audio data on an audio CD, or "Red Book" audio (named after the color of the cover on the original audio CD specification) is stored in a special PCM audio data format—not the .WAV file or any other standard PC audio file format.

In fact, downloading one three-minute song on a 56K modem from a CD would take you a long time—nearly two hours. For all but the most discerning owners of a very high bandwidth Internet connection, this is unacceptable.

TIP

The way you determine how much music can be stored on a compact disc is actually quite simple. It's a matter of figuring out the number of bits all the pieces add up to. This is done by multiplying the number of samples per second by the number of bits per sample by the number of channels (in the case of CD audio, separate samples are taken for both the left and right speakers to provide stereo, so the number of channels is two). Here's how it tallies up for CD audio:

44,100 x 16 x 2 = 1,411,200 (bits per second)

Since 8 bits equal one byte, and a kilobyte is a 1,000 bytes, 1.4 million bits per second is 176 KB per second. If a song is three minutes long, then it consumes almost 32 MB of space on the CD!

NOTE

We won't cover WAV, AIFF files, or MIDI files in this chapter—you can find all of the excruciating details in chapters 9 and 10, respectively, as well as numerous other places in the book. But just in case you're skipping around, here's the quick skinny:

WAV files are the highly popular Windows-based, non-compressed audio format. The WAV file format supports many types of audio data including 8-bit and 16-bit, mono and stereo audio. If you're working with Windows, you'll probably use the WAV format for almost all of your audio work, and almost all Windows-based sound and music software uses this format. WAV files have the .WAV file extension and are as good as or better than CD-quality sound.

AIFF files are practically the Macintosh twin of a WAV file, and you'll see them with both the .AIF and .SND file extensions. It's an excellent all-purpose file format and almost all sound and music software for the Macintosh platform employs it.

The MIDI file format is used by musicians extensively, as well as in many popular PC games and entertainment software, and there are loads of MIDI files available on the Internet. A MIDI file does not capture and store audio data; instead, it manages a list of events which describe the specific steps that your sound card or computer must take to generate the music. MIDI files are tiny compared to digital audio files and are easy to edit, allowing the music to easily be rearranged, recorded, and played in real time.

MP3: It's All in the Algorithm

With the MP3 file format, it takes less than ten minutes to download an average three-minute song at a modem speed of around 50 Kbps, which doesn't require the patience of a saint! MP3 does this by using an algorithm that compresses, or *encodes,* the audio data, wadding the entire chunk of audio data up kind of like the way you might crumple a sheet of paper into a ball.

Of course, in order to listen to the music once your download is complete, it must be decompressed, or *decoded,* on your computer—kind of like un-wadding that paper ball. This is done with an MP3 player, such as Winamp, Windows Media Player, Sonique, MusicMatch—the list goes on and on. The kicker is that decoded audio will not sound quite as good as the original, uncompressed recording. Think of that paper ball: When you unfold it, it has creases in it, so that anything written on the paper will not be quite as clear as it was when the paper was smooth and crease-free.

In the case of MP3, there are enough creases to keep the file size manageable, but not so many that the audio quality suffers too much. An average MP3 file actually compresses at a ratio of about 12 to 1, so think of twelve creases. This is not far from CD-quality.

A Nickel Tour of MP3 History

MP3 stands for "Moving Picture Experts Group, Audio Layer 3." It began as far back as the 1980s, when the German Fraunhofer Institut set out to create a high-quality, highly compressed audio file format. Fraunhofer was granted a patent for MP3 in Germany in 1989 and subsequently submitted MP3 to the International Standards Organization (ISO).

It wasn't until around 1997, however, that a commercially acceptable MP3 player was created. Dubbed the "AMP MP3 Playback Engine," it quickly became the basis for the creation of Winamp, the first widely adopted MP3 player to hit the Internet. Winamp was developed by two university students, Justin Frankel and Dmitry Boldyrev.

Since then, there have been many new versions of Winamp, while a slew of other players have emerged offering different playback options, EQs, effects, graphic visualizations, and other features and improvements. New tools, encoders, and CD rippers have also been developed, spurring an exciting—and competitive— marketplace. "MP3" has become the most popular search term at search engine sites, and portable MP3 players now let music lovers take their music with them wherever they go.

If that weren't enough, there's Napster, the tool that allows users to connect to each other's hard drives to share MP3 files. Shortly after Napster was released in 1999, it spawned a community of music junkies that grew like gangbusters.

Another compelling aspect of the history of MP3 (you *could* arguably call it the revolution of MP3) is the fact that music in MP3 format has always been free and void of security features. This has in no small way attracted the attention of the RIAA (the Recording Industry Association of America), which represents the major recording labels. The RIAA views MP3 as a significant piracy threat and has tried more than once to stop its unsecured use, including filing lawsuits against Napster and MP3.com.

MP3 Encoding

So how do you get your music made over into an MP3 file? How do you go about encoding it? There are numerous tools available, and it is not the aim of this chapter to cover them all. Table 19.1 lists some of the most popular programs that will encode MP3 files.

Table 19.1
MP3 Encoding Software

Name	Web Site	Platform(s)
Audioactive 2.0	audioactive.com	Win95/98/NT
MP3 Producer	opticom.de	Win95, NT 4.0
MP3 Strip_It!	digitalcandle.com	Win95/98/NT/2000
MP32WAV	rjpa.net	Win9.x/DOS
MPEG DJ Encoder	xaudio.de	Win95/98/NT/2000
MusicMatch 6.0	musicmatch.com	PC/Mac/Linux
RealJukebox	real.com/jukebox	Windows
XingMPEG Encoder 2.2	xingtech.com	Win9.x, NT

Table 19.1 is by no means a definitive list, and the features of these programs vary widely. RealJukebox and MusicMatch, for example, are full-featured MP3 players in their own right, while MP32WAV (a command-line program, by the way—and not for the faint of heart) and DJ Encoder are built explicitly for encoding.

In addition, most of the digital audio recording software available provides the ability to encode MP3 files, including SONAR and Sound Forge 5.0. With SONAR, the process is handled by simply exporting the file to the MP3 format, as shown in Figure 19.1. All you have to do is select File > Export Audio from the menu bar and choose MP3 from the Files of Type drop-down box.

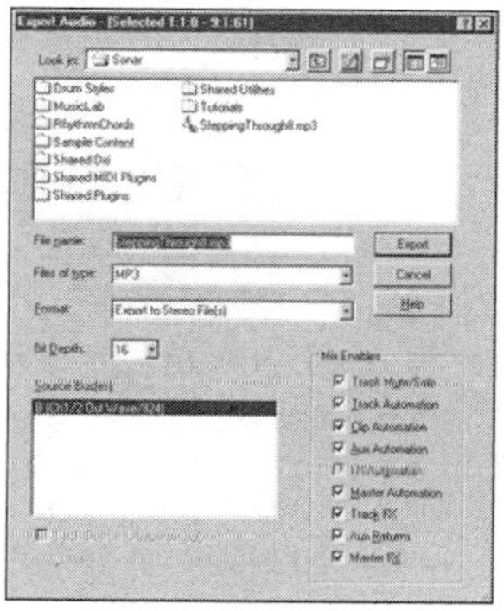

Figure 19.1
MP3-encoding your
composition in SONAR
is built-in and easy.

Sound Forge is just as simple, allowing you to open and save MP3 files as you would any other file through the use of the Sonic Foundry MP3 plug-in.

Bitrates and Compression Techniques

Good MP3 encoding software will actually give you more than one option when it comes to converting your music to MP3. The reason for this is that the format itself was designed to support different degrees of compression, as shown in Table 19.2.

CHAPTER 17

Table 19.2
MP3 Performance Comparison

Sound Quality	Bandwidth	Mode	Bitrate	Compression Ratio
CD	16 kHz	Stereo	112-128 Kbps	12:1
Near-CD	15 kHz	Stereo	96 Kbps	16:1
FM radio	11 kHz	Stereo	64 Kbps	24:1
AM radio	7.5 kHz	Mono	32 Kbps	24:1
Short-wave	4.5 kHz	Mono	16 Kbps	48:1
Telephone	2.5 kHz	Mono	8 Kbps	96:1

NOTE

Technically speaking, 96–128 Kbps is not strictly CD quality, though it sounds so close in most common listening environments that for popular music, it is, practically speaking, CD quality. The ambient noise characteristic of listening outdoors, in your car, or on a CD Walkman will mask the deficiencies. However, for highly dynamic genres like classical music, compression is less suitable.

Note the numbers in the Compression Ratio column. These are in reality approximations—the actual compression rate that can be achieved during encoding can vary by a few digits higher or lower. For example, although 12:1 is an average compression rate to maintain CD quality, it could wind up anywhere from 11:1 to 14:1.

That's the reason for the numbers in Bitrate column: Because compression ratios are not always an exact measurement, a bitrate is calculated to accurately track compression strength. A bitrate is the average number of kilobits (Kbps) that 1 second of audio data will consume. One kilobit is 1,024 bits.

We learned earlier that a digital audio signal from a CD runs at 1,378,125 bits per second. Translated into a bitrate, this is approximately 1,378 Kbps! With MP3, CD-like sound quality can be achieved by compressing the audio down to a bitrate of 96 Kbps.

The question is: How far can you go without sacrificing too much quality? This is not an unusual question in the online world. For instance, Web designers struggle with optimizing images and image formats all the time. The two most widely used image files are the GIF and JPEG formats, and each of them uses compression algorithms. For that matter, if you've ever downloaded a Zip file, you've encountered compression as well—a Zip file format can compress just about anything, from text to binary executable files to images, as well as audio files.

TIP

There aren't really that many instances where you'll want to go below 96 Kbps. If you are doing a lot of singing and/or have a lot going on musically, anything lower than 96 Kbps will not sound good. Also, some of the Web sites that allow you to post your MP3s also require that the bitrate be at least 128 Kbps, including MP3.com.

In a few cases, lowering the bitrate might make sense; for example, if you're doing a lot of spoken word or if instrumentation is sparse, you may not lose any noticeable quality while reducing the file size. The best way to find out is to experiment with different bitrates.

For audio, to make a good compression algorithm technique, the MP3 format uses something called *perceptual noise shaping*. The idea is simple: The encoding algorithm uses psychoacoustic modeling—certain known facts about how humans hear—to determine how to compress the data.

NOTE

The psychoacoustic model of the human auditory system is more or less the sensitivity of the human ear to sound frequencies. With some variation, most of us are very sensitive to frequencies between 2.5 and 5 kHz, and our perception drops pretty rapidly for frequencies lower or higher than this range.

For example, sound frequencies that the human ear can barely detect or not hear at all can be eliminated during the compression process, while sound frequencies that are heard better than others are "punctuated"—especially if two sounds occur at the same time, in which case the loudest frequencies can be left untouched at the expense of softer frequency levels.

The bottom line is that, by eliminating some of the less common frequencies and inaudible elements of an audio signal, audio can be scrunched up into a manageable size.

Other compressed audio file formats work in a similar fashion, and there are two worth mentioning: Windows Media and Real Audio.

Windows Media

Windows Media was developed by Microsoft and is particularly suited to streaming audio files over the Internet. It more or less offers the same bitrate and quality options as MP3. Any computer running Windows and a player that handles WMA or ASF files (Windows Media Player or MusicMatch, for example) can play Windows Media. Windows Media also supports video data.

Another part of Windows Media is Microsoft's ASX file format—text files that manage the streaming of other audio files. They are very small because they contain no audio data, just information about and links to audio data.

CHAPTER 17

If you're concerned about how widely your music is distributed via the Internet (see the section later in this chapter, "Intellectual Property What?"), the ASX format provides a minimal level of security inherent in the way that it is used. For example, when a user clicks a link to an ASX file, the browser downloads it to the cache directory, launches Windows Media Player, and then starts streaming the audio file that the ASX file points to—meaning casual listeners would have to dig a little deeper to find the audio file itself, write it to their drive, and distribute it at their own discretion.

If you want to find out more about the Windows Media format, go to **http://www.microsoft.com/windowsmedia/.**

Real Audio

If you spend any time at all surfing the Internet, then you've certainly heard of Real Audio. As the audio-only part of the RealMedia file format, Real Audio is well suited to very high compression rates and streaming audio.

This means that even on a slow modem (like a 28.8 Kbps modem) you can almost immediately start listening to a song as it downloads rather than having to wait for the whole file to download to your computer's hard drive. This makes Real Audio ideal for previewing songs online, but less than desirable if you want to provide near-CD quality—unless you use Real's newer G2 format, which provides more options and much better quality compression. To find out more about Real Audio, surf on over to **www.real.com.**

Getting Your Music Out There

You understand how MP3 files and other Internet audio file formats work now. You've downloaded a suitable MP3 encoder and converted all your recordings to MP3.

You're ready for the next step—getting the music up there, out there, and online-there—and it's only a matter of time before Amazon.com picks up your music for distribution.

Sound far-fetched? Maybe. Maybe not—artists are starting to make money and truly are getting exposure on the Internet now. Go read some of the success stories over at MP3.com if you're skeptical.

It is going to take some work, though. You need to put the guitar down, don your marketing hat, think of what you want to say about your music and the "image" you want to project, and decide where you want your music to be available online. The rest of this chapter will guide you through these steps, starting with setting up your own Web site.

If you want to be noticed, you need a dedicated Web presence for your music. No bones about it, and there's no objection you can make that holds water, unless you don't have the money—and that one almost doesn't cut it, since Web sites are mighty cheap these days.

Even if your strategy is only to get your music hosted on other Web sites (such as MP3.com), you still need a "home base." Why? Let's look at few reasons.

Timing is Everything

Internet time is very similar to an MP3 file in that it's highly compressed. News, events, new content—these things *can* happen almost instantly when you have the ability to communicate almost instantly. With your own Web site, you can post new music whenever you want, as quickly as you want. You can upload news about the band, your lyrics, gig dates—anything and everything you want to say about the music—in less time than it takes to make your morning coffee. You can also get feedback on your music through the use of a bulletin board, guest book, or your own online chat.

You can do these things through a music site that will host your music—and many of them do a very good job of providing these kinds of services. However, it's not instant: A professional music host site has to accommodate thousands of artists and will need to categorize, verify, and read whatever changes you make to your site. This takes time—from hours to days.

The Look is Important

With your own site, you are completely in charge of the look and feel—the image you want to project to the world. Now, this could be a bad thing if your visual sense is only slightly better than a bat's, but it can be a very good thing if you have a good feel for color and design (or someone you love does!)

Alternatively—presuming you don't have the money to hire a working designer—there are lots of artists on the Web who are looking to add to their resumes. Go to **www.deja.com** and search the discussion areas for Web designers. Make a pot of coffee. By the time you've finished the brew, you'll probably have located a half-dozen students or fledgling designers willing to have an e-mail or two with you.

Don't Limit Yourself

Another downside to keeping your music hosted with an online music service is size. You are limited to how many pages you can have and what formats you can use. While having your own site will come with some limitations, too, they will be far less restrictive than what you'll find at MP3.com or Garageband.com, for example.

Make It Official

Let's face it—having your own Web site adds a certain legitimacy to your music. The world sees it as your gig and yours alone. Though you may have your music on a half-dozen other music sites (and indeed you should, as we'll discuss later), fans have one "official" place to go to get the music or read what's happening with the band, provide feedback, and get the latest tunes. And your business cards and demos are far more impressive with "www.thebeatles.com" on them than "www.mp3.com/thebeatles."

A Little Remuneration, Please

There's also the potential for earning some money from your site. If you choose, you can charge money for downloads, or, more likely, you can participate in link exchange programs, merchandise selling programs, or paid advertisements. You won't get rich by any means, but you may make a few bucks—enough to offset the purchase of that new effects box or DirectX plug-in you've been wanting.

Designing a Web Site

There are very large books—many of them completely worthless and a handful of them very useful—that say an awful lot about Web design. There are books on color theory, user interfaces, understanding the user path, optimizing graphics, and Web programming. There are books on designing in Shockwave, Flash, Dynamic HTML, and JavaScript. There are books on using client-side Java, and there are books on using HTML. Amend that: There are a TON of books on both Java and HTML.

Suffice it to say, all those books exist because a well-designed Web site is not the easiest thing in the world to, well, design. Therefore, this section is not going to attempt to teach you how to become a professional Web designer. What it will do is provide you with a quick, cheap, useful roadmap for putting together your own site by showing you the tools you'll need and a little bit about how to use them.

FrontPage 2000

First things first. If you have a burning desire to understand the inner workings of Figure 19.2, then you do not need to read this section. You may skip it and instead purchase the book *Mastering HTML 4, Premium Edition*, by Deborah and Eric Ray (Sybex, 1999, ISBN 0782125247).

The figure shows an example of the source code behind a typical Web page—in this case, a small part of the HTML source code behind one of the Web pages on David Bowie's Web site. There are two things to notice about this figure: First, the figure shows only a small portion of the source code behind one page—the sign-up page—of the site; and second, there are several thousands of other Web pages very similar to this one that make up **www.davidbowie.com**.

Figure 19.2
This a small part of the HTML source code for BowieNet's sign-up page.

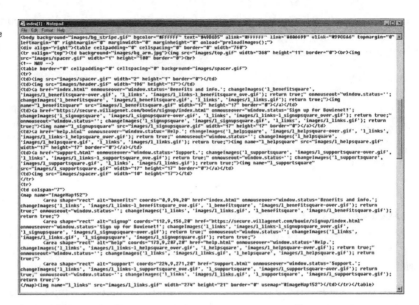

The point here is that you need a tool—a tool to hide all of this source code from you because you do not want to deal with it.

There are a number of tools on the market from which to choose, but we're going to focus on one in particular—a Microsoft product called FrontPage 2000—because it's one of the least expensive, is full-featured, and is the easiest to learn how to use. For example, Figure 19.3 shows the same page on BowieNet loaded into FrontPage 2000, all ready for editing. A little easier to stomach, don't you think?

Figure 19.3
FrontPage 2000 makes Web page editing about as easy as it can possibly be.

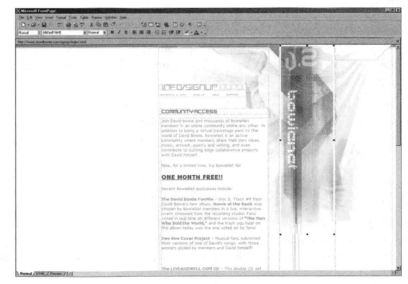

CHAPTER 17

FrontPage is a WYSIWYG (What-You-See-Is-What-You-Get) Web editor. You use it just like you use a word processing program—entering text, adding images, creating links—and the pages you edit look almost exactly the way they're going to look in a Web browser.

NOTE

FrontPage 2000 is available on the shelf at your local software chain or you can buy it online at **http://www.microsoft.com/frontpage/**. At the time of this writing, it can be bought for $149 as a standalone product or it can be purchased as part of the Microsoft Office 2000 suite.

An Overview of FrontPage

After obtaining a copy of FrontPage, you'll be led through an installation wizard and, in a few clicks, it will be installed on your PC. FrontPage is well documented and includes a number of tutorials which will get you started using the software in a matter of minutes.

That said, there's a lot to the program. I recommended the following two books—they're written in plain English and cover all you could possibly want to know about FrontPage:

▶ *Sams Teach Yourself Microsoft FrontPage 2000 in 21 Days*, by Denise Tyler (Macmillan Computer Publishing, 1999, ISBN 0672314991)

▶ *Complete Idiot's Guide to Microsoft FrontPage 2000*, by Elisabeth Parker (Macmillan Computer Publishing, 1999, ISBN 0789718065)

The FrontPage interface excels in the way it allows multiple views of a given Web page: You can view the Web page the way it looks, yet edit its text and images on the spot (using "Normal" Mode), view and edit the dreaded HTML source in HTML Mode, and preview the page in Preview Mode.

FrontPage Features

You can also view all the files that make up your Web site, run reports to find slow pages and older files, set up your site's navigational structure, and very easily keep track of the pages you're creating.

For example, you can create and edit Web pages in Page View, adding tables and links, graphics, thumbnail images, frames, search forms, hit counters, and numbered or bulleted lists. You can then use Folders View to see all the content on your Web and set up how your pages link to each other in Navigation View.

FrontPage also comes with more than sixty pre-designed "themes," most of which are tacky and unusable but a few of which you might actually find appealing.

FrontPage Basics: A QuickStart Tutorial

To give you a feel for how easy it is to get up and running with FrontPage, this section will walk you through getting started with the FrontPage editor—probably the most useful part of the software and the one you'll use the most.

Figure 19.4 shows the basic editing interface you'll see when working in FrontPage. To the left is the Views Bar, which allows you to quickly change to different views of your Web page, such as the Navigation View for creating navigation buttons and viewing the navigational structure of your site or the Tasks View for adding tasks to your project.

Figure 19.4
The FrontPage 2000 editing interface is similar to a typical word processing program.

When you're working in the FrontPage editor, you really don't need to have the Views Bar up. You can hide it very easily by selecting the View menu on the menu bar and simply removing the check in front of the Views Bar selection, as shown in Figure 19.5.

Figure 19.5
Removing the Views Bar is easy.

With the FrontPage editing interface staring us in the face, let's type in some text and do something key to the whole concept of the Web: create a link.

A link (short for "hyperlink"), as you probably know, is the connection you make between Web pages. When you click on a link in your Web browser, the browser interprets that link as the location of another Web page either on your site (a local link) or another Web site (an external link). You can embed a link in text or in images on your Web pages.

Let's add some links! We'll start by adding a link to another Web site—we'll use BowieNet—and then add a link to what could be another page on your own site.

To create the first link:

1. Type in the text: Check out BowieNet! It's a very cool site and Bowie rocks!

2. Highlight "BowieNet."

3. From the Insert menu on the menu bar, select Hyperlink to open the Create Hyperlink dialog box (see Figure 19.6).

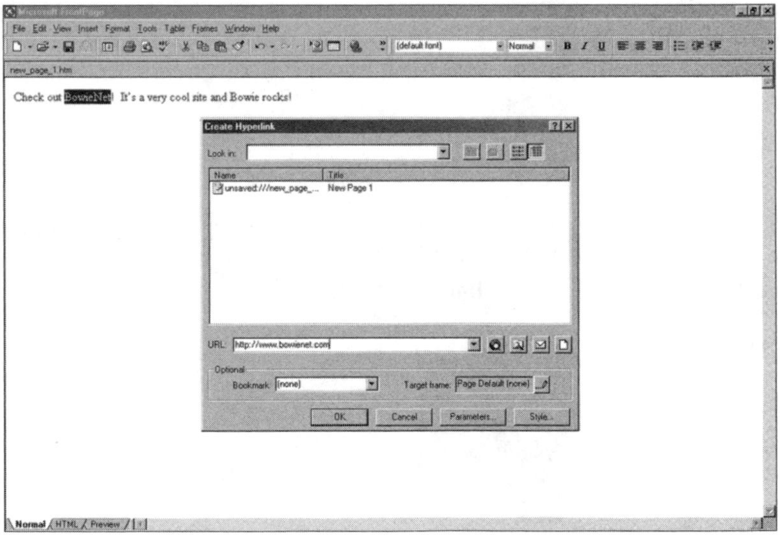

Figure 19.6
Make a link to BowieNet using the Create Hyperlink dialog box.

4. In the URL textbox, after the "http://" prefix, enter the following text: www.bowienet.com

5. Select OK to close the dialog box and save the link.

6. Hit the Return key on your keyboard and type in the following text: Click here for my other Bowie links.

7. Highlight the word "here."

8. This time, right-click on the highlighted word and select Hyperlink (see Figure 19.7) to open the same Create Hyperlink dialog box.

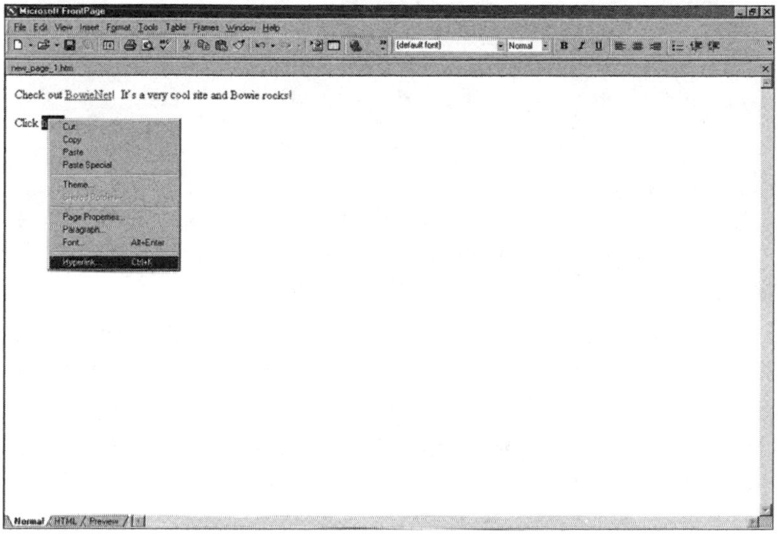

Figure 19.7
You can right-click on a highlighted word to access the Hyperlink dialog box.

9. In the URL textbox, highlight the "http://" prefix, delete it, and type: mybowielinks.html

10. Select OK to close the dialog box and save the link.

Notice this time that you didn't need the "http://" part of the link, since you are (for the purposes of this example) linking to a *local* page on your site—not another Web site. Linking to a local page on your own site only requires that you enter the name of the file, not the full Internet-prefixed address. Now click the Preview tab in FrontPage Editor. This is how your Web page will look to the world (see Figure 19.8).

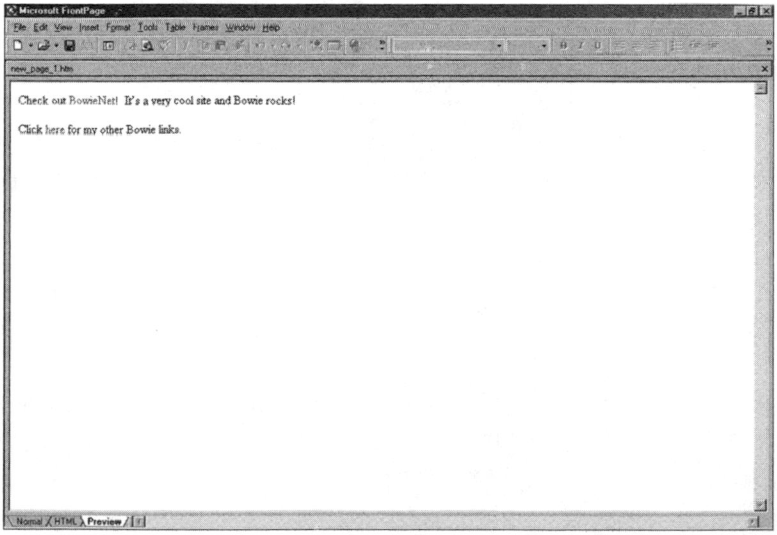

Figure 19.8
Working links for Web visitors to click on.

Not terribly exciting, but you get the idea. If you click on the BowieNet link, it will take you to BowieNet (if your Internet connection is active). On the other hand, if you click on your "here" link, you'll generate a "This page cannot be displayed" error. Don't worry—this is only because you haven't created the page mybowielinks.html yet!

Web Graphics

Now that you have a taste of how easy it is to add a link to a Web page, you'll be happy to know that adding an image to your Web page is just as easy. That's the good news. The bad news is that creating good-looking images is not nearly so easy.

Creating compelling images requires that you have a good software application for drawing and working with your images, and that program should also support exporting those image to Internet-ready formats—mainly GIF and JPEG image files.

If you buy FrontPage, it comes with an excellent image editing application called Image Composer, shown in Figure 19.9.

Figure 19.9
Image Composer is excellent for manipulating Web graphics.

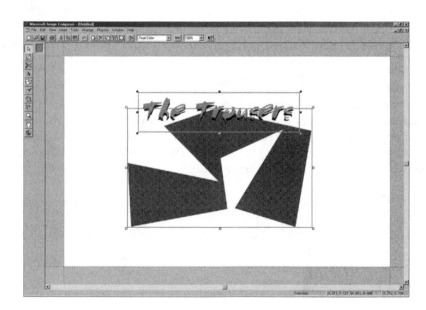

Another inexpensive, yet very powerful, graphics application is Paint Shop Pro. A free, 30-day evaluation of Paint Shop Pro is available for download (**www.jasc.com**), and the full version can be purchased for about $100, at the time of this writing, from Jasc online or from your local software retailer.

Paint Shop Pro (Figure 19.10) is particularly good for drawing Web graphics and is very good at optimizing your graphics in the GIF and JPEG formats.

There are a number of resources available for working with Image Composer (**www.microsoft.com/frontpage/**) and, as luck would have it, Muska & Lipman has a book available which covers all the ins and outs of Paint Shop Pro 7. The book is *Paint Shop Pro Web Graphics, Third Edition*, by Andy Shafran and Lori J. Davis, (2000, ISBN 1-929685-13-0) and is comprehensive and well written.

Figure 19.10
Paint Shop Pro is one of the most popular graphics programs on the Web.

Web Hosting

Once you've created your Web pages, the next step is to find a place to put them—a server where you can store your Web site for access by anyone with an Internet connection.

This is a process that involves several steps. The first one is to locate a reputable hosting company that you can afford to host your site. The second step is to decide if you need your own Web site address or if you're happy using the base Web address of the hosting company. The third step is to learn how to upload your files to your new site.

CHAPTER 17

Hosting Services

Web hosting is simply paying for space on another computer that has a Web server and a high-speed connection to the Internet. The host computer will "serve" your Web site to your adoring fans.

There are hundreds of reputable Web hosting services these days and perhaps a few that aren't so reputable. Plans and prices can sometimes vary by quite a bit, so it's worth doing some research to see what kinds of deals are available.

At the time of this writing, a typical plan costs about $20 per month and looks something like this:

- 125 MB of disk storage
- 3 GB data transfer per month
- 25 e-mail accounts
- 24-hr FTP access
- CGI-BIN + free scripts
- Graphical statistics and raw logs
- Real Audio/Video support
- 99.9 percent up-time guarantee

As you can see, an average plan gives you some limitations on how much storage space you can have for Web pages, how active your site can be (for example, no more than 3 gigabytes of data transfer—or "thruput"—per month is allowed), how many e-mail accounts you can have, and so on.

The best approach is to start off small and see where it leads you. In the above example, 125 MB of disk space and 3 GB of thruput is plenty of storage and bandwidth to get your started, and you'll probably have to think for awhile to figure out how you can use twenty-five e-mail accounts.

Probably the most important thing to look for is reputation. What you want to avoid is hosting with a company that has a lot of technical problems with its equipment, uses sub-standard equipment, or has bad customer service.

Budgetweb.com and The Ultimate Web Host List (**webhostlist.internetlist.com**) are both excellent sites for researching Web-hosting services, and Yahoo! also maintains a long list of companies.

Make sure you go out to Deja (**www.deja.com**) and search for information in the discussions area about different Web hosting companies. In addition to being a consumer product review site, Deja publishes and updates messages from thousands of newsgroups, and you're very likely to find information on the companies you're curious about.

There are also a number of free hosting services available. The most used are:

- GeoCities (**www.geocities.com**)
- Tripod (**www.tripod.com**)
- Angelfire (**www.angelfire.com**)
- FreeTown (**www.freetown.com**)
- ACMEcity (**www.acmecity.com**)

Free hosting services will typically offer chat, e-mail, and Web pages, but they have far greater limitations on space and bandwidth.

Domain Names

When it comes to a domain name, there are essentially two choices:

▶ Your own unique domain name, e.g. www.yourname.com, which you purchase through a domain name provider. A list of all the domain name providers is available at **www.icann.org**. Many Web hosting companies will also register the domain for you. The cost is currently around $35 per year or less.

▶ A "piggyback" URL, i.e., www.yourwebhost.com/yourname, or possibly yourname.yourwebhost.com, which doesn't require registration and can be set up on virtually any Web host. This is the format that free Web-hosting companies use as well.

It almost goes without saying that, if you can afford it, go with a unique domain name.

Uploading Your Site

Once you've enlisted a Web hosting company to host your site, you'll typically be given an FTP account with which to upload files and manage the files that are on your site. FTP stands for file transfer protocol, and it's the standard for uploading and downloading files to and from a Web site.

NOTE

FrontPage 2000 also includes an alternative to using standalone FTP software, by allowing you to "publish" your site directly to the server, as long as your host server has FrontPage extensions installed. The process is very simple and akin to copying and pasting files in Windows Explorer!

To use FTP, you'll need a piece of software that knows FTP commands. Several good ones exist, and the two very good ones are LeechFTP (freeware) and WS-FTP (inexpensive shareware). Both can found at **www.stroud.com**.

The process of FTP is really as simple as copying files in Windows Explorer—and, in all reality, that's exactly what you're doing, copying files. The only difference is, you're copying files from your computer to another computer, instead of copying them from one folder to another on the same computer.

Intellectual Property What?

This chapter wouldn't be complete without a few words concerning intellectual property rights as they pertain to the Internet. It's a bit of a touchy subject, for a couple of reasons.

First, just how concerned should you be? Do you need to worry about someone making claim to your work—or making money from it—once it's available to anyone with a connection? Second, how do you protect your work, and what kind of protection do you need?

The Law

You may be aware of the changes made to U.S. copyright law in 1978. On January 1 of that year, a completely new copyright statute, the Copyright Act of 1976 (Public Law 94-553), came into effect in the United States, superseding the Copyright Act of 1909. The law applies to creators of "original works of authorship," including literary, dramatic, musical, artistic, and certain other intellectual works.

The law protects both published and unpublished works, and the protection exists from the time the work is created in fixed form; that is, it is an "incidence of the process of authorship." The copyright in the work of authorship immediately becomes the property of the author who created it. Only the author or those deriving their rights can rightfully claim copyright.

So, the bottom line is that, technically speaking, U.S. law provides the ability for you to establish grounds with which to seek redress if someone rips off your work.

The Reality

You can practically throw copyright law out the door when it comes to the Internet and your music. To begin with, although a number of other countries (Japan, the U.K., and Germany, for example) do recognize copyrights—even if the copyright for a particular work is not registered in their home country—not every country does. So that's one risk: On the Internet, your work is available to the whole world.

The reality is that, once your music is online, you'll be hard-pressed to decide who can download it and who can't—and even then, you ultimately have no idea where it will end up. And if that weren't enough, there is a lot of debate going right now about what is legal and what is not in the online music world. Recent lawsuits over the rights of recording artists, the RIAA, Napster, and MP3.com have shown that there are no clear answers yet.

You'll need to decide how much the issue of protecting your own work means to you. Perhaps the best advice is to not worry about it—to just let it happen—it's hard enough just to get the music noticed, let alone worry about who "owns" it and who doesn't. On the other hand, you may not feel comfortable with the openness of Internet—in which case, about the only thing you can truly do is not to participate at all.

If you do participate, here are a few tips for watching your music's backside:

- ▶ Post copyright notices on your Web site, using the © symbol and specifying that you own your own work.
- ▶ Make sure that when you encode your music for the Internet, your name and the copyright mark © are included. This is done through the ID3 tagging format for MP3 files—almost all of the MP3 software available allows you to tag your music with ID3.
- ▶ Read the license agreements carefully when you sign up to post your music on other Web sites. If you feel uncomfortable at all about the legalese, get a lawyer to check the verbiage for you.
- ▶ Check the sites where your music is available on a regular basis. See how they're approaching the delivery of the site's content and ensure that you're comfortable with their practices and policies.

18

Promoting and Marketing Your Music

If you want your music to be heard, you'll have to know a thing or two about marketing and promoting it. This chapter will show you the basic ropes and dive into the details where it makes sense, including coverage of these topics:

▶ The basics of promoting your music

▶ Marketing your music using the Internet

▶ Using search engines and directories

▶ Advertising and affiliate programs

Promoting Your Music

Promoting your music is a big topic, and there are several good books that have been written on it. *All You Need to Know About the Music Business*, by Donald S. Passman and Randy Glass (Simon & Schuster, 2000, ISBN 0684870649) is excellent, as is *This Business of Music Marketing and Promotion*, by Tad Lathrop and Jim Pettigrew (Billboard Books, 1999, ISBN 082307711X).

Although it would be impossible to try to distill the kinds of insights and details these books bring to the table, we'll touch on some fundamental tips for how to promote your music.

Have a Marketing Plan

You don't have to be a marketing manager at Proctor & Gamble to know the basics. First, write down some clear and practical goals you have for distributing your work. You'll be amazed at how useful writing it all down can be: It brings the reasons why you want to promote your work into focus.

Think about your own "hot buttons" as a consumer of music: What makes you spend your own money on a new recording? What attracts you most to music you'll pay money for? Is it the radio, television, the Rolling Stone review, live performances, the Internet? Write down the areas in which your CDs will have the best chance of being noticed, then prioritize which ones you can tackle.

CHAPTER 18

If you live near a college town, for example, getting a little radio time may not be all that difficult. Many college towns will set aside time to play local artists on fairly regular basis. The same is true for college newspapers—in fact, if you have any writing skills at all, penning an article about the CD and your music yourself and pitching it to the paper could be the slight edge you need to get the word out.

A Little Airplay Would Be Nice!

Radio airplay remains the defacto method for promoting popular music. Do a little research and find out where the radio stations in your area are located. Prepare a CD and print a bio sheet describing your music and either mail or hand-deliver your music to stations that you think would be interested in playing your style.

Local radio stations sometimes do compilation CDs of local artists as well. Look at the check-out counters of local music stores to see if any have been offered in your area, or ask the stations themselves.

Another option is public broadcasting. Many public television stations still set aside TV airtime for local announcements as well as locally produced programs. It wouldn't be unusual to get a music video played on one of these stations.

Send Press Releases

Send press releases to all local media about your new CD. Talk about the CD, talk about the tracks, and give a short bio about yourself. Keep press releases short and to the point. Even small radio and TV stations receive a slew of press releases every day, so a pithy, well-written release stands a greater chance of being used. Send a copy of your CD along with the press release, and if you're playing gigs, note any upcoming live performances.

Believe it or not, large books have been written about press releases. Take a trip down to the library and get a handle on standard press release formats—you'll stand a much better chance that way of getting them noticed by the media.

Marketing Your Music

Guess what? Once you establish your Web presence, transfer your Web site's files to the host server, and choose a Web address, you're halfway home! Okay—maybe a little more than halfway—but that depends on how much stock you put in the idea of marketing and advertising your music online.

One thing's for sure—if you don't take the time to advertise yourself, you're not going to create a lot of fans. It's the irony of being a home recording artist rearing its ugly head again: Sometimes you have to spend so much time doing things that have nothing to do with the music that the music almost becomes secondary.

Still, using the Internet to boost your audience is not difficult—only time-consuming. All of the resources in this section are easy to grasp and many of them are free or cheap, so the only thing that can potentially keep you from making yourself known is how much time you can devote to it. And that's a long way from where home studio enthusiasts were a few years ago, when there was a lot more time than money (and there wasn't much money, then, either).

Music Sites That Want You

There are a number of Web sites that want your music available to their listeners, and many of them attract huge numbers of visitors per day—far more listeners than you'll likely ever get to your home site.

These sites are your number-one source for online marketing, and they represent the best kind of marketing, because the focus is almost always on the music.

MP3.com

MP3.com is the mother of all music Web sites for getting your music heard. Make no mistake about it—if you're a home recording artist, you should be on MP3.com. Because of its huge traffic (more than 10 million visitors per month, at the time of this writing), joining MP3.com is almost a guarantee that your recording will be heard by thousands of music lovers (potentially millions).

MP3.com also has a number of tools—from online radio stations to a daily ranking system—to help you market yourself effectively online as well as earn money. It's free to join, and there are no maintenance fees.

MP3.com provides Web pages for your music, showcases tunes on a daily (sometimes hourly) basis, allows for pictures and other artist information, and allows you to update your pages fairly quickly. The site also has a large and very active online bulletin board system, so getting feedback on your latest recording can be very swift.

MP3.com also has a unique program that enables it to make CDs of your music and sell them online. So far, the deal has always been a straight-up 50/50 split, which is very reasonable, considering that they cut and manufacture the CDs, market them, and handle all of the accounting. Most artists get a check for a few dozen dollars every quarter—but some have made thousands, and a few have made hundreds of thousands of dollars from the online sale of their CDs.

Garageband.com

Garageband.com is a fascinatingly cool concept: You can upload your tunes only after you've reviewed other songs. In turn, other artists review your tunes for the same reason. Pretty neat, hey? The result is that you get a lot of constructive (and occasionally not-so-constructive) criticism (see Figure 18.1) about your music, the mix, the lyrics—everything—from other musicians as well as the listening public, who may also do reviews.

Figure 18.1

A typical listing of a band's reviews by Garageband.com listeners.

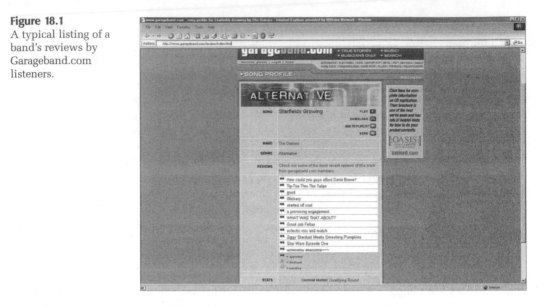

Songs that consistently get high rankings may get promoted to "The Final Countdown," a final round of reviewing to determine a winning artist, who will earn a $250,000 recording contract from Garageband.com for a stated review period. The process claims to be 100 percent merit-based and 100 percent-driven by the reviews of music lovers, and it appears to be a very fair way to decide which new artists get big breaks.

Oh, yeah, one other thing: Garageband.com also claims that there's always the potential for one of its advisory board members to jump in and offer a deal to an artist on the spot. This is not necessarily a major claim, until you look at their list of advisory board members, which reads like a Who's Who list of recording producers and engineers. Names like Sir George Martin, Brian Eno, and Steve Earle are enough to make you think twice about the possibilities.

RollingStone.com

Rolling Stone magazine has thrown its hat into the online music ring, too, with a well-developed section for home recording artists called MP3 & More. The site lets you post and update your bio, photos, lyrics, and tour schedules, and it tracks the number of downloads your music receives.

There is also a chance to get your music heard by Rolling Stone's roster of music critics. Rolling Stone editors will listen to MP3 tracks, rate ten they like the best every couple of weeks, and highlight them on the front page of MP3 & More. This is a very cool opportunity considering that, just a few years ago, there was only one way to get reviewed by Rolling Stone—if you were signed to a major record label.

IUMA (iuma.com)

The Internet Underground Music Archive is an excellent place to gain exposure to your music. You get a Web address with your band name first (for example, daisies.iuma.com for the band "The Daisies") and a custom Web page where you can post all your band info and MP3s, sell CDs, create message boards and fan lists, and get e-mail from fans. The service is free.

The IUMA interface is very well designed, and navigating the site is intuitive and easy. Artists are categorized by the musical genres you'd expect. Visitors can do a full-text search (see Figure 18.2), sample tunes in Real Audio, and then download the MP3s when they find something they like. There is also a large community and message board area, as well as streaming IUMA Radio.

Figure 18.2
A search result for "The Daisies" on IUMA.

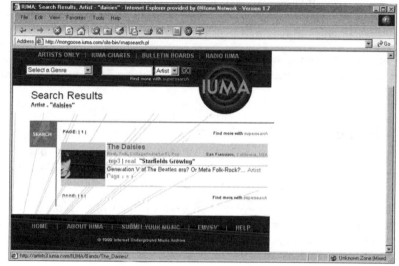

CMJ

www.cmj.com

CMJ (which stands for College Media Journal) offers a wide array of services for artists, including your own Web site, e-mail, a personalized domain name, and subscription discounts for their magazines. The site is well designed and quick to load.

Though you're limited to uploading three songs, CMJ claims that your uploads will be reviewed by their A&R staff who have "solid contacts throughout the music industry."

It definitely can't hurt.

MusicBuilder.com

MusicBuilder has a number of features similar to MP3.com and is completely free as well. The site offers you your own artist page, a fan mail manager, similar artist search, location search, and a searchable gig calendar.

Like MP3.com, you can setup an Artist CD, and MusicBuilder will handle all of the manufacturing (and distribution, if you like). They will burn the CD, professionally print the CD and the cover art provided by you, add a printed tray card, slip it all into a jewel case, and ship it. The site requires that you sell the CD for a minimum of $5.95—they take the first $4.95 to pay for it all and the rest is your profit.

MusicBuilder also runs promotions where you can earn free banner advertising on their site, and there are no limits to how many songs you can post. Statistics and reports about your site's visitors are also very well done.

Listen.com

Listen.com isn't quite as easy to get listed on. Click on the "Add Artist" link from the main page and you can fill out a form requesting to be included on the site. Listen.com staff reviewers will review your music and decide if it gets listed.

The site doesn't provide artist services to speak of, but it does do a solid job of listing bands and reviews, and it's worth mentioning here for its high traffic numbers—which are, incidentally, very high.

Search Engines and Directories

Sites that specialize in searching and cataloging the Web are some of the most heavily used sites on the Web themselves. In fact, most "top ten" lists of the largest Web sites will include many of the search engine and directory sites.

This is no surprise, really—the Web comprises millions of Web pages and it's hard to know what's out there without someone to index it all for you. The great thing about these sites is that you can get listed on them—thereby increasing traffic to your site—and, in most cases, it's totally free.

This section lists the sites you'll want to register with, and they fall into two categories: search engines and directories.

A search engine site employs applications (often called "spiders" or "Web bots") that crawl Web sites twenty-four hours a day, following links and taking notes. These spiders then funnel the information back to the search engine site to be index and published. A directory doesn't use spiders; instead, real people surf the sites, follow links, and write summaries about them to be indexed. The advantage to search engines is that they uncover more pages and are more up-to-date. Directories, on the other hand (Yahoo!, for example), generally do a better job describing what a Web site is really all about.

Although search engines and directories have different approaches to how they index the Web, they don't vary nearly as much in their submission practices and requirements. Almost all of them expect you to have a few key things before you submit your Web address.

▶ **Describe Yourself.** Write a brief description of your site that reflects what it's about. Spend some time on this, and keep it short— less than twenty-five words. Though you'll want to accurately describe what's on the site and make your site appealing to users, stray away from clichés and "marketing" words, like "the future of rock and roll" or "amazing musical sound quality" and the like. Get to the heart of what your site—and your music—is.

▶ **Keywords and Keyword Phrases.** Submit or suggest keywords that describe the site. These are words that a prospective visitor would type in to find you. For example, if your songs are country songs that sound like Johnny Cash, your keyword phrases might include the name of your band, "Johnny Cash," "Country Music," and so forth. In general, try to keep the list of keyword phrases a short one. Four to six phrases are plenty for a given Web page.

▶ **Make the Page Match the Content.** Write copy on your pages that accurately reflects the content. For example, if you have a lyrics page, preface the lyrics with a paragraph or two explicitly describing what's on the page and where the lyrics come from. Though it may seem like overkill, the search engines love it— which makes sense, because search engines need to be able to describe the page before a new user gets to it.

NOTE

Web pages can also contain something called "metatags," which are really just hidden keywords and a description of the page to help spiders when they index it. It's a good idea to put metatags in all of your Web pages, and as a minimum it's good practice to use the same description and keywords you might submit to the search engine and directory sites.

If you're using FrontPage 2000, adding metatags is easy:

1. In Page view, right-click the page and then click Page Properties on the shortcut menu.

2. Click the Custom tab.

3. Under User variables, click Add.

4. In the Name box, type the name of the metatag. For a description, type "Description." For keywords, type "Keywords."

5. In the Value box, type the your description and keywords, respectively.

CHAPTER 18

Yahoo!

www.Yahoo!.com

Yahoo! is the Web's most popular directory service and has a well-deserved reputation for helping users find information easily. Yahoo! is the largest human-compiled guide to the Web and employs hundreds of editors in its efforts. With more than one million sites listed, it's one of the best, and you definitely want a listing on Yahoo!.

Yahoo! is the oldest major Web site directory, having launched in late 1994, and so the site has had a lot of time to figure out what works and what doesn't. The number-one rule when submitting to Yahoo!—submit only your primary domain name or main page, and do it only once.

Open Directory

www.dmoz.org

Open Directory uses volunteer editors to catalog the Web, and the company pledges that anyone and everyone may use information from the directory through an open license arrangement. Several sites, including Lycos, AOL Search, AltaVista and Hotbot, currently feature Open Directory categories within their results pages.

Open Directory is less picky than Yahoo! about the strength of your site, its description, and your keywords, but a listing in the Open Directory is just as important because of its open license approach.

GoTo

www.goto.com

Unlike the other search engines, GoTo sells its listings, meaning you can pay money to be placed higher in the search results, which GoTo feels improves relevancy. It does have non-paid search results, however. GoTo launched in 1997 and incorporated the former University of Colorado-based World Wide Web Worm.

GoTo is listed here because it garners a large amount of traffic, but you may want to put this one on the shelf until you see how well you do with the other, free services.

AltaVista

www.altavista.com

AltaVista is one of the largest search engines on the Web in terms of quantity. Its comprehensive coverage and power searching capabilities have made it particularly popular among experienced Web users. It also offers a number of features designed to appeal to basic users, such as "Ask AltaVista" results, and it also provides directory listings from the Open Directory.

If you only have time to list with one search engine, this is the one.

Excite

www.excite.com

Excite is one of the most popular search services on the Web. It has a medium-sized index and integrates non-Web material such as secondary sources of information and sports scores into its results to provide more descriptive listings. Excite was launched in late 1995 and grew quickly in prominence, even buying two of its competitors (Magellan in July 1996 and WebCrawler in November 1996).

Go.com

www.go.com

Go is mainly a portal site produced by Infoseek and Disney, but it also provides search services. Go is very good at providing high-quality and relevant search results, thanks to the type of search algorithms it uses, but it also has an impressive human-compiled directory of Web sites as well.

LookSmart

www.looksmart.com

LookSmart is yet another human-compiled directory of Web sites. In addition to being its own independent Web service, the company provides directory results to MSN Search, Excite, and other partners. AltaVista provides LookSmart with search results when a search fails to find a match from among LookSmart's reviews.

Google

www.google.com

Google is a search engine that makes heavy use of "link popularity" to rank Web sites. The idea is that the more popular a site is, the more other pages will link to it. This can be especially helpful in finding good sites in response to general searches for music, because users across the Web have upped the results rankings by linking to them.

The success of Google is good reason to get your site listed on as many other services and Web sites as possible.

HotBot

www.hotbot.com

HotBot is similar to AltaVista and is revered for its large index of the Web and its power-search options. The site also gets directory information from the Open Directory. HotBot was purchased by Lycos in 1998 but continues to be run as a separate search service.

Lycos

www.lycos.com

Lycos started out as an independent search engine, indexing its own search results. In 1999, it shifted to a directory model similar to Yahoo!. Its main listings come from the Open Directory, but secondary results come from its own spidering of the Web.

Lycos is very popular and well worth a listing. It's a good site to list multiple pages, provided each page has distinct content.

CHAPTER 18

Northern Light

www.northernlight.com

Northern Light features a very large index, can categorize documents by topic, and is very well designed. When you submit to Northern Light, you submit only your top-level or primary domain name, and no other pages. Their spider is good enough to find all of the pages on your sites.

Northern Light also sells pay-per-view information that is not typically accessible to search engine spiders. These are documents from other sources, such as newswires and magazines. You can search the collection for free, but, at the time of this writing, Northern Light charges up to $4 to see individual documents.

Search Engine Watch

www.searchenginewatch.com

Search Engine Watch is not actually a search service, but it is listed here because it is far and away the best place on the Web to learn more about the whole business of search engines and directories. The site keeps up with everything that's happening in the search engine "community" on a daily basis and offers a number of informative, detailed articles about how to use search services more effectively. The site is maintained by Danny Sullivan, an experienced editor and professional journalist.

Advertising

As your Web site grows, there are a few things you can do to earn revenue from your Web site—and there are a number of opportunities to spend money getting the word out.

You may have heard about "ad engines" or ad services such as Double-Click or AdForce. While buying and selling advertising to support your music is a beautiful idea, the reality that it's big business, big money, and not something you should invest any brain cells in until your site is well over the 10,000-visitor-per-day mark. And unless you're planning on launching your own dot-com, that isn't going to happen any time soon.

Still, there a few things you can do. One of them is looking for inexpensive banner space deals on small to mid-sized sites that might be happy to take anything you can offer. They might even offer you banner space in exchange for a link or banner on your site.

This can be an effective means of advertising if you can get exposure across many sites—and it will also help your rankings on Google.com, as discussed in the last section. Look for small- to mid-sized Web sites that have visitors who would be interested in your site's content. Sometimes this means more than just your music. For example, if you are a highly lyrical songwriter, cross-listing your site with poetry Web sites by pointing to your lyrics page could be a clever way to get new listeners interested in your music. And there a large number of small zine and journal sites that focus on poetry.

Another example might be the kind of recording equipment you use. If you've become the definitive expert on your DAW setup, why not write an article about it and post it on your Web site? Sites that do equipment reviews (like **www.harmonycentral.com**, for example) or sites that sell gear (**www.zzounds.com**, or **www.musiciansfriend.com**) might just find your article interesting enough to link to you, and this ultimately means more exposure to your recordings.

If you do any linking or advertising on other sites, it pays to put together some banner ads to put on those sites. Having a banner ad is much more effective than just a text-based link.

NOTE

Using e-mail is one of the most powerful (and cheap) online tools available to you. An excellent way to advertise is through the use of an e-mail newsletter, either your own homegrown, periodic updates (using any e-mail software) or by buying ad space in an existing newsletter that reaches people in your audience. E-mail advertising typically generates a higher response than any other online advertising method.

Banner Ads

While you can hire a designer to create a banner ad for you, if you've acquired even basic Web or graphics skills, creating your own banner isn't too difficult. In fact, there is even ad creation software that can make it easy for you to create banners whether you're artistic or not.

A banner ad can vary widely in its design—it can really be just about anything you want it to be—but most sites will require that the size of the banner be one of several specific sizes, as shown in Table 18.1. In addition, banner ads almost always have technical requirements. For example, a banner ad is typically several frames of animation, so its format must be the GIF file format (the JPEG format doesn't support animation). There are also limitations on the size of the GIF: generally, it should be less than 15 Kb for a full-sized banner to less than 3 Kb for a button-sized ad, though many sites have even tighter file size restrictions.

Table 18.1
Banner Ad Sizes

Banner Type	Pixel Size
Full Banner	468×60
Half Banner	234×60
Square Button	125×125
Button Style	120×90 or 120×60
Small Button	88×31
Vertical Banner	120×240

What Makes a Good Banner Ad?

Just like a memorable pop song that has a "hook," a well-designed banner ad should also hook viewers into wanting to click it. For example, you could feature your most creative song title in the ad, or your most interesting band photo.

The graphics should generally be bold and clear—not subtle and muted. This is because your ad will be competing with all the other content on a given page, and possibly other ads as well. Try to keep the animation limited to three or four frames, but pause the frames long enough so that the viewer has plenty of time to read them or to "get it."

CHAPTER 18

Here are some other tips:

▶ Obtain some good GIF animation software for creating banner ads. Microsoft makes a plug-in for Image Composer called Microsoft GIF Animator (**www.microsoft.com/imagecomposer/**), and Paint Shop Pro comes with an excellent program called Animation Shop (**www.jasc.com**). Another good choice is Adobe's ImageReady application, which works on both Mac and Windows (**www.adobe.com**).

▶ Use simple, readable fonts—not fancy spaced-out characters.

▶ Always include your Web address in the ad. If the viewer doesn't click through to your site, you at least want her to remember the address!

▶ Create a static version in addition to the animated one, since some sites don't accept animated ads (usually due to file size).

The Medium is the Message: Audio Advertising

An increasingly interesting option these days is audio and radio advertising via the Internet. It's getting to be popular and is particularly well-suited to online music.

The simplest example of doing audio advertising is to mix an audio message referring to your Web site in the song itself—either at the beginning or end of the song. Something like, "Visit thebeatles.com to hear more!" works just fine. Then, as you sign up with music sites and make your material more widely available, listeners have an immediate reference to where to find more. Of course, this approach could also be potentially irritating to the listener—it's up to you to decide how far you can go with it.

There are also a slew of Internet broadcasting sites that do audio advertising, usually inserting ads before the music starts that run 10-15 seconds long. Broadcast.com, for example, has been doing this for some time.

These "lead-in" advertisements can be implemented in any file format, but the tools that come with both RealMedia and Windows Media are better suited for it. In fact, RealMedia has created an extension to its RealServer product for this purpose. See **realnetworks.com/products/update/advertising.html** for details.

NOTE

For a comprehensive primer on online broadcasting, see the book, *Online Broadcasting Power!*, by Ben Sawyer and Dave Greely (Muska & Lipman, 2001, ISBN 0-9662889-8-X). The book discusses everything from the technical aspects of broadcasting online to the legal issues, teaches you how to promote your station, and covers the latest software, such as SHOUTcast, icecast, RealAudio, Windows Media Audio, and myCaster.

Bringing in a Little Income

It's worth mentioning that you can bring in some extra income from your Web site by participating in affiliate programs. Affiliate programs—or "associate stores," as they're sometimes called—allow you to earn a commission by sending visitors from your site to the Web retailer sponsoring the affiliate program. If one of your site's viewers ends up making a purchase, you get the commission, usually a small percentage of the sale.

But What About the Music, Man?

Affiliate stores are not everybody's gig. Some people feel funny about making over their site into a virtual storefront, just to make a few extra bucks. And you will ultimately be giving your listeners one more reason to jump from your site to somewhere else—potentially before they've decided to bookmark it.

On the plus side, you may need a way to help pay your monthly Web hosting fees or offset the cost of your Internet connection or the upgrades you invariably will have to make to your computer.

The most obvious route to consider, since your gig is music, is to offer links to online music stores. You can put up direct links to artists' pages or even to specific albums, which isn't a bad thing if you're a music enthusiast and you want to encourage other people to check out what you think is hot.

You can also add some legitimacy to your links by doing album reviews and making recommendations. In this way, you're not only increasing the likelihood that you'll pick up a sale but also adding something to the dialog by providing useful information to your visitors in any case.

Join affiliate programs that you like—sites that you respect, have used yourself, and that have good customer service. You want every visitor to be a return visitor, and becoming an associate store for a site with a questionable reputation or bad customer service will ultimately reflect poorly on your Web site.

The technical aspects of joining an affiliate program are fairly simple: You typically provide the URL of your Web site and receive pieces of HTML code to embed in the links that go to the retailer's site. These pieces of code contain a unique ID that lets the retailer know that it was you who sent them the customer.

Most affiliate programs will pay you up to 15 percent of the sale, though you are usually required to earn a minimum amount per month (or per quarter) before they cut you a check. That said, the following sections list some of the better programs available.

Amazon.com

www.amazon.com

Amazon.com, originally a small online bookstore, is now the largest e-commerce site on the Web. Though its core business is still books (and, to an increasing degree, music), it now sells or brokers just about everything.

Amazon handles all of the customer service, fulfillment, shipping, and tracking of sales. You can link to Amazon by recommending specific products, by placing an Amazon search box on your site, or by linking to the Amazon home page. There is no charge to join and you can earn up to 15 percent on books featured on your site and 5 percent on all other items. You can check you earnings and traffic reports online at any time.

Barnes & Noble

www.bn.com

Barnes & Noble has been selling books for years and now has a thriving online business. It pays 5 percent for sales of music, software, videos, and gift certificates and up to 7 percent on books and magazines. You can link to the Barnes & Noble main page, featured subject areas, Bargain Book Store, Music Store, and specific title pages or put a Barnes & Noble search box on your site.

Tracking your progress is easy with a number of online reports that allow you to see impressions (how many people viewed your Web page and how often), click-through (people who actually clicked on your ad), orders, shipments, and your commissions.

Borders

www.borders.com

Borders is yet another bookstore that has established an online component to their business. Borders pays up to 7 percent of sales, though you have to produce one million dollars in sales to reach the 7 percent mark. They start paying you when your commissions exceed $50.

CDNow

www.cdnow.com

CDNow sells music and videos, and you can become involved with two different types of affiliate programs.

The first one, Cosmic Credit, is geared toward music lovers, fan sites, and artist sites, and you can make from 7 to 15 percent on purchases made through your links—with a minimum of $100 in earnings needed before CDNow will send you a check.

The second one—dubbed the C2 Program—is a bit different—it's a "co-branding" type of affiliate program. This means that you can link to CDNow content, and participate in special promotions, sales, and contests to provide more than just links to music and videos. In return, it's an exclusive program, according to their site. Both programs are free to join.

TowerRecords.com

www.towerrecords.com

Tower Records is one of the largest record chains in the country, and it is also fast becoming a large online retailer of music and video. TowerRecords.com pays you a straight-up 4 percent on CDs, videos, and DVDs and has no sales quotas. You can recommend titles, add a TowerRecords.com search box to your site, or use a TowerRecords.com banner to link directly to its home page.

Appendix
Home Studio Recording Resources on the Web

The focus of this book has been to get your home studio up and running in a real-world, practical way. The aim has been to show the reality of setting up a home studio and making it all work so that you can start recording, mixing, and distributing your work as soon as possible. The book is comprehensive, but it doesn't—and doesn't attempt—to cover everything.

If you want to take your skill and knowledge further, stay up on the newest equipment and techniques, and communicate with other home recording artists, you'll find several places on the Internet for doing just that. This appendix lists several of the best sites at the time of this writing.

Harmony Central

http://www.harmony-central.com/

Figure A.1

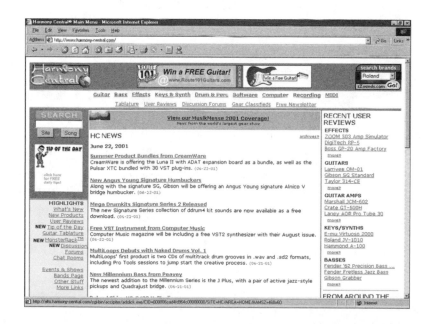

Harmony Central is probably the single best source of information for musicians on the Web right now. Especially popular is its extensive (highly extensive—it would take you weeks to go through its databases) equipment reviews from regular musicians.

The site is very well maintained and updated, just as it has been from its inception in 1995. Harmony Central also reports daily on the music and recording industry. The site is divided into departments: Guitar, Bass, Effects, Software, Recording, MIDI, Keyboard and Synths, Drums and Percussion, Computers and Music, and Bands. It will take you about five minutes to figure out that you need to bookmark this site.

MP3.com

http://www.mp3.com/

Figure A.2

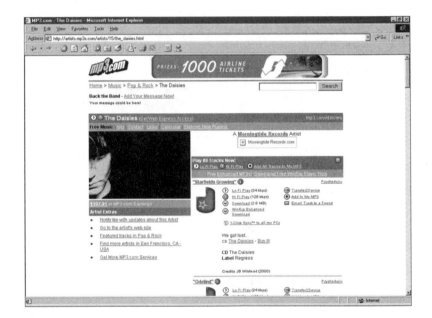

MP3.com is still the mother all online resources for the homegrown recording artist. If you're a home recordist, it's almost a given that your work should presented here, and it's still free.

MP3.com's messageboards boast some of the heaviest activity on the Internet, and they offer free artist pages, Web radio stations, and the cost-free means to market, distribute, and collect real money for your music.

ProRec

http://www.prorec.com/

Figure A.3

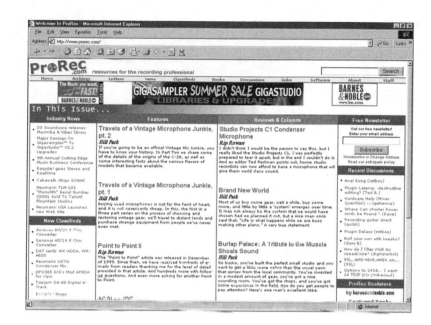

ProRec delivers the goods for pro, semi-pro, and home recording artists geared toward PC digital audio software and hardware. This prolific site contains hundreds of very useful (and entertaining) articles on almost all aspects of digital recording.

ProRec's staff is composed of engineers and producers with extensive knowledge and experience with PC digital audio recording. These guys know what they're talking about, but they haven't forgotten what it was like when they were doing everything out of their garages. In fact, some of them are still doing it from the garage.

Home Recording at About.com

http://homerecording.about.com/

Figure A.4

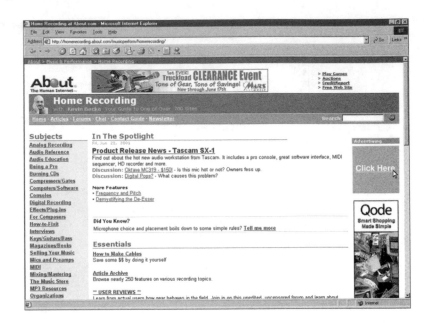

Kevin Becka, a recording engineer, writer, editor, and musician, maintains About.com's comprehensive Web site on Home Recording.

According to Kevin:

"The recording scene has changed dramatically in the last ten years, with modular digital multitrack and hard disk recording decentralizing the industry. The line between consumer and pro audio gear is getting hazier each day, and it's becoming easier to have a great recording studio on a tight budget. I base the site around cutting edge recording techniques along with user reviews, news, an active forum, and a great chat room."

The nice thing about Kevin's comment is that he's right on. The site is updated frequently and provides a large number of home recording articles, online forums, chat, and a newsletter. An excellent resource!

Epanorama.net

http://www.epanorama.net/

Figure A.5

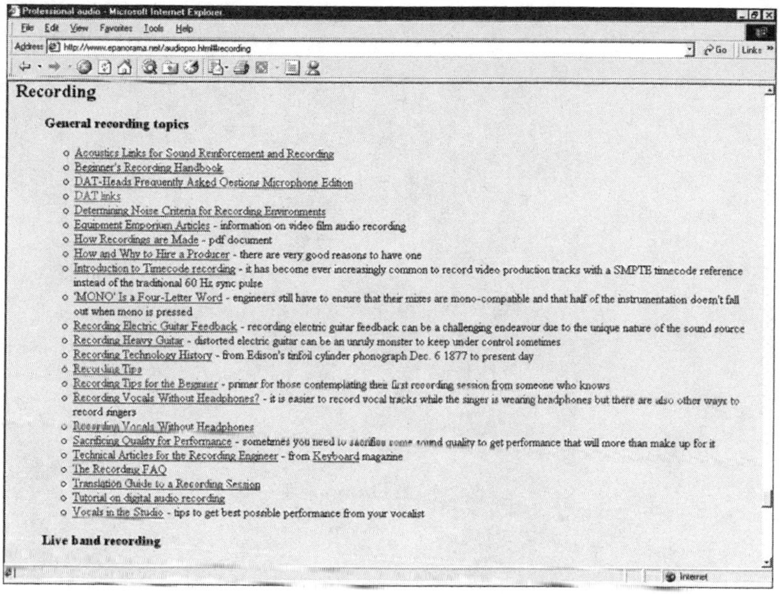

Epanorama.net is an ultra-huge collection of links, articles, and FAQs on anything and everything electronic. The site has very, comprehensive sections on audio, MIDI, and music and oscillator circuitry. This prolific site also has a great deal of information on home electronics and PC hardware. Not to be missed.

Synth Zone

http://www.synthzone.com/

Figure A.6

Synth Zone has been around almost since the Web began and contains rich sources of information about MIDI, synthesizer, and music production. The site is especially well known for its links to synthesizer software patches, manuals, and additional software. There's at least one active link for just about any synth you can name, as well as links to discussion groups, classifieds, auctions, and software downloads.

Scott Garrigus Web Sites

http://www.garrigus.com/

Figure A.7

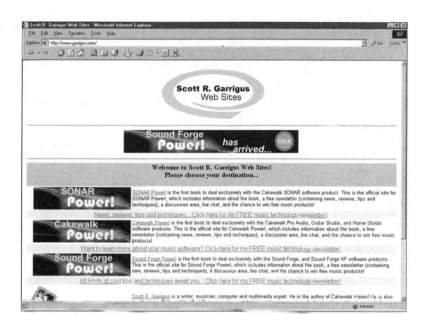

Fellow Muska & Lipman Publishing author Scott Garrigus has put together sites that provide articles, discussion areas, chat, and a monthly music technology newsletter for both SONAR and Sound Forge 5.0. This expert author has the two latest books for both these applications: *SONAR Power!* (2001; ISBN 1-929685-36-X) and *Sound Forge Power!* (2001; ISBN 1-929685-10-6).

The Recording Website

http://www.recordingwebsite.com/

Figure A.8

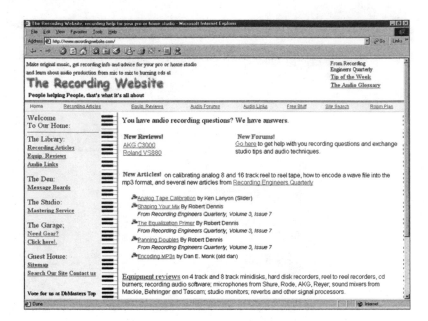

The Recording Website is a growing collection of articles and equipment reviews. The site has an active messageboard with tons of posts. The articles on the site tend to be fairly short but are well worth reading for their accuracy and level of detail.

What is a Synthesizer?

http://hem.passagen.se/tkolb/art/synth/intro_e.htm

Figure A.9

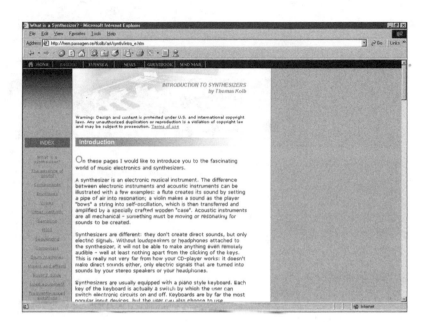

This Sweden-based Web site (the English is excellent), written and maintained by Thomas Kolb, is a wonderful exploration of details behind synth components, sampling, MIDI, computer-based recording, mixing, and effects. The articles are very rich and very well written.

CRMAV.com

http://www.crmav.com/

Figure A.10

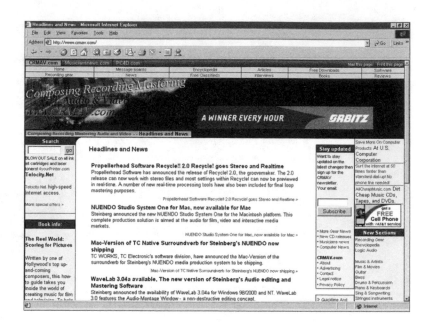

CRMAV.com is a Webzine and news site for anyone interested in **C**omposing, **R**ecording and **M**astering of **A**udio and **V**ideo. (Don't you just love baked-up acronyms?)

The site has articles, a messageboard, and classified ads, but it shines in its links to online resources as well as additional books on recording, music and audio. CRMAV.com is also part of a larger network of music and technology sites, all stemming from (**Musiciansnews.com**.)

Cakewalk

http://www.cakewalk.com/

Figure A.11

The Cakewalk homepage is the first place to look for more information on SONAR. The site contains a lot of information, with extensive FAQs, product updates, technical specifications, and an online store.

You also can find tips, techniques, and tricks and hook up with the Cakewalk newsgroup, Cakewalk User's Guild, and various Cakewalk mailing lists. You can also find support for the software and get in touch with Cakewalk's Tech Support group from the site.

Sonic Foundry

http://www.sonicfoundry.com/

Figure A.12

For updates, discussion, product information, and specifications, Sonic Foundry, the makers of Sound Forge, have developed a well-worn and deep Web site. In addition to excellent support of Sound Forge, it also provides support and documentation for all of its other products—including Vegas and ACID.

The site is very well done and is what you'd expect.

Index

INDEX

INDEX

INDEX

INDEX

INDEX

Sound Forge POWER!

Sound Forge Power! is a valuable resource for musicians and music hobbyists who want to record and edit their music and get the full benefit of Sound Forge's various features. Sound Forge is used for professional audio postproduction, designing sound, creating music, and multimedia authoring. Written for both the beginning and intermediate user, *Sound Forge Power!* discusses the many features of Sound Forge, including recording and playback, special effects, using Sound Forge with MIDI, and how to use additional audio tools.

Complete Coverage of Sound Forge 5.0
and Sound Forge XP 5.0

Sound Forge POWER!

Scott R. Garrigus

ISBN 1-929685-10-6
$29.95 U.S. $44.95 CAN

Key Features
- The first book to deal exclusively with Sound Forge 5.0, the popular music editing software by Sonic Foundry
- Written by the author of Cakewalk Power! and SONAR Power!
- Includes thorough discussions and many examples in clear language
- Special appendices cover how to use Sound Forge with ACID, how to burn files to a CD, how to back up files, and how to find Sound Forge resources on the Web

MUSKA & LIPMAN

http://www.muskalipman.com

MUSKA&LIPMAN

Order Form

Postal Orders:
Muska & Lipman Publishing
P.O. Box 8225
Cincinnati, Ohio 45208

Online Orders or more information:
http://www.muskalipman.com
Fax Orders:
(513) 924-9333

Title/ISBN	Price/Cost
Cakewalk Power! 1-929685-02-5	
Quantity _____	
	× $29.95
Total Cost _____	
SONAR Power! 1-929685-36-X	
Quantity _____	
	× $29.95
Total Cost _____	
Sound Forge Power! 1-929685-10-6	
Quantity _____	
	× $29.95
Total Cost _____	

Title/ISBN	Price/Cost
CD Recordable Solutions 1-929685-11-4	
Quantity _____	
	× $29.95
Total Cost _____	

Subtotal _____

Sales Tax _____
(please add 6% for books
shipped to Ohio addresses)

Shipping _____
($6.00 for US and Canada
$12.00 other countries)

TOTAL PAYMENT ENCLOSED _____

Ship to:

Company _____

Name _____

Address _____

City _____ State _____ Zip _____ Country _____

E-mail _____

Educational facilities, companies, and organizations interested in multiple copies of these books should contact the publisher for quantity discount information. Training manuals, CD-ROMs, electronic versions, and portions of these books are also available individually or can be tailored for specific needs.

Thank you for your order.